Violence and Trauma in the Lives of Children

Violence and Trauma in the Lives of Children

Volume 2: Prevention and Intervention

Joy D. Osofsky and
Betsy McAlister Groves,
Editors

PRAEGER™

An Imprint of ABC-CLIO, LLC
Santa Barbara, California • Denver, Colorado

Library of Congress Cataloging-in-Publication Data

Names: Osofsky, Joy D., editor. | Groves, Betsy McAlister, editor.
Title: Violence and trauma in the lives of children / Joy D. Osofsky and Betsy McAlister Groves, editors.
Description: Santa Barbara, California : Praeger, an Imprint of ABC-CLIO, LLC, [2018] | Includes bibliographical references and index.
Identifiers: LCCN 2017061841 (print) | LCCN 2018004154 (ebook) | ISBN 9781440852596 (ebook) | ISBN 9781440852589 (set : alk. paper) | ISBN 9781440852602 (vol. 1) | ISBN 9781440852619 (vol. 2)
Subjects: LCSH: Psychic trauma in children. | Psychic trauma in adolescence. | Psychic trauma in children—Treatment. | Psychic trauma in adolescence—Treatment. | Child psychotherapy.
Classification: LCC RJ506.P66 (ebook) | LCC RJ506.P66 V54 2018 (print) | DDC 616.85/2100835—dc23
LC record available at https://lccn.loc.gov/2017061841

ISBN: 978-1-4408-5258-9 (set)
978-1-4408-5260-2 (vol. 1)
978-1-4408-5261-9 (vol. 2)
978-1-4408-5259-6 (ebook)

22 21 20 19 18 1 2 3 4 5

This book is also available as an eBook.

Praeger
An Imprint of ABC-CLIO, LLC

ABC-CLIO, LLC
130 Cremona Drive, P.O. Box 1911
Santa Barbara, California 93116–1911
www.abc-clio.com

This book is printed on acid-free paper ∞

Manufactured in the United States of America

Contents

Acknowledgments

Violence and trauma take an often-unrecognized toll on children of all ages. Exposure to trauma occurs so often that many people have come to expect to hear about violence in their everyday lives. A problem that comes up frequently is how to find the appropriate language to talk to children about the violent events that have occurred in their families, communities, and their world. These handbooks are designed to expand knowledge not only about the types of traumas that occur at the individual, family, community, and national levels but also to educate the reader about ways to build resilience in children. In addition, policy issues related to violence prevention are crucial to make a difference for children.

The editors of these handbooks have come to the trauma field through somewhat different paths. Joy D. Osofsky, throughout her career, has had a strong commitment to prevention and intervention. With that passion came the recognition that more innovative and concentrated interventions were needed to help children exposed to violence and trauma. Through her early efforts to partner with police in the community and during summer programs for youth, the Violence Intervention Program in New Orleans represented a positive way to reach out to attempt to reduce and prevent youth violence. While she was working with the police and in schools, nine-year-old James Darby wrote a letter to President Clinton asking him to stop the violence because he was afraid that he would be killed. Unfortunately, his fears turned out to be well grounded as he was killed shortly after he wrote the letter. That experience and others influenced her work throughout many years in establishing prevention and intervention programs and helping those impacted by violence and trauma.

For Betsy McAlister Groves, her early work in child-care settings with children in the child protection system taught powerful and sobering lessons about the impact of trauma in early childhood. These experiences led to the founding of the Child Witness to Violence Project, providing clinical intervention and advocacy for children under age eight and their families. This program was one of the first in the country to specifically focus on young children and exposure to violence. Funded since 2001 by the National Child Traumatic Network as one of four sites in the Early Trauma Treatment Network, the Child Witness to Violence Project has provided training and consultation nationally and internationally on early childhood trauma and intervention.

The editors want to express appreciation to the many individuals who supported us through the process of developing and editing *Violence and Trauma in the Lives of Children*. We give special thanks to Lucy S. King, a gifted young woman who is a graduate student in psychology at Stanford University, for her enormous help and editing skill working with us to bring the volumes to completion. We want to express much appreciation to Debbie Carvalko, senior acquistions editor at ABC-CLIO/Praeger Publishers, who provided continual availability and assistance every step along the way toward publication. We also want to extend heartfelt thanks the authors, all leaders in the field, who despite their many commitments for time and expertise, contributed very significantly to these volumes.

Both of the editors wish to acknowledge the professional and personal relationships that have been fostered over the past 18 years by the National Child Traumatic Stress Network (NCTSN), funded by the Substance Abuse Mental Health Services Administration. Over half of the authors who wrote chapters for these Handbooks, as well as the editors, have been funded through the NCTSN, a network that by encouraging collaborations and connections has contributed substantially to our knowledge about the effects of violence and trauma on the lives of children shared in these volumes.

Joy D. Osofsky expresses special appreciation to colleagues in the Department of Psychiatry at Louisiana State University Health Sciences Center for their collaborative efforts to support children exposed to trauma and violence and helping me learn from their experiences. Finally, I could not do this work with trauma so effectively without the continual encouragement and support from my husband, Howard, who is not only always available to think things through with me but also endlessly patient with my long work hours. He is both a loving partner and a consistent believer in my work and contributions. I also want to add special thanks to my grown wonderful children, Hari, Justin, and Michael who taught me so much not only about being a parent, but also the importance of love and nurturing in families.

Betsy McAlister Groves thanks her students at Harvard's Graduate School of Education, who have challenged her to think more broadly about the cultural dimensions of research and intervention in this field. Appreciation also goes to my colleagues in the Department of Pediatrics at Boston Medical Center and at the Child Witness to Violence Project, who continue to inspire me. Finally, and most important, I thank my family—my husband Tim, an educator with extensive child-focused experience, and my daughters, Jeanie and Rebecca, who, along with Tim, have patiently accompanied me in the two-year evolution of this book project.

Hopefully, this book will contribute to making a difference in the lives of children, adolescents, and families now and in the future.

CHAPTER 1

Introduction

Betsy McAlister Groves and Joy D. Osofsky

The history of systematic research on the subject of child and adolescent trauma in the United States has included denial and minimization of the fact that children can be irreparably harmed by traumatic events. Elyssa Benedek, a child psychiatrist, described a meeting in the late 1970s of professionals who conducted research on victims of terrorism (Benedek, 1985, in Eth & Pynoos, 1985). As part of that meeting, Lenore Terr presented findings on her work with a group of children who had been buried alive. She had followed these children for four years after this event, carefully documenting their short- and long-term responses. Her presentation was met with skepticism by many people and even with hostility by some who questioned her methodology and findings. Benedek was surprised by the intensity of the criticism, and at first, she assumed that because Dr. Terr was the only woman on the panel, the others were showing bias against a female researcher. However, as she later discussed her observations with the presenter, she came to believe that the subject itself was to blame. It was too painful to know that children could be affected in the ways that were described. It was easier to attack the research than to accept the fact that children might carry the scars of trauma with them throughout their lives. Dr. Terr went on to become a pioneer in the study of the effects of trauma on children, and her groundbreaking study, "The Children of Chowchilla," was published in 1979 (Terr, 1979).

In 1980, posttraumatic stress disorder (PTSD) was included for the first time in the *Diagnostic and Statistical Manual of Mental Disorders* (*DSM*).

However, the diagnostic classification was based mainly on research with male Vietnam veterans, and children were not included. Attention to the field of child trauma changed in 1985, when Eth and Pynoos laid the groundwork for the burgeoning field of research in child trauma with their publication by the American Psychiatric Association of the book *Post-Traumatic Disorder in Children* (Eth & Pynoos, 1985).

Now, more than 30 years later, child trauma is a large and well-established field. The *DSM IV* included the diagnosis of PTSD for children and in the 2013 edition of the DSM-5, a diagnosis of preschool PTSD appeared (Scheerenga & Zeanah, 1995). Recognizing that children were impacted by trauma and that these diagnostic categories should be included were the results of years of research and clinical practice, affirming the extent to which children—even very young children—could be impacted by dangerous and threatening events. Paralleling this research was the evolution of trauma-focused treatment with its emphasis on rigorous outcome evaluation and research. These advances have led to the development of a wide range of evidence-based treatments for children and adolescents. The chapters in Volume I of this series describe the kinds of traumatic experiences that children and adolescents may encounter; the effects at the individual, family, and community level; and the types of interventions being used to help them. The focus is on the individual child, with attention paid to developmental stage. There are also chapters that describe theoretical perspectives on trauma, brain development, and the long-term impact of trauma on child and adolescent physical and mental health.

Volume II broadens the scope of research and practice to consider an expanding range of topics related to children affected by trauma. The content goes beyond the individual child to include the larger social context of the child and family. The volume begins with a chapter describing ways that the concepts of "trauma" and "healing" have different meanings across cultures (Lewis, McConnico, & Anderson, Chapter 2). Symptoms or reactions are expressed differently, and there are diverse ways that families seek or accept help from various sources. The cultural dimensions of trauma are broad, requiring practitioners, and the systems in which they work, to be aware of biases and limitations in their understanding of the ways that others practice. This chapter focuses on three ethnic and racial groups that are disproportionately affected by historical trauma, disparities in care, and the role of culture as an agent of healing for these children and their families.

Chapters 3 and 4 examine resilience and posttraumatic growth, respectively. The chapter on resilience (Narayan & Masten) is a powerful reminder that trauma does not impact everyone in the same way and that acknowledging and building upon children's resilience is important. In Chapter 4, Armstrong, Basquin, and Tedeschi define "posttraumatic growth" and differentiate it from the concept of resilience. They describe the potential for children and adults not only to survive or endure traumatic events but also to develop new perspectives on their lives and to experience psychological or spiritual growth.

Chapters 5–9 focus on the systems in which children and families live and interact. Bronfenbrenner's seminal work on the ecology of human development is a foundation for this focus, looking beyond the individual to consider the child in the context of his or her environment. These authors emphasize how family, community, and larger ecosystems impact the child's development (Bronfenbrenner & Ceci, 1994). Given the ubiquity of child exposure to trauma, there is great interest in focusing on the systems that impact the child and family and whether they support a child's efforts to recover from trauma or impinge upon those efforts. As was mentioned in the introduction to Volume I, in 2014, a monograph was published by the U.S. Services Administration for Mental health and Substance Abuse that defined "trauma-informed systems" and outlined the core components of a trauma-informed response (SAMHSA, 2014). This publication was offered as a guide to create trauma-informed systems and reflected the developing national interest in better understanding the core components of such a system.

Chapter 5 (Wissow & Groves) describes a trauma-informed pediatric primary care system—one in which parents and children establish trusting relationships with staff and providers. With this approach, trauma is viewed as an important health issue that is respectfully acknowledged and assessed, and referrals are carefully made with input from families. The importance of training and supporting clinic staff is also emphasized. Chapter 6 (Blodgett) focuses on trauma-informed schools, and Chapter 7 (Harden & Duncan) addresses the child welfare system. Chapter 8 (Osofsky, Osofsky, Speier, & Hansel) presents a macrosystems approach to responding to terrorism and disaster. The authors describe risk factors that are unique to disasters—the length of time of community recovery after a disaster or an act of terror, the extent to which children are exposed to media coverage—and discuss a tiered model of intervention.

Chapter 9 (Cohen & Osofsky) highlights the judicial response to children affected by abuse and domestic violence and describes changes that have occurred in the past decade in knowledge and perspectives for juvenile judges by integrating a trauma-informed and collaborative approach into the courts. The authors present an illustrative example of an innovative program for young children, Safe Babies Court Teams, to show how trauma-informed changes have been made in juvenile courts to support young children exposed to violence and trauma.

Chapter 10 (Tullberg & Muradwij) shifts the focus by considering "the cost of caring" (Figley, 1995). This chapter centers on the workforce within systems and the ways in which their exposure to and interactions with traumatized children and families can affect them. Case studies direct the reader's attention to the personal and professional costs of secondary trauma and offer ideas for support and intervention.

Chapter 11 (Pinderhughes & Davis) considers the impact of trauma on communities, examining the link between individual trauma and community health. From this perspective, they suggest that trauma cannot be addressed at the individual level only, but must also be focused on at the population level. The authors describe community-level interventions that have been developed in several cities in the United States.

Volume II ends with two chapters addressing public policy and legislative efforts to address child and adolescent trauma in the United States. In Chapter 12, Gerrity, Elmore Borbon, and Strain provide an overview of landmark federal laws related to child trauma and violence. They focus on high-risk populations, such as victims of sex trafficking, refugees and immigrants, LGBTQ youth, and adolescent substance abusers. They review laws related to health and mental health insurance coverage, access to care for children and adolescents, and funding to address the opioid crisis. These authors also identify several pressing policy gaps and remind readers about the importance of individual advocacy. They conclude their chapter with practical tips about how to effectively communicate with lawmakers.

In Chapter 13, authors Oser, Cohen, Cole, Huddleston, and Usry focus on the needs of children from birth to age five, highlighting the critical importance of these years for addressing mental health needs. They propose a framework for considering policies to address early childhood trauma and discuss potential policy solutions and opportunities at the federal, state, and community level. These authors highlight the importance of supportive family policies as key determinants of young children's well-being. They also present policy case examples to describe systemic responses to trauma and the growth of trauma-informed practice approaches. The chapter ends with a proposal for trauma-informed early childhood policies.

Together, Volumes I and II reflect a broad and complex picture of child and adolescent exposure to violence and other traumatic events. The authors remind us of the importance of context: family, community, culture. They challenge us to think, not only of the individual child or of a single traumatic experience, as for many children, the traumas are cumulative and exposure may be chronic. Both children and their caregivers may encounter systems that have further impact, either positively by providing support or negatively by intensifying their stress.

Our authors also remind us about the importance of focusing on resilience and the opportunities for posttraumatic growth. The majority of children who are exposed to a potentially traumatic event are not adversely affected, and there is much to learn from their experiences. In the 38 years since Lenore Terr published her first paper, our understanding of the vulnerability of children—especially young children—has changed dramatically, leading to advances in identification, treatment, universal prevention programs, and broader child health and mental health policy. While groundbreaking research on the brain has led the way, others have followed with ideas about the importance of trauma-informed interventions, treatments, and systems change. The authors of the last two chapters in this volume encourage us to be bold and optimistic in envisioning a future that better supports families and reduces exposure to violence and trauma. There is cause for hope and optimism that our understanding of trauma will continue to evolve with new horizons of research and intervention, and a renewed focus on prevention.

References

Benedek, E. P. (1985). Children and psychic trauma: A brief review. In S. Eth & R. Pynoos (Eds.), *Post-traumatic stress disorder in children* (pp. 1–17). American Psychiatric Association Press, Inc.

Bronfenbrenner, U., & Ceci, S. (1994). Nature-nurture reconceptualized in a developmental perspective: A bioecological model. *Psychological Review, 101*, 568–586. doi:10.1037/0033-295X.101.4.568

Eth, S., & Pynoos, R. S. (1985). *Post-traumatic stress disorder in children*. American Psychiatric Association Press, Inc.

Figley, C. R. (1995). Compassion fatigue: Toward a new understanding of the costs of caring. In B. H. Stamm (Ed.), *Secondary traumatic stress: Self-care issues for clinicians, researchers, and educators* (pp. 3–28). Baltimore, MD: The Sidran Press.

SAMHSA. (2014). *SAMHSA's concept of trauma and guidance for a trauma-informed approach*. Retrieved from https://store.samhsa.gov/shin/content/SMA14-4884/SMA14-4884.pdf

Scheerenga, M., & Zeanah, C. (1995). Symptom expression and trauma variables in children under 48 months of age. *Infant Mental Health Journal, 16*, 259–270.

Terr, L. (1979). Children of Chowchilla. *The Psychoanalytic Study of the Child, 34*, 547–623.

CHAPTER 2

Making Meaning from Trauma and Violence

The Influence of Culture, Traditional Beliefs, and Historical Trauma

Marva L. Lewis, Neena McConnico, and Riana Elyse Anderson

> If you wish to be a diagnostic center then you focus on pathology. But if you wish to become a change center, then you focus on strengths. (Minuchin, Colapinto, & Minuchin, 1998)

Culture, defined as the language, traditions, values, and practices of a group, may offer mental health practitioners and researchers the opportunity to focus on the strengths of children and their families exposed to trauma and violence. The meaning of trauma and violence to young children and their families can be filtered through three developmental perspectives: *psychological, relational*, and *environmental*. These interlocking levels of systems provide a basis for a multilayered understanding of how trauma impacts a child's development. Typically the focus has been on the pathological impact of trauma on children who play, live, and learn within neighborhoods, cities, villages, and communities around the world. However, this is a limited view that overlooks the protective role of culture.

In this chapter, we refer to three groups of children who are disproportionately represented in many indexes of health and well-being—young children of color. Three racial and ethnic groups of children—African American children—American Indian children, and Hispanic/Latino children, have been exposed to centuries of violence targeted at their cultural and ethnic groups in the United States (e.g., Tribal Behavioral Health Agenda, 2016). Their families' experiences of chronic historical trauma included slavery, genocide, and treacherous immigration experiences. Each of these experiences included violent physical atrocities, legal segregation, and group humiliation of well-known stereotypes based on their physical features. The decades of subjection by a dominant colonizer or slave holder began with the decimation of the group's culture, language, and separation from their homeland and systematic erosion of their ethnic identity (Schwab, 2010). Yet, currently each of these groups—African Americans descended from the enslaved Africans; Native Americans who survived the genocide and boarding schools that separated children from families; and Hispanic Americans who survived escape from countries marred by decades of political violence—managed to survive and raise children against all odds.

This chapter will also focus on the role of culture as an agent of healing for children and their families. We will discuss how cultural socialization provides psychological, relational, and environmental mechanisms that may serve to nurture and heal children and their families exposed to violence and trauma. We present an analysis of culturally based responses that may mitigate trauma-based developmental processes. For practitioners, we present guidelines to use for talking with children about violence and trauma. Finally, we discuss how storytelling, an ancient cultural practice known around the world, may serve as a vehicle for healing from the legacies of historical trauma or the modern-day challenge of war, immigration, and acculturation in a strange environment (Tuwe, 2016).

The Developmental Niches of Young Children

Super and Harkness (1997) created a universal conceptual approach that incorporates transcultural and ecological factors that facilitate an understanding of the influence of culture on a child's development. They identified three levels of the developmental niche to explain individual differences in children's development: the psychology of the child's caretaker; the customs of child care in which the child is socialized, including the unique cultural practices; and the physical and social settings where the child grows and develops.

"Young children grow up embedded in the physical and social niches of caregiving environments . . . They grow and develop physically, cognitively, and emotionally within a network of human relationships" (Lewis & Ghosh Ippen, 2004, p. 11). The psychology of the caretaker is shaped in part by the childhood experiences of that person and the experiences of having been parented. Attachment theory (Bowlby, 1969) describes the concept of *internal working models* of the caregivers' early relationships with their parents. The parents' earliest emotions of felt security, love, and acceptance formed their feeling of confidence that a primary adult caregiver would provide the basic necessities to insure their very survival. These earliest memoires form the emotional template that shapes the quality of their attachment relationship with their child and ability to provide nurturing parenting.

In looking at the developmental niche of child care and cultural practices, Lewis (2000) argues that distinctions must be made in differentiating the concept of culture from the concepts of ethnicity and race. Individuals are typically born into a specific ethnic group and are socialized into the language and culture of that group. During their later developmental processes of identity formation, their ethnicity becomes a subjective choice. Racial group membership, on the other hand, is a limited sociopolitical external classification of individuals based on arbitrary physical characteristics such as skin color or physical features. Thus, a child born in Mexico who immigrates to the United States may have Spanish cultural roots and speak Spanish as a first language and identify ethnically as Mexican but in the United States be classified racially as "Hispanic." In the United States, the developmental niches include not only culture but also race, historical trauma, and modern-day traumas such as authority-based shootings of African American males associated with racial group membership (Ashing, Lewis, & Walker, 2017; Lewis, Noroña, McConnico, & Thomas, 2013).

Historical Trauma in the Developmental Niche

For infants and children of color, their development and early home and urban community experiences may include distinct experiences of violence and trauma (APA, Stress and Discrimination, 2016; Tribal Behavioral health Agenda, 2016). In this chapter, we discuss the psychological impact of one form of violence that is not often recognized as having a potential psychosocial impact on young children—historical trauma.

Historical trauma, defined by Brave Heart (2003, p. 247), as "a cumulative emotional and psychological wounding over the lifespan and across generations emanating from massive group trauma experiences," adds an invisible layer of intensity to understanding the meaning of a child's experiences with violence and trauma. Social groups whose history includes experiences where they have been targeted for violence by a dominant social group within the same culture or nation may experience traumas such as war, enslavement, or genocide. Experiences of decades of the legally sanctioned genocide of Native American men, women, and children and relegation of their surviving members to distant boarding schools and reservations by European settlers in the United States; of the horror of the Holocaust systematic extermination and murder of Jews by Nazi Germany in Europe; and the mid-90s genocide and slaughter of Tutsui ethnic group families by the Hutu ethnic group within the country of Rwanda in Africa, will be embodied in the collective memories of their descendants for generations (Bar-On et al., 1998; Boszormenyi-Nagy & Spark, 1973; Brave Heart, 2002).

The experience of trauma reverberates throughout the caregiving environments of young children, their caregivers, families, and cultural groups. The intergenerational transmission of historical trauma in young children is a powerful thread in the tapestry of culture that creates the developmental niches of young children. Social learning theory and John Bowlby's theory of attachment help us understand the parental messages, behaviors, and beliefs that have their roots in what Maria Yellow Horse Brave Heart identified as a *historical trauma response* (2000). The process of cultural socialization that is handed down through the customs of child care may incorporate historical trauma responses in parenting practices that become part of the practices, beliefs, fears, and strengths that led to the survival of the group (Brave Heart, 2000). These unrecognized intergenerational traumatic parenting practices, beliefs, and behaviors that originated in previous generations of the group that directly experienced the historical trauma even may contribute to risk and vulnerability as their children form attachment relationships (Sotero, 2006). For example, unresolved grieving practices may have been passed down through generations in response to a historical trauma event such as genocide (Brave Heart, 2000). The caregiver may have grown up with a modeled response to grieving the loss of a family member with a ritualized or prescribed manner of behavior and specific expression and duration of emotions. The emotional preoccupation with grieving may result in the caregiver's emotional unavailability. Thus, the caregiver may miss important attachment cues communicated by the developing infant or young child.

As a child listens to and witnesses older family members process events of historical trauma (e.g., "they murdered all of our women!") with strong emotions of anger or rage focused on a dominant "other," the message that the child may absorb is that "bad things happen to our group."

It is also important to understand the families' themes, myths, and heroes that are passed on through generations related to experiences of historical trauma. Families and cultural groups may have prescribed responses to death, mourning, and coping. For example, in Latino families who have lost family members to political violence in their home countries and have immigrated to the United States, is there permission to acknowledge and grieve the recent loss of a loved one? Or does the cultural practice dictate that family members remain stalwart and stoically move forward? Is there fear that providing details of the loss to the children in the family will overwhelm them because of the ties of the event to well-known historical events?

Figure 2.1 depicts this expanded view of the developmental niche to broaden an understanding of the role of historical trauma and violence to children and their families. Each layer of a child's developmental niche helps us unpack what might be unique factors that contribute to the child's understanding of trauma. At the center, the *first level* of this embedded developmental niche is the child's unique temperament and physical, cognitive, and emotional developmental status. The formation of an attachment relationship of the child and caregiver and caregiving environment (Lewis, 2000) will be the main source of the developmental trajectory for this growing infant and young child. Further, this relationship sets the stage for individual differences in the personality development of the child and the formation of resilience to future traumatic experiences.

The *second level* of the niche includes the caregivers' experiences of direct trauma and violence. This level includes the parent's internal working model of attachment relationships that serves as the psychic mechanism for the intergenerational transmission of trauma. An example is the depressed mood of a Jewish caregiver as he or she reenacts his or her grandparents' unresolved grief responses or survivor guilt as they relate the hushed stories of the horrors of the Holocaust. This second level may include the direct historical trauma response of a Native American grandparent's recurring nightmares of experiences of being abruptly and helplessly separated from family and community and shipped to boarding school. From a relational perspective, the meaning of hearing the rat-a-tat-tat of gunfire by young children may be determined by the frightened look they decode from their primary caregiver's facial expression.

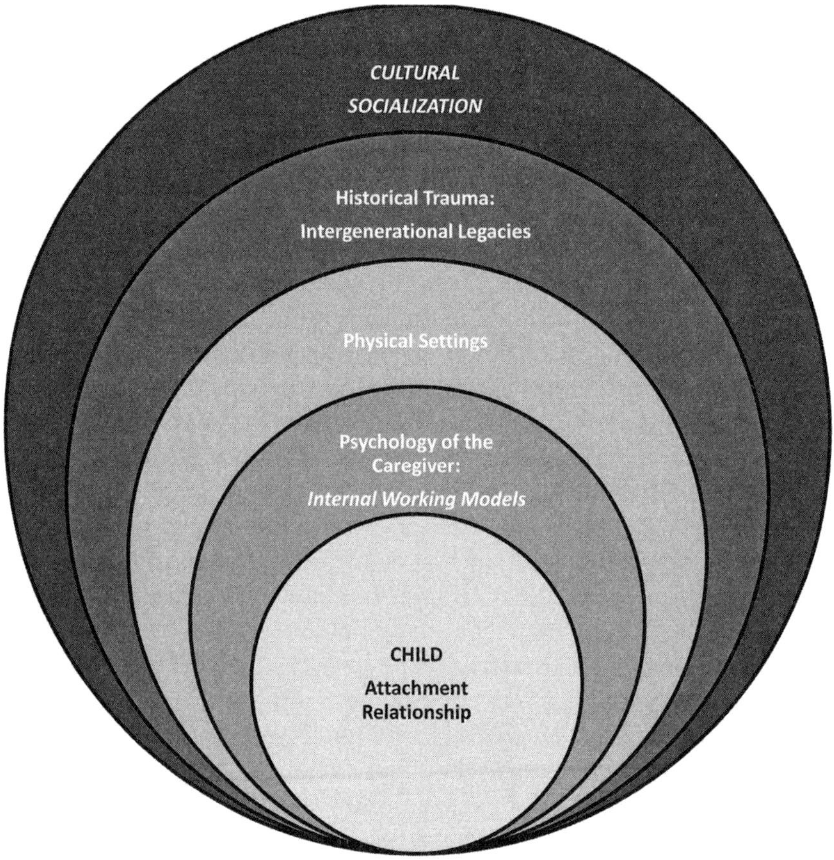

Figure 2.1 An Expanded View of the Developmental Niche: The Role of Historical Trauma

Note: Multiple factors at each of these levels help us understand how the broader concept of culture shapes the meaning of children's responses to violence and trauma.

The *third level* of the developmental niche, as originally conceptualized by Super and Harkness (1997), includes the physical environment and childcare settings. From a trauma framework, this level may include traumatic memories of the physical setting of trauma, such as the African American families sheltered in the Superdome during the collective trauma of Hurricane Katrina in 2005 that took place in New Orleans, Louisiana.

The physical setting of child care includes environmental contributions to the meaning of violence and trauma to a child that may come from the chronic gunshots that occur in the neighborhood in which the young child lives. Living in distressed urban environments or with decades of war between ethnic groups may create a kind of "normalcy" to expect gunfire in the everyday lives of some young children. Recent research suggests that children who grow up in environments where they don't feel safe may have elevated responses to threat (Wilkins, Tsao, Hertz, Davis, & Klevens, 2014). One study found that children living in environments where safety is constantly threatened by violence may misinterpret neutral facial expressions such as anger. These children may be more likely to respond with the connections in their brain to survival skills if they are continually exposed to violence (fight) or running away (flight) than children who grow up in safe, stable, and nurturing environments.

The *fourth level* of cultural socialization within the framework of the developmental niche directly identifies the caregiver's group's experience of historical trauma. The intergenerational legacies of historical trauma, as noted in the examples previously, may be the unrecognized factors of risk and vulnerability in caregiver–child relationships (Lewis et al., 2013).

The *fifth level* of the niche is the broad concept of culture and the associated socialization practices by the caregiver with children. The caregivers' beliefs about their role as parents, the beliefs about children and childhood and adolescence, and the values they hold for family and relationships are determined at this level. The most critical contribution at this level is the emotional socialization of the child. This level structures the parent–child relationship through cultural rules and standards for emotional displays. For example, is it acceptable for young boys to cry? At what age should boys be "tough" and not show fear? Is holding a newborn infant throughout the day going to "spoil" the child? How long should a mother breastfeed her infant or toddler: six months, one year, or, as is true in some cultures, three years? These questions are typically answered by cultural norms, standards, and rules for behaviors. Culture then helps parents and caregivers make meaning of their everyday world (Lewis, 2000; Super & Harkness, 1997).

Cultural, Ethnic, and Racial Socialization

Cultural socialization refers to implicit and explicit messages that emphasize cultural pride, heritage, and ancestral legacy and is associated with positive developmental outcomes, including academic and psychological well-being and identity development. Several studies have used the term "cultural socialization" to include ethnic and racial socialization processes. For example, cultural socialization, that includes ethnic and racial practices associated with academic achievement, is a positive predictor of grade point average, educational aspirations, and cognitive engagement (Wang & Huguley, 2012).

In a review of the literature on racial and ethnic socialization protective factors, Neblett, Phillip, Cogburn, and Sellers (2006) proposed a conceptual model of the mechanisms of psychological protection of children that included ethnic–racial socialization and cultural orientation in a broader model of culture-informed promotive and protective factors of socialization (p. 299).

In their (2006) review of studies focused on urban African American youth, they found that self-worth messages were associated with higher levels of academic curiosity and persistence. For example, they found that when youth received positive messages about the significance and meaning of a behavior, such as persistence and being a member of a racial or ethnic minority group, the youth reported higher levels of feelings of competence across multiple domains (e.g., academic, social, and behaviors).

Findings also show that parental involvement and messages on cultural heritage and preparation for bias work together to offset poor academic adjustment for youth with low public regard (McGill, Hughes, Alicea, & Way, 2012). Furthermore, Neblett, Rivas-Drake, and Umaña-Taylor (2012) highlight ethnic/racial identity, ethnic/racial socialization, and cultural orientation as protective factors that are interrelated to help youth develop self-concept, cognitive appraisal skills, and coping skills for psychological wellness. Cultural socialization has also been associated with greater optimism and fewer depressive symptoms (Liu & Lau, 2013) and indirectly associated with fewer depressive symptoms through racial pride (Neblett, Banks, Cooper, & Smalls-Glover, 2013). Gatson (2011) found that cultural socialization and egalitarianism messages were associated with less avoidant coping. Additionally, Murry, Berkel, Brody, Miller, and Chen (2009) found an association between the receipt of cultural socialization messages and positive racial identity development. Finally, child and parent gender add to our understanding of cultural socialization messages in that parents of girls were more likely to emphasize cultural socialization whereas those of boys were likely to emphasize a combination of cultural socialization, coping skills, and promotion of mistrust (Peck, Brodish, Malanchuk, Banerjee, & Eccles, 2014). Suizzo, Robinson, and Pahlke (2008) indicate that mothers have a great desire for more educational material and supports to aid in racial socialization, particularly for cultural socialization and preparation for bias.

For example, the ongoing events of authority-based shootings of black youth by police have become part of the "talk" and preparation for bias the black parents use with their male children. They prepare them with how to behave and respond to police officers based on a larger preparation for racial socialization of the realities of racial profiling (Ashing, Lewis, & Walker, 2017; Thomas & Blackmon, 2014).

The Influence of Culture, Traditional Beliefs, and Historical Trauma

A cultural focus on the resilience of children and their families living with legacies of historical trauma is an underrecognized source of strength in health and healing from trauma. In her seminal work with the Lakota Indians, clinician Maria Yellow Horse Brave Heart (2000) observed symptoms in contemporary clients that she identified as a historical trauma response. She observed that a group of clients displayed symptoms directly related to the massive group trauma of the 1890 Wounded Knee Massacre of the Lakota Indians. She noted that these descendants displayed an identifiable array of symptoms—survivor guilt, complicated and unresolved grief response, and what is termed "transposition," where one lives simultaneously in the past and the present with the ancestral suffering as the main organizing principle in one's life.

In the Lakota culture Brave Heart identified individuals who were the descendants of historical trauma survivors and were called *Wakiksuyapi*. These "memorial people" (p. 248) carried the grief and whose lives provide a testimony to the lost ancestors maintained a connection with the spirit world and identification with ancestors from their historical past. Using a cultural practices approach, Brave Heart (2000) created a clinical strategy to help these individuals heal from historical trauma. Called "a return to the sacred path," she created a culturally congruent four-day psychoeducational intervention designed to initiate grief resolution that had its origins in historical trauma from previous generations. The research conducted with this model yielded healing themes of these survivors that were categorized as *coping strategies*, *ideas about healing*, and *transforming the past*.

In different cultural groups, practices within the groups have served as a vehicle for healing from past trauma and creating resiliency in current generations. For example, Jewish Holocaust descendants who maintain the collective generational trauma of lost ancestors light "Memorial Candles" (Fogelman, 2003). The ancient Jewish culture has many cultural practices such as the practice of "Passover", reverently lighting seven candles of remembrance each year and repeating the stories of the Angel of Death saving Jewish firstborn sons from the death decreed by Caesar, which are faithfully taught from generation to generation.

African American families utilize and value egalitarianism as a socialization strategy. Egalitarianism is defined as a principle of equality and flexibility of family roles within the nuclear and extended family structures. For example, this role flexibility and egalitarianism allow for men in the father role to be responsible for child care with no threat to their masculinity. Sociologist Robert Hill (1972) identified this concept of egalitarianism as a core strength of black families. Research by Anderson et al. (2015) found that the egalitarianism comes second in frequency only to cultural socialization practices (Hughes et al., 2008). While some research indicates a high frequency of messages involving racial equality (86%; Coard, Wallace, Stevenson, & Brotman, 2004), other studies find that this frequency is moderated by sociodemographic characteristics. For example, White-Johnson, Ford, and Sellers (2010) found that parents who are at least high school graduates are less likely to use egalitarianism messages than other socialization strategies. However, they also found that parents use egalitarianism and preparation for bias strategies more with their sons than their daughters, whom they are more likely to socialize with cultural pride messages. The extant literature also shows that there are positive outcomes associated with egalitarianism when used with other racial socialization strategies. Specifically, Neblett et al. (2012) found a positive association between egalitarianism and young people's self-concept when used with cultural socialization. Egalitarianism is also associated with higher racial centrality for youth when used with cultural socialization and preparation for bias in racial socialization.

In Table 2.1 we briefly present how intergenerational, relationship-based cultural practices may serve as a protective or risk factor for young children experiencing violence and trauma.

Ubuntu Storytelling: An Everyday Template for Families to Heal from Historical Trauma

The cultural practice of storytelling can be enlisted by families to help children make meaning of historical trauma. Further, this essentially narrative therapy technique can help families confront and re-story legacies from the past that no longer serve them.

The African oral tradition of *Ubuntu* open-ended storytelling provides a no-cost, culturally informed template for families to use with young children to address the legacies of historical trauma of their cultural, ethnic, or racial group. Ubuntu means "I am what I am because of you." The concept is centered on people or humanity (Carson, 1998; Mandela, 1994). These stories offer explanations of natural phenomena, teach morality, provide African people with a sense of identity, and are entertaining as well as instructive.

Storytelling with young children is a practice easily incorporated into the everyday routines of families with young children. Practitioners may

Table 2.1 Cultural Socialization: Protective Practices, Risk and Vulnerabilities for Children

Developmental Processes	Protective Cultural Socialization Practices	Cultural Risk and Vulnerabilities
Sense of safety	Secure attachment	Vigilance for experiences of targeting for violence, bullying, racism, oppression, microaggressions, and discrimination
Ability to regulate emotions of anger and aggression	Storytelling depicting a wide range of emotional responses, conflict, and roles for the expression of emotions	Reward and selective attention to cultural prescriptions for violence. For example, misquoted Bible verse, "spare the rod, spoil the child." Emphasis on obedience based on need for survival of historical trauma. Refined use of passive–aggressive methods to express anger and communicate rage. Learned helplessness as member of a devalued, powerless group. Internalized oppression
Self-concept	Cultural pride, heritage, and rituals that give meaning to everyday experiences	Participation in empty rituals that no longer serve the greater collective good
Ethnic identity and belonging	Ancestral legacies, family and ethnic identity formation. Development of cognitive appraisal skills and coping skills for psychological wellness	Legacies of hatred leading to radicalization in opposition to other cultural groups. Use of stereotypes of members who do not belong to your group

help families identify experiences and behaviors that have origins in historical trauma such as unresolved grieving patterns (Brave Heart, 2000) or acceptance or rejection of children based on skin color in African American families (Lewis et al., 2013). Family systems therapists have well-developed techniques for supporting families to address the eradication of unhealthy coping or family myths that impact their relationships (Boszormenyi-Nagy & Spark, 1973).

These stories may help families to reclaim their ethnic identity and culture with a sense of pride and excitement. Stories can help children to identify historical ways of coping that can be transformed into modern experiences of resilience. For example, the method of collective storytelling of the humorous trickster stories about the smart strategies employed by the small rabbit to outwit the larger bear told by the enslaved Africans can be easily adapted to help a young frightened child from a minority group cope with bullies using racial hatred from a dominant racial or religious group on the playground or in their classroom.

We recommend strategies parents may use to talk with children about experiences of violence or trauma. Whether the trauma occurred in past generations or in the recent past or even currently, these general strategies will help parents help their children to make sense of experiences of violence or trauma.

Nine Recommendations for Talking to Children about Violence or Historical Trauma

1. **Be open and willing to have a dialogue**: As difficult as it may be to talk about racism and race-based violence with children, it is imperative that adults be willing to have the conversation. This provides modeling for the child and gives them permission to speak about something that they perhaps think is "unspeakable" and therefore silenced about. Allowing space for dialogue also takes away some of the power of such race-based encounters and demonstrates to children that their experience is not so insurmountable that it cannot be talked about or tolerated by others. Talking about racially charged events is not easy, and it is important to recognize that conversations will be ongoing—not able to be neatly wrapped up in one sitting.
2. **Engage in self-reflection and examine your own biases**: In order for adults to be effective and impactful in race-based interactions with children, they must be honest and authentic about the beliefs, biases, and assumptions that influence their practices and actions with others. Taking time to reflect on the sociopolitical underpinnings of racism, oppression, privilege, and the interconnection to the philosophy of the American education and judicial systems of care that are structured around the values and beliefs of the dominant culture is crucial. Awareness of mainstream dominant culture and the influence of one's own belief system can help with identifying, processing, and addressing race-based violence.
3. **Be open and honest**: Give children the truth by providing them with developmentally appropriate answers to their questions and about encounters they

experience. While we may believe that we are protecting children by avoiding answering questions, giving placated responses, or making up a story to shield them from the harsh realities of the truth, this is often more detrimental than telling the truth. When children lack answers to the questions they have, they often create a story that can be far worse than what actually transpired and can lead to confusion and distrust of adults. Young children will benefit when provided with simple concrete answers, while older children will need more details to help them process and make sense of the situation.

4. **Expect to be uncomfortable**: Experiencing discomfort is inevitable and is at the cornerstone of every difficult conversation. While it may be something you strive to avoid, it is pivotal to invoke change and serves as an example to children that despite your discomfort, you choose to listen and bear witness because they matter and their experience matters. There is hope in knowing that race-based conversations are filled with many "teachable moments" for all involved.
5. **You do not need to have all the answers**: Just like any other conversation, it is not necessary to have all the answers to children's questions. In fact, children will appreciate your honesty and authenticity and be more willing to engage in conversation when you are forthcoming about your limitations. Examples of how to respond in this situation are "Let me think about that one." "I don't know, but it's important, so let's figure it out together."
6. **Listen to children and hear their story**: Being the victim of a racist encounter or being witness to such an encounter by media exposure or the reactions and conversations of others can make an individual feel invisible and powerless. Allowing children to tell their story without judgment, without fear and without correction can help mitigate this feeling as doing so allows children to feel seen and safe. Resist the temptation to tell children what they meant to say or are really trying to say because it makes you uncomfortable or it may not be politically correct. Listen empathically and ask for clarification first before engaging in "teachable moments."
7. **Get clarification from children**: It is important to remember that children often do not have the same understanding of words nor do they interpret experiences and the actions of others the same way that adults do. When talking with children about race relations, it is important not to project your thoughts and feelings onto the child. You should not assume that you know what the child meant or what he or she is trying to say, but instead ask clarifying questions regarding the child's thoughts, feelings, rationale, and interpretations.
8. **Allow children to have negative emotions**: While adults may become uncomfortable and nervous when children express strong feelings of anger and hate and display aggressive behavior, it is part of the process that children must go through as they try to make sense of the experience they had or witnessed. Being granted the opportunity to release these negative

emotions can be cathartic for children and should be permitted as long as the child is not physically hurting himself or herself or others.

9. **Practice creating a solution or plan of action**: Help children identify something they can do about the situation. Help children and adults feel better and counter against complacency. Doing so fights against the feeling of being immobilized and disempowered. Being solution-focused helps to rechannel anger, aggression, and extreme sadness to drive change and allows one's voice to be heard.

Conclusion

In this chapter we have focused on culture as a source of strength for children and families exposed to violence and trauma. We presented a conceptual approach proposing that trauma and violence must be filtered through multiple interlocking levels of systems to provide a more nuanced understanding of the meaning of trauma and violence to children and their families. Each of the systems at the psychological, relational, and environmental levels makes distinct contributions to the developing child's experience of trauma as well as resilience in a context of violence and trauma. We add the level of historical trauma and discuss the intergenerational legacies of parenting practices that may become incorporated as normative child-rearing practices by groups targeted with violence over generations.

Finally, we present culture as a source of strength and a protective factor as well as a potential risk factor and source of vulnerability for children and their families. Using this broader framework of culture allows practitioners, researchers, and policy makers to provide supports and services that build on the strengths of children and their families.

References

American Psychological Association (2016). *Stress in America™: The Impact of Discrimination*. Retrieved from http://www.apa.org/news/press/releases/stress/index.aspx

Anderson, A. T., Jackson, A., Jones, L., Kennedy, D. P., Wells, K., & Chung, P. J. (2015). Minority parents perspectives on racial socialization and school readiness in the early childhood period. *Academic Pediatrics,15*(4), 405–411. doi:10.1016/j.acap.2014.11.002

Ashing, K. T., Lewis, M. L., & Walker, V. P. (2017). Thoughts and response to authority-perpetrated, discriminatory, and race-based violence. *JAMA Pediatrics,171*(6), 511.

Bar-On, D., Eland, J., Kleber, R.J., Krell, R., Moore, Y., Sagi, A., . . . Ijzendoorn, M.H. (1998). Multigenerational perspectives on coping with the Holocaust experience: An attachment perspective for understanding the developmental sequelae of trauma across generations. *International Journal of Behavioral Development, 22*(2), 315–338. doi:10.1080/016502598384397

Boszormenyi-Nagy, I., & Spark, G. (1973). *Invisible loyalties: Reciprocity in intergenerational family therapy.* New York, NY: Harper & Row.

Bowlby, J. (1969). *Attachment and loss: Attachment* (Vol. 1). New York, NY: Basic Books.

Brave Heart, M.Y. (2000). Wakiksuyapi: Carrying the historical trauma of the Lakota. In M.J. Zakour (Ed.), *Disaster and traumatic stress research and intervention* (Vol. 21–22, Winter/Spring, pp. 245–266). New Orleans, LA: Tulane University, School of Social Work.

Carson, C. (1998). The *autobiography of Martin Luther King, Jr.* New York, NY: Grand Central Publishing.

Coard, S.I., Wallace, S.A., Stevenson, J.H., & Brotman, L.M. (2004). Towards culturally relevant preventive interventions: The consideration of racial socialization in parent training with African American families. *Journal of Child and Family Studies, 13*(3), 277–293. doi:10.1023/b:jcfs.0000022035.07171.f8

Gatson, J.D. (2011). *Racial socialization, racial discrimination and mental health among African American parents* (Unpublished doctoral dissertation). University of California, Los Angeles.

Hill, R.B. (1972). *The strengths of black families.* Lanham, MD: University Press of America.

Hughes, D., Rivas, D., Foust, M., Hagelskamp, C., Gersick, S., & Way, N. (2008). How to catch a moonbeam: A mixed-methods approach to understanding ethnic socialization processes in ethnically diverse families. In M. Quintana & C. McKown (Eds.), *Handbook of race, racism, and the developing child* (pp. 226–277). Hoboken, NJ: John Wiley & Sons Inc.

Lewis, M.L. (1996). Trauma reverberates: Psychosocial evaluation of the caregiving environment of young children exposed to violence and traumatic loss. In J. Osofsky & E.S. Fenichel (Eds.), *Islands of safety: Assessing and treating young victims of violence* (5th ed., Vol. 16, pp. 21–28). Washington, DC: Zero To Three.

Lewis, M.L. (2000). The cultural context of infant mental health: The developmental niche of infant-caregiver relationships. In C.H. Zeanah Jr. (Ed.), *Handbook of infant mental health* (2nd ed., pp. 91–107). New York, NY: Guilford Press.

Lewis, M.L., & Ghosh Ippen, C. (2004). Rainbows of tears, souls full of hope: Cultural issues related to young children and trauma. In J.D. Osofsky (Ed.), *Young children and trauma: Intervention and treatment* (pp. 11–46). New York, NY: Guilford Press.

Lewis, M. L., Noroña, C. R., McConnico, N., & Thomas, K. (2013). Colorism, a legacy of historical trauma in parent-child relationships: Clinical, research, and personal perspectives. *Zero to Three, 34*(2), pp. 11–23.

Liu, L. L., & Lau, A. S. (2013). Teaching about race/ethnicity and racism matters: An examination of how perceived ethnic racial socialization processes are associated with depression symptoms. *Cultural Diversity and Ethnic Minority Psychology, 19*(4), 383–394. doi:10.1037/a0033447

Mandela, N. R. (1994). *A long walk to freedom: The autobiography of Nelson Mandela*. Boston, MA: Little, Brown & Company.

Mcgill, R. K., Hughes, D., Alicea, S., & Way, N. (2012). Academic adjustment across middle school: The role of public regard and parenting. *Developmental Psychology, 48*(4), 1003–1018. doi:10.1037/a0026006

Minuchin, P., Colapinto, J., & Minuchin, S. (1998). *Working with families of the poor.* New York, NY: Guilford Press.

Murry, V. M., Berkel, C., Brody, G. H., Miller, S. J., & Chen, Y. (2009). Linking parental socialization to interpersonal protective processes, academic self-presentation, and expectations among rural African American youth. *Cultural Diversity and Ethnic Minority Psychology, 15*(1), 1–10. doi:10.1037/a0013180

Neblett, E. W., Banks, K. H., Cooper, S. M., & Smalls-Glover, C. (2013). Racial identity mediates the association between ethnic-racial socialization and depressive symptoms. *Cultural Diversity and Ethnic Minority Psychology, 19*(2), 200–207. doi:10.1037/a0032205

Neblett, E. W., Jr., Philip, C. L., Cogburn, C. D., & Sellers, R. M. (2006). African American adolescents' discrimination experiences and academic achievement: Racial socialization as a cultural compensatory and protective factor. *Journal of Black Psychology, 32*(2), 199–218. doi:10.1177/0095798406287072

Neblett, E. W., Jr., Rivas-Drake, D., & Umaña-Taylor, A. J. (2012). The promise of racial and ethnic protective factors in promoting ethnic minority youth development. *Child Development Perspectives, 6*(3), 295–303. doi:10.1111/j.1750-8606.2012.00239.x

Peck, S. C., Brodish, A. B., Malanchuk, O., Banerjee, M., & Eccles, J. S. (2014). Racial/ethnic socialization and identity development in black families: The role of parent and youth reports. *Developmental Psychology, 50*(7), 1897–1909. doi:10.1037/a0036800

SAMHSA. (2016). *The national tribal behavioral health agenda* (National Tribal Public Health Summit, Rep.). Retrieved from https://store.samhsa.gov/shin/content//PEP16-NTBH-AGENDA/PEP16-NTBH-AGENDA.pdf

Schwab, G. (2010). *Haunting legacies: Violent histories and transgenerational trauma*. New York. Columbia University Press.

Sotero, M. (2006). A conceptual model of historical trauma: Implications for public health practice and research. *Journal of Health Disparities Research and Practice, 1*(1), 93–108.

Suizzo, M., Robinson, C., & Pahlke, E. (2008). African American mothers socialization beliefs and goals with young children. *Journal of Family Issues, 29*(3), 287–316. doi:10.1177/0192513x07308368

Super, C. M., & Harkness, S. (1997). The cultural structuring of child development. In J. W. Berry, P. R. Dasen, & T. S. Saraswathi (Eds.), *Handbook of cross-cultural psychology* (2nd ed.), *Vol. 2: Basic processes and human development* (pp. 1–39). Boston, MA: Allyn & Bacon.

Thomas, A. J., & Blackmon, S. M. (2014). The influence of the Trayvon Martin shooting on racial socialization practices of African American parents. *Journal of Black Psychology, 41*(1), 75–89. doi:10.1177/0095798414563610

Tuwe, K. (2016). The African oral tradition paradigm of storytelling as a methodological framework: Employment experiences for African communities in New Zealand. In *Proceedings of the 38th AFSAAP Conference: 21st Century Tensions and Transformation in Africa,* Deakin University, October 28–30, 2015.

Wang, M., & Huguley, J. P. (2012). Parental racial socialization as a moderator of the effects of racial discrimination on educational success among African American adolescents. *Child Development, 83*(5), 1716–1731. doi:10.1111/j.1467-8624.2012.01808.x

Wardi, D. (1990). *The memorial candles: Dialogues with children of Holocaust survivors.* Jerusalem: Keter (in Hebrew)

White-Johnson, R. L., Ford, K. R., & Sellers, R. M. (2010). Parental racial socialization profiles: Association with demographic factors, racial discrimination, childhood socialization, and racial identity. *Cultural Diversity and Ethnic Minority Psychology, 16*(2), 237–247. doi:10.1037/a0016111

Wilkins, N., Tsao, B., Hertz, M., Davis, R., & Klevens, J. (2014). *Connecting the dots: An overview of the links among multiple forms of violence.* Atlanta, GA: National Center for Injury Prevention and Control, Centers for Disease Control and Prevention. Oakland, CA: Prevention Institute.

CHAPTER 3

Resilience in the Context of Violence and Trauma

Promotive and Protective Processes of Positive Caregiving

Angela J. Narayan and Ann S. Masten

For decades, child psychologists and developmental scientists have emphasized the primary role of caregivers in shielding children from the harmful effects of adversities, including maltreatment, violence victimization, and exposure to large-scale atrocities such as war and disasters (e.g., Gewirtz, Forgatch, & Weiling, 2008; Masten & Narayan, 2012; Rutter, 1987). Historically and currently in the resilience literature, positive caregiving practices have been deemed among the most critical factors that protect children from harm and promote positive adjustment despite exposure to severe adversity (Luthar, Crossman, & Small, 2015; Masten, Narayan, Silverman, & Osofsky, 2015; Wright, Masten, & Narayan, 2013). Universal aspects of positive caregiving, such as warmth and acceptance, appear to function as fundamental indicators of resilience in ways not explained by sociodemographic advantages, such as better education, more money, or place of residence (Masten, 2001; Narayan, 2015). These basic features of high-quality care serve to organize and maintain healthy adjustment and well-being in children at multiple levels, including neurodevelopmental, cognitive, emotional, and behavioral functioning (Bowlby, 1969/1982; Cicchetti, 2010; Sroufe, Egeland, Carlson, & Collins, 2005).

This chapter highlights common yet classic patterns of resilience supported by empirical accounts of positive caregiving practices in action during child exposure to violence and trauma, with a focus on direct maltreatment of children (physical, sexual, and emotional abuse and neglect of children, as well as physical/corporal punishment), exposure to family conflict and violence (verbal and psychological conflict in addition to physical and sexual aggression), exposure to community violence (witnessing of and victimization by crime), exposure to war (experiencing armed conflict or terrorism, serving as a child soldier, and viewing media coverage of war), and exposure to natural disasters (earthquakes, floods, tornadoes, hurricanes, tsunamis, and wildfires). Prior comprehensive reviews have noted the role of parenting practices and parent–child relationships following child exposure to violence and trauma; however, these reviews have encompassed a broader range of adversities (e.g., poverty, homelessness, parental psychopathology; Labella & Masten, 2017; Luthar et al., 2015; Masten & Cicchetti, 2016), or a broader range of caregiving, including negative parenting (Gewirtz et al., 2008; Howell, 2011; Masten & Narayan, 2012). Here, we provide a focal review that specifically delineates pathways of resilience characterized by positive aspects of caregiving or interpersonal relationships that foster children's adaptive development in contexts of maltreatment and exposure to violence in families, communities, and societies. We focus on this question: How does positive caregiving protect child development in the context of violence and trauma?

There are several reasons for the specific focus on caregiving processes associated with resilience. Targeted reviews on the promotive and protective role of caregiving in specific types of child adversities are scarce (Narayan, 2015). Another compelling reason for the emphasis on positive caregiving processes is because parent–child dyads, families, and communities are often implicated and endangered during the types of violence and trauma covered here, making the protective functions of caregiving capacity all the more important (Narayan & Masten, 2012; Wright et al., 2013). Thus, in addition to focusing specifically on caregiving processes linked to resilience, we also include support from relatives, nonbiological kin, and larger communities in addition to biological parents. The chapter concludes by extending the discussion of positive caregiving practices in resilience to the prenatal period. Case examples highlight how pregnant women may draw on childhood memories of positive experiences with caregivers, despite severe childhood adversities, to avert transmission of risk to offspring in the next generation.

Definitions of Resilience and Prevalence of Violence and Trauma

Variations in definitions of resilience and the types of processes associated with resilient pathways have evolved over time (Luthar et al., 2015; Masten, 2001; Rutter, 1987). We endorse a systems definition of resilience that can be applied in many fields of science and practice, including studies of resilience in systems at the level of individuals, families, communities, health systems, emergency and other social service systems, and ecological systems (Masten, 2014a, 2014b). Resilience refers to the capacity of a system to adapt successfully to challenges threatening its function, well-being, or future, through processes that draw on resources and relationships inside and outside the system (Masten, 2011, 2014a, 2014b; Masten & Cicchetti, 2016). The results of resilience processes in the lives of individual children are manifested when we observe pathways of positive adaptation and recovery in the aftermath of challenging experiences, including violence and trauma (Masten, Best, & Garmezy, 1990; Masten & Narayan, 2012). Observations of "manifested resilience" require not only that an individual is functioning well, but also that he or she was exposed to a significant threat to health or well-being (Luthar, Cicchetti, & Becker, 2000; Masten, 2001). In contrast, observations of manifested *competence*, reflecting positive adaptation or development by specified criteria, do not require exposure to risk or challenges (Wright et al., 2013).

A key aim of this chapter is to specify the type of processes—e.g., promotive and protective—by which caregiving behaviors or relationships may account for resilient outcomes. *Promotive factors* are associated with better child development or adjustment in contexts of violence or trauma, regardless of the level of risk. These factors may indicate adaptive processes that promote good outcomes under wide-ranging circumstances, including advantaged or low-risk environments. Typically, promotive factors are identified by statistical main effects. In contrast, *protective factors* refer to apparent moderators of risk that suggest buffering processes, with greater significance when risk levels are high. Statistical interactions suggest the possibility of moderating functions indicative of protective factors

(Masten & Cicchetti, 2016; Masten & Narayan, 2012; Narayan, 2015; Sameroff, 2000). Because of the specific emphasis here on contexts in which some type of adversity in the form of violence or trauma exposure is present, it is important to consider how processes by which parenting functions to shield children may differ by severity of exposure (Rutter, 1987).

Over the decades, one of the most consistent findings that emerged from quantitative as well as case studies on resilience in development was the observably high prevalence of resilience pathways even among individuals exposed to severe adversity (Masten, 2001; Masten & Narayan, 2012). This observation is particularly striking given the prevalence rates of violence and trauma documented in the literature. It also continues to be apparent in present day.

Rates of Maltreatment

Globally, millions of children experience maltreatment and exposure to violence on any given day. The Center for Disease Control and Prevention (CDC) recently estimated that approximately 1 billion children, half of the children on the planet, experience maltreatment each year, including emotional/verbal, physical, and sexual abuse (CDC, 2016a). According to the CDC's Violence against Children Survey (VACs; CDC, 2016a), between 22 and 73 percent of children ages 0–18 experienced physical abuse alone in the non-U.S. countries surveyed, with prevalence rates likely tied to factors such as developed versus developing country, cultural and societal norms, and urban versus rural region. In 2014 in the United States alone, Child Protection Services (CPS) received reports of maltreatment for almost three-quarters of a million children; however, it is estimated that as many as one in four total U.S. children experience some type of abuse or neglect throughout childhood and adolescence (CDC, 2016b).

Rates of Exposure to Intimate Partner Violence

Rough estimates in U.S. prevalence rates of direct maltreatment and children's exposure to intimate partner violence (IPV) seem to be comparable. The National Survey of Children's Exposure to Violence (NatSCEV; Hamby, Finkelhor, Turner, & Ormrod, 2011) approximated a 25.6 percent lifetime exposure rate of IPV in U.S. children ages 0–17. Here, IPV included both verbal and psychological violence, such as breaking, punching, throwing things, and threatening physical harm or property destruction, in addition to physical violence, defined as observations of parents, parents and siblings, or adult relatives pushing, hitting, slapping, and choking each other. Moreover, the 2011 NatSCEV found that approximately 11.7 percent of children had directly witnessed an assault to one of their parents (Hamby et al., 2011).

Rates of Exposure to Community Violence

Accurate estimates of youth exposure to community violence in the United States are difficult, as these experiences include being directly involved in gang and gun violence or victimized by robbery and mugging, hearing gunshots, and being indirectly affected (e.g., losing a family member to homicide) from crime and violence in neighborhoods and communities. In 2008, the NatSCEV reported that 19.2 percent of youth ages 0–17 witnessed an assault in their community (Finkelhor, Turner, Ormrod, Hamby, & Kracke, 2009). Furthermore, a CDC survey on youth's direct involvement in violence found that almost one-third (32.8%) of U.S. high school–aged youth (ages 0–19) had been in a physical fight in the last year, and 16.6 percent of youth indicated that at least once in the past month they had carried a weapon, such as a knife, gun, or club (CDC, 2016c).

Rates of Exposure to War and Disaster

Rates of youth exposure to global violence, including terrorism, war, and armed conflict, are also exceedingly high and continually rising. In 2011, the United Nations (UN) estimated that conflict and disasters forcibly displaced approximately 14 million children (UN, 2014), and by 2015, it was estimated that 1 in 10 children lived in regions with ongoing armed conflict (UNICEF, 2015). Additionally, as of 2013 global estimates of child soldiers ranged from 250,000 to 300,000 (UNICEF, 2013). Furthermore, thousands of children are born directly exposed to the consequences of war, displacement, and deprivation. UNICEF reported that in 2015, approximately 70,000 children were born to parents living in refugee camps (UNICEF, 2015).

Global estimates of children's exposure specifically to disasters are also quite high. In 2011, the UNICEF estimated that up to 175 million children experienced some consequence of disasters (UNICEF, 2011a). Typically, these include direct exposure, displacement, or material or emotional loss (Masten & Narayan, 2012). During 2011, there were estimated to be approximately 1 billion children living in regions deemed "high seismic risk" for earthquakes (UNICEF, 2011b). Taken together with the above rates of exposure to war, UNICEF estimated that as of 2016, 535,000 million children (approximately one in four children globally) live in regions characterized or affected by disaster or armed conflict (UNICEF, 2016).

Overview of Promotive and Protective Caregiving in the Context of Violence and Trauma

The following review provides a summary of existing research on positive caregiving practices, parent–child relationships, and extrafamilial (e.g., kin, community) supports associated with resilient patterns of child development in contexts of violence and trauma. Studies indicate that caregiver-specific factors, such as extent of parental exposure, distress, and symptomatology, are so important for child functioning that they often partially or even fully mediate the effects of children's exposure on child outcomes. For example, children in grades 4 through 12 had a higher likelihood of developing symptoms of anxiety or depression following the 9/11 attacks, not only if they themselves were directly exposed but also if they had a parent or family member who was exposed (Hoven et al., 2005). Similar findings were observed following disasters. The link between exposure to an earthquake and four- to five-year-old preschoolers' distress was fully mediated by parental distress for boys and partially mediated for girls (Proctor et al., 2007). These findings underscore the salience of parental function for children experiencing trauma (Gewirtz et al., 2008; Masten & Narayan, 2012). Explanatory processes include the general importance of parenting for child adaptation and the role of social referencing by parents, in which children look to their caregivers for cues about the danger of situations.

These patterns also pertain to more proximal family violence and emphasize the potency of parental psychological functioning for child functioning above and beyond the parent–child relationship. For mothers victimized by IPV and preschoolers exposed to it, mothers' posttraumatic stress disorder (PTSD) symptoms were a more robust mediator of maternal total life stress exposure and child total behavioral problems than the quality of the mother–child relationship (Lieberman, Van Horn, & Ozer, 2005b). How a parent functions following exposure to trauma is critical to child well-being and often directly portends child outcomes (Masten, 2001).

While the review in this chapter is not exhaustive due to space constraints, our goal is to illustrate evidence for a range of caregiving and relational resilience processes in action. Importantly, in line with previous conceptualizations of resilient functioning, we define positive outcomes as those that reflect higher levels of positive child behaviors or manifest functioning, as well as lower levels of child symptoms or impairments (Masten, 2001; Narayan, 2015). As much as possible, we have specified the subtype of violence or trauma in question (e.g., which subtype of maltreatment the child experienced, whether the youth witnessed or was directly victimized by community violence), the ages of children under investigation, if findings were sex-specific, and the particular child outcomes that were assessed. We have also strived to specify whether promotive or protective processes were involved and describe the characteristics of the caregiving behaviors, relationships, or external supports underlying these processes. Finally, we have acknowledged examples when expected or hypothesized positive effects of caregiving or relationships were tested but not found to be significant.

Maltreatment

Several studies conducted on samples of children who have been maltreated or experienced corporal punishment indicate the protective or buffering effects of positive parenting for child adjustment. In school-aged children (ages 7–10) who had experienced physical, sexual, or emotional abuse or neglect, children's more secure perceptions of relatedness with mothers, including better emotional quality and closeness, buffered the association between maltreatment and children's emotion regulation difficulties (Alink, Cicchetti, Kim, & Rogosch, 2009). Similarly, higher levels of maternal sensitivity protected very young children (ages 1–3) who had received mothers' commanding and physical discipline from heightened levels of aggression (Alink et al., 2008). Evidence also suggests the importance of the interplay of positive and negative parenting behaviors for positive child adjustment. In a study of parenting in eight countries (China, Colombia, Italy, Jordan, Kenya, Philippines, Thailand, and the United States), higher levels of maternal warmth buffered the association between corporal punishment and children's anxiety and aggression levels, unless corporal punishment was also high, in which case children displayed higher levels of anxiety (Lansford et al., 2014). All three of these studies emphasize that protective qualities of positive caregiving can work in tandem with, and for some child outcomes, even compensate for, negative, physical, or maltreating parenting behaviors.

Studies have also emphasized the role of paternal and extended kin in buffering or deterring effects of maltreatment, as well as the long-term effects of positive parenting. Maternal as well as paternal warmth buffered fifth- and sixth-grade children from the effects of harsh physical discipline on children's internalizing problems (McKee et al., 2007). In a longitudinal sample of children at high risk for maltreatment, several of whom already had documented physical and sexual abuse and neglect, more support during early childhood (ages 0–64 months), including higher quantity, quality, and more consistent interactions with a second caregiver (usually the biological father, a grandparent, or other relatives), was directly associated with (promotive of) lower levels of teacher-rated internalizing and externalizing behaviors in first grade (Appleyard, Egeland, van Dulmen, & Sroufe, 2005). In the same longitudinal study, higher levels of maternal sensitivity during toddlerhood predicted greater academic achievement (e.g., better reading and math performance across grade school) and higher educational attainment, even into early adulthood (Sroufe et al., 2005). In another large sample of children followed to adulthood, children who were maltreated but perceived either parent as caring had lower levels of psychopathology (e.g., mood, anxiety, eating, or substance use disorders) in adulthood (Collishaw et al., 2007). In both of these longitudinal studies, aspects of parenting were promotive of better school and psychological functioning even many years later.

Exposure to IPV

In contexts of child exposure to IPV, both promotive and protective effects of positive caregiving have been documented. Following episodes of escalating conflict between parents, including verbal and physical aggression, parents' sensitivity and supportiveness buffered 8–12-year-old children's self-blame (DeBoard-Lucas, Fosco, Raynor, & Grych, 2010). Similar with maltreatment, however, the interplay of positive and negative caregiving continued to be important. For the same children, parents' punitive, dismissive, and coercive behaviors toward children directly related to children's higher self-blame following parental conflicts (DeBoard-Lucas et al., 2010). Buffering effects of positive caregiving were also found in other studies of younger children. Parenting of 5-year-old children characterized by high levels of warmth, scaffolding, and praise completely buffered children with heightened parental conflict from greater observed negative affect with peers and behavioral problems in school three years later. Parenting that was also stronger in meta-emotion (awareness and coaching of emotions) completely buffered these children's negative affect with peers and academic difficulties at age 8 (Katz & Gottman, 1997). Similar protective effects in specific contexts of parental physical aggression were observed for parental warmth as a buffer of 7–9-year-olds' externalizing problems (Skopp, McDonald, Jouriles, & Rosenfield, 2007).

Relationships with fathers were also effective in the case of parental conflict, as they were in contexts of maltreatment. Fourteen to 19-year-old adolescents with greater closeness to mothers reported lower perceptions of threat following parental conflicts, whereas adolescents with greater closeness to fathers reported lower self-blame (Grych, Raynor, & Fosco, 2004). Closeness to either parent directly and uniquely promoted adolescent adjustment.

These promotive and protective patterns held in increasingly violent and impoverished contexts. Homeless parents who were warmer toward preschool-age children buffered children's peer relations in school despite verbal aggression and physical violence at home (Narayan, Sapienza, Monn, Lingras, & Masten, 2015). Here, warmth exerted a risk-activated protective effect (Masten, 2001), such that as the level of IPV rose, parents' warmth also seemed to increase to predict better peer relations in a subset of kids exposed to the most severe violence (Narayan et al., 2015). Two other studies found promotive rather than protective effects of positive caregiving in families who had all been exposed to IPV. Mothers with more positive observed relationship quality during play had two to five-year-old preschoolers with lower internalizing and externalizing problems (Lieberman et al., 2005b). Similarly, mothers who displayed more positive involvement, as well as less inconsistent or corporal punishment, had four- to six-year-old preschoolers with better emotional regulation and prosocial skills (Howell, Graham-Bermann, Czyz, & Lilly, 2010).

Exposure to Community Violence

In contexts of community violence, including witnessing and being a victim of crime, the protective role of positive caregiving has emerged more frequently than the promotive role across a range of youth ages and often in both sexes. One study did report sex-specific findings pertaining to the positive role of male youth's perceived support from parents. Middle school-aged males (grades six to eight) who perceived greater parental social support were buffered from the effects of witnessing community violence (but not from the effects of being directly victimized by it) on subsequently perpetrating physical violence themselves (Brookmeyer, Henrich, & Schwab-Stone, 2005). Protective effects specific to witnessing but not being a victim of community violence were also found in another study. Higher levels of parental monitoring buffered the effects of witnessing community violence (but not being victimized by it) on older adolescents' (ages 16–19) depression and anxiety symptoms. Alternatively, however, higher levels of monitoring were effective in buffering the effects of direct victimization of community violence, but for a different outcome. Both male and female adolescents had lower antisocial behavior if they had high levels of parental monitoring despite being victims of community violence (Bacchini, Miranda, & Affuso, 2011).

Similar findings emerged for younger adolescents. For both males and females, more positive family functioning characterized by higher cohesion, structure, and positive parenting behavior protected both younger and older adolescents (ages 11–21) from perpetrating physical violence if they had either witnessed or been a victim of violence or who had a family member who had been attacked, robbed, injured, or had died from violence (Gorman-Smith, Henry, & Tolan, 2004). Finally, higher levels of 9–13-year-old male and females' perceived acceptance from caregivers buffered them from elevated internalizing symptoms following experiences of witnessing and being victimized by community violence, but only when violence was at low to moderate levels (Kliewer et al., 2004). This latter finding illustrates a protective-reactive effect, whereby the protective effect becomes less effective when the level of risk surpasses a particularly (high) range (Luthar et al., 2000).

War and Disaster

In global contexts of youth exposure to violence and armed conflict, parenting shows similar protective effects as discussed earlier in this chapter for exposure to community violence. For instance, higher levels of positive caregiving practices, including more effective discipline, buffered the association between 8 and 14-year-olds' exposure to ethnopolitical violence in Israel and Palestine, and their subsequent PTSD symptoms (Dubow et al., 2012). These effects extended to youth activism in the conflict, in addition to youth exposure. For 11–12-year-old Palestinian youth, higher levels of traumatic event exposure were associated with higher levels of political activism, which in turn were associated with poorer psychological adjustment; however, higher levels of positive parenting, such as parental affection and parent–child intimacy, attenuated the association between greater activism and maladjustment (Punamäki, Qouta, & El Sarraj, 1997). Similarly, both male and female 14-year-old youth who reported high levels of parental acceptance were protected from the negative effects of activism in the Palestinian Intifada on antisocial behavior and depressive symptoms (Barber, 2001).

In addition to protective effects of parenting during war and armed conflict, several studies documented promotive effects, particularly pertaining to aspects of children and adolescents' perceived coping ability and support from families and communities. Illustrating a direct promotive effect of social support, adolescents aged 12–16 years who reported higher levels of perceived support from parents were less likely to have a diagnosis of PTSD following exposure to violence and conflict in the Gaza Strip (Thabet, Ibraheem, Shivram, Winter, & Vostanis, 2009). For 15-year-old youth, higher levels of adolescent-reported coping advice from their parents, including positive reframing, emotional expression, acceptance, planning, and help-seeking, were promotive factors for adolescents' lower levels of distress following direct or indirect exposure (e.g., media coverage) to the 9/11 attacks (Gil-Rivas, Silver, Holman, McIntosh, & Poulin, 2007). Importantly, direct advice from parents about strategies to cope was the "active ingredient" here. Adolescents who perceived their parents as supportive but avoidant of discussions (e.g., because of worry about upsetting youth) reported higher levels of distress in the months following the attacks. These "active ingredients" appear to change across contexts and, at times, have different effects for fathers versus mothers. In another study, higher levels of perceived parental support from fathers, but not mothers, were associated with higher levels of 15-year-olds' positive affect one year after the World Trade Center attacks (Gil-Rivas, Holman, & Silver, 2004).

Family support and direct communication are also helpful for younger children's postconflict adjustment. Lebanese preschool children aged three to six years who were exposed to high levels of shelling attacks but who had a more supportive family environment had lower levels of behavioral problems (Zahr, 1996). For younger children in particular, media exposure to coverage of war and terrorism has potential to be very harmful and distressing because young children may mistakenly view repetitive news coverage and perceive the events as recurring (Masten et al., 2015). However, for two- to six-year-olds who were indirectly exposed to the 9/11 attacks via media coverage, higher levels of family expressiveness were associated with lower levels of PTSD symptoms in preschoolers (Otto et al., 2007).

In addition to supportiveness and coping advice from nuclear families, extended support from peers and communities had promotive effects during exposure to war and involvement as a child soldier. For example, higher levels of perceived support from peers, in addition to parents, were promotive factors for lower depression in 15–19-year-olds following exposure to the war in Sarajevo (Duraković-Belko, Kulenović, & Dapić, 2003). For youth returning to their communities following serving as child soldiers, higher levels of family connectedness and social support were directly associated with lower levels of emotional distress and better psychological and social well-being (Annan, Blattman, & Horton, 2006). Illustrating the promotive role of the broader community, higher levels of community acceptance were associated with lower levels of depression in 10–18-year-old returning child soldiers from Sierra Leone (Betancourt et al., 2010).

Regarding exposure to natural disasters, promotive patterns of caregiving that emphasize parent and family support mirror findings from the literature on war and armed conflict. Mothers' more positive relationship quality with adolescents was directly associated with lower levels of PTSD and depression symptoms in families exposed to the Thailand tsunami (Wickrama & Kaspar, 2007). Furthermore, for children in grades 7–12 exposed to a wildfire in Greece, higher levels of social support, including from parents, were associated with lower levels of children's PTSD and depression symptoms (Papadatou et al., 2012). Finally, one study tested promotive versus protective factors against each other to understand specific mechanisms at play. While greater perceived family support in youth in grades 3–12 exposed to Hurricane Katrina was directly associated with lower levels of youth depression, illustrating promotive effects, the protective (moderating) role of family social support was not significant (Banks & Weems, 2014).

Summary of Findings on Positive Caregiving in the Context of Violence and Trauma

Collectively, the findings reveal several compelling and overarching patterns regarding the processes and mechanisms associated with child resilience following maltreatment and exposure to various types of violence, war, and disaster. A striking observation across several of these contexts is that aspects of positive caregiving or parent–child relationships may often compensate or "make up for" the effects of substantial contemporaneous adversity. For instance, following maltreatment or corporal punishment, parents who displayed positive behaviors, such as sensitivity and warmth, and who prioritized closeness, often had children with better adjustment (e.g., less anxiety or aggression) even when the maltreatment or physical punishment may have come from the same parents (Alink et al., 2008, 2009). Similarly, following parental conflict, parents who in turn were able to show sensitivity, warmth, and awareness of child emotions were able to protect children against self-blame and maladjustment at school (DeBoard-Lucas et al., 2010; Katz & Gottman, 1997). Compensating patterns were also observed for mothers whose positive involvement and effective discipline helped to promote young children's better behavioral, emotional, and peer skills following maternal victimization by IPV (Howell et al., 2010; Lieberman et al., 2005b).

Importantly, however, negative or harsh parenting that co-occurred with warm or sensitive parenting seemed to undo or negate these positive effects on children (DeBoard-Lucas et al., 2010; Lansford et al., 2014). Often times, other caregivers, including fathers or extended kin, were able to step in and promote or protect children's positive adjustment (Appleyard et al., 2005; McKee et al., 2007). These findings indicate that even though maltreatment or violence may occur in the home, having at least one parent who is supportive or reliable may be associated with higher potential for child resilience (Collishaw et al., 2007). Broadly, these findings underscore that childhood adversity and supportive assets are often relatively orthogonal, with support able to offset the long-term effects of adversity on maladaptation (Narayan, Rivera, Bernstein, Harris, & Lieberman, 2018).

In contexts of child exposure to violence outside the home, such as in the community or during political conflict, a remarkable pattern emerged regarding the potential for positive caregiving to buffer youth from engaging in violence or aggression themselves. In several studies on community violence, aspects of positive parenting, such as greater support, better monitoring, and more cohesion and structure protected youth with exposure to community violence from perpetrating physical violence themselves or engaging in antisocial behavior (Bacchini et al., 2011; Brookmeyer et al., 2005; Gorman-Smith et al., 2004). Importantly, however, these protective caregiving processes varied in strength depending on whether youth had witnessed community violence or had been directly victimized by it, indicating the unique interplay of caregiving with different types of exposure. Barber (2001) also reported that parental acceptance was an effective buffer against youth's higher antisocial behavior following Intifada activism. Taken together, it is very promising to note that aspects of positive caregiving in these extremely adverse contexts might be particularly effective for buffering cycles of violence perpetration and antisocial behavior from continuing.

Another key theme observed was the general effectiveness of perceived support from family, as well as peers and the broader community, in both promoting and protecting child and adolescent adjustment following maltreatment, community violence, and exposure to war and terrorism (e.g., Annan et al., 2006; Appleyard et al., 2005; Brookmeyer et al., 2005; Duraković-Belko et al., 2003). Broadly, these findings suggest that biological parents or nuclear families are not the only ecological systems that can foster the positive well-being of youth following severe adversity. Some findings also went further to suggest that aspects of parents' direct ability to facilitate youth's emotional communication and coping strategies may be particularly helpful for youth's psychological well-being, while parents' passive support in the absence of acknowledging or discussing traumatic experiences may be counterproductive (Gil-Rivas et al., 2007). Generally, these promising findings on social support encourage further consideration of broader ecological systems that encompass youth, as well as continued search for "active ingredients" that promote or protect youth's well-being.

Finally, it is crucial to weigh the observation that several studies expecting promotive or protective effects of positive caregiving in contexts of violence or trauma did not find them. For example, two studies on preschoolers' exposure to IPV did not find that more positive or effective parenting moderated or mediated the effects of exposure and positive socioemotional adjustment (Levendosky, Huth-Bocks, Shapiro, & Semel, 2003; Martinez-Torteya, Anne Bogat, Von Eye, & Levendosky, 2009). Furthermore, another study failed to find that either parental or peer support buffered emotional functioning in 11–16-year-olds following witnessing or victimization by community violence (Jain, Buka, Subramanian, & Molnar, 2012). Finally, neither 12–16-year-old youth's perceptions of more parental support nor less harsh discipline from parents differentiated youth's PTSD symptoms following exposure to the Palestinian conflict (Khamis, 2015). Notably, each of these findings is directly contrary to the main themes discussed here regarding the compensating role of positive caregiving or support. However, together, they serve as an important reminder of the complexities not only in how distinct aspects of parenting affect children differently depending on age, developmental stage, cultural factors, and many other influences but also of the complexities regarding the nature, severity, and unique features of the exposure itself (Masten & Narayan, 2012).

Furthermore, caregiving behaviors that have positive intentions might not actually have positive effects. This is evident in findings of adolescent distress when supportive parents did not openly discuss the 9/11 attacks for fear of upsetting the youth (Gil-Rivas et al., 2007). In another study, adolescents of mothers who were too protective following a flood in Poland had higher PTSD symptoms (Bokszczanin, 2008). More work is needed to sharpen these findings; determine other "active ingredients" in positive caregiving across different types of exposures, cultures, and ages of youth; and clarify why certain types of positively intentioned parenting might not actually be effective.

Prenatal Protective Processes for Resilience in Contexts of Violence and Trauma

The studies described in this chapter reflect several promotive and protective processes for youth resilience in contexts of violence and trauma for children ranging in developmental stages from early childhood to late adolescence. Notably, very few studies have focused on infancy, with the earliest ages of children under investigation at approximately one to two years old (Alink et al., 2008; Lieberman et al., 2005b). Moreover, no studies examined promotive or protective processes that might be present during the prenatal period. How might this be accomplished?

One method to assess protective processes during pregnancy is to assess pregnant women's memories of positive, loving, or supportive experiences with childhood caregivers that occurred amid violence or trauma. These positive memories have been conceptualized by Lieberman and her colleagues (Lieberman, Padrón, Van Horn, & Harris, 2005a) in terms of "angels in the nursery" because they serve to help parents with histories of childhood trauma and violence to recreate positive moments of loving care with their offspring. These positive memories are hypothesized to offset the negative effects of "ghosts in the nursery." The latter negative memories represent lingering emotions of fear and rage from childhood experiences of trauma and violence that are redirected toward the self, unconsciously carried forward to the next generation, and reenacted with children (Fraiberg, Adelson, & Shapiro, 1975; Lieberman et al., 2005a).

Angels in the nursery (nicknamed "angel memories") were initially recognized in clinical work with parents and preschoolers exposed to IPV. Several victimized mothers reported drawing on childhood memories of love, protection, and safety that served as guiding lights amid the victimization and helped them to maintain warmth and sensitivity with their young children (Lieberman et al., 2005a).

Angel memories are assessed using a brief, semistructured, audiorecorded interview ("Angels in the Nursery Interview") that asks traumatized parents to "think of a time when you were little when you felt especially loved, understood, or safe" (Van Horn, Lieberman, & Harris, 2008). Several standardized prompts follow to gather details about the memory, including associated sensory experiences (e.g., sights, smells, sounds, or other sensations connected to the memory), ages during which the memory occurred, and secondary memories with other caregivers. Responses are later coded by trained raters for memory quality, with higher scores reflecting memories that are more specific, elaborated with details, and that link sensory details or concrete emotions (e.g., feeling loved, protected, comforted) to the experiences described. The following case examples illustrate the salience of these angel memories for pregnant mothers who have experienced childhood maltreatment, exposure to violence, and natural disasters.

Jessica

Jessica's angel memories were assessed during a clinical research study on intergenerational pathways of risk and resilience through the prenatal period (Narayan, Rivera, et al., 2017). Jessica was 23 years old and pregnant with her second child. During the life events portion of the study interview, Jessica described a childhood characterized by maternal, emotional, and physical maltreatment; paternal abandonment; and community violence exposure, including several relatives' homicides from gang-related activity. In response to the opening prompt on the Angels Interview about feeling loved, understood, or safe, Jessica responded, "My grandma shared a room with me for a few years when I was seven or eight. She was always there for me when my parents were not. On Sundays if we couldn't make it to church because it was raining or it was too cold, we would just have church in our room and she would be the pastor. We would listen to gospel music, and she would read the Bible to us. I remember feeling warm and cozy as I cuddled with her under the blankets." Jessica's response would receive a high score on angel memory quality because it is not only specific and elaborated, but it is also accompanied by the sensory experience of feeling physically warm.

In the latter portion of the Angels Interview, parents are asked to describe how they would use these childhood positive memories to sustain them or help them as they raise their own children. These questions are meant to directly elicit positive caregiving strategies rooted in mothers' childhood memories that can be brought to conscious awareness and referenced during parenting. Jessica responded, "My grandma taught me how to parent. When I got home from the hospital with my first daughter, she showed me how to help my daughter latch and breastfeed, bathe her gently, and change her diapers. My mom wanted me to have an abortion; she thought I was too young, but my grandma supported me in my decision to have the baby. I always think about the Bible, how the Pharaoh had all the babies dumped in the water, but Moses was the only one who was saved. My grandma used to call my older daughter 'Moses' up until the day my grandma died because my daughter made it through the 'Pharaoh' my mom was trying to be. Even though my grandma is not with me anymore, I still remember everything she taught me about being a good mother, so this new baby will benefit from that."

Samantha

As part of the same clinical research study, Samantha, age 29, completed the Angels Interview while pregnant for the first time. In her angel memory narrative, she described two different memories, one of which occurred in the context of childhood exposure to a natural disaster, the 1989 San Francisco earthquake. Similar to Jessica, Samantha experienced parental abandonment, in this case, by her mother. During the Angels Interview, she said, "I remember playing in my championship soccer game and my dad was yelling and cheering on the sidelines. He would always run down the field as I raced towards the goal. To this day I can still hear him cheering for me in my head. He was always there for me." Then, during the prompt about secondary memories, she said, "I also distinctly remember what happened right after the '89 earthquake. My dad was a mechanic so he was under his truck working on it when the earthquake started. I remember looking out the window as the house started shaking and I could see that his truck had fallen off the stand. I ran to the stairs to go make sure he was okay, but by the time I got to the top of the stairs, he was already coming up to get me." When asked about how she will use these memories to sustain her as she raises her baby, Samantha added, "I will always be there for my kid like my dad was for me. Always cheering for me, always alongside me knowing what I needed to feel safe and secure. I want my child to feel that way, too."

Summary of Case Examples

Both Jessica and Samantha's "angel memories" contain key elements that echo empirical findings described earlier in this chapter. For Jessica, the emotional support and physical guidance from an extended family member, her grandmother, were powerful, benevolent forces in promoting and shaping her positive parenting practices, despite enduring childhood maltreatment and abandonment from both of her biological parents, as well as community violence in her surrounding neighborhood. For Samantha, the consistency and support in daily activities, such as sports involvement, as well as the salient episodic memory of her father rescuing her during the earthquake and reassuring both of their safety, guided her goals to promote the same sense of support, love, and reassurance in with her new baby. Jessica and Samantha's responses reflect the enduring compensatory role that a second parent or extended family member can have in promoting resilience and protection against harm when one or both biological parents are the sources of pain and abuse. This is a common theme in many of the angel memory narratives and is often illustrated by responses such as: "I always felt safe with my mother; she protected and comforted me when my father was violent towards her, or when he was trying to take his anger out on me."

These narratives assessed with the Angels in the Nursery Interview suggest that positive memories may serve to protect against the intergenerational transmission of violence and trauma by countering negative memories that reenact painful childhood experiences. Preliminary empirical evidence indicates that higher quality angel memories buffer elevations in PTSD symptoms in mothers with childhood maltreatment histories (Narayan, Ghosh Ippen, Harris, & Lieberman, 2017). In the ongoing study of 101 pregnant women described previously (Narayan et al., 2017), the next step is to empirically test whether angel memories also have protective effects against the intergenerational transmission of negative or punitive caregiving.

Implications and Conclusions

Research and case examples reviewed in this chapter suggest several promising directions for future research, practice, and policy aiming to promote child resilience in contexts of violence and trauma. Further research is needed to sharpen understanding of the exact ways that promotive and protective processes of caregiving operate differently across different situations and ages. More studies are needed of children during the first year of life and also during the prenatal period.

Measurement improvements also are needed. A notable limitation in many of the aforementioned studies is the reliance on parental self-report to assess parenting practices or aspects of the parent–child relationship. Obvious biases pertaining to social desirability or state- or trait-related parental factors affecting self-reporting likely exist. Future studies should continue to employ objective methods to assess positive caregiving or relational processes, such as observational assessments of parenting or coder-rated methods from audio-recorded parental responses, as is done in the Angels Interview.

In terms of implications for practice, there are several highly effective, well-established parenting or parent–child relationship-focused interventions designed to promote child, parent, and family resilience following experiences of trauma and violence. Examples include Child Parent Psychotherapy (CPP) for parents and young children, including infants, toddlers, and preschoolers exposed to IPV, maltreatment, and community violence (Lieberman, Ghosh Ippen, & Van Horn, 2006; Toth, Maughan, Manly, Spagnola, & Cicchetti, 2002); Steps for Effective, Enjoyable

Parenting (STEEP) and the Attachment-Biobehavioral Catch-up (ABC), both of which are also for maltreated children and those in foster care (Dozier, Peloso, Lewis, Laurenceau, & Levine, 2008; Erickson & Egeland, 2004); a mother-child intervention to promote warmth and support in Bosnian refugee families with young children (Dybdahl, 2001); and several parent-focused interventions to promote positive parenting and effective discipline in families who have experienced violence and military deployment (Gewirtz et al., 2008). The field of implementation science continues to expand with growing knowledge on best scalable practices to access, understand, and disseminate interventions in violence-ridden environments, disaster-prone areas, and war zones.

It is our hope that the current evidence and progress will expand to include interventions for the prenatal period. Notably, there is clinical evidence to suggest that positive memories of traumatized mothers are malleable to treatment and may be more strongly recalled and retained with the help of pregnancy-focused interventions such as a perinatal adaption of CPP (Lieberman, Díaz, & Van Horn, 2009; Narayan, Oliver Bucio, Rivera, & Lieberman, 2016). Policy efforts should incorporate these findings not only to prioritize parenting, relational, and family-focused interventions for children following violence and trauma but also to consider the prenatal period as a window of opportunity. Prenatal development offers a promising window for interventions leading to positive parenting in the next generation. There are a wealth of exciting potential avenues for future research and translational work to be done with families exposed to maltreatment, victimization, war, and disasters. These opportunities offer reason for optimism that resilience can be facilitated despite severe and acute exposure to violence and trauma while also underscoring the importance and feasibility of striving to avert or mitigate adversity exposure.

References

Alink, L. R., Cicchetti, D., Kim, J., & Rogosch, F. A. (2009). Mediating and moderating processes in the relation between maltreatment and psychopathology: Mother-child relationship quality and emotion regulation. *Journal of Abnormal Child Psychology, 37*, 831–843.

Alink, L. R., Mesman, J., Van Zeijl, J., Stolk, M. N., Juffer, F., Bakermans-Kranenburg, M. J., . . . Koot, H. M. (2008). Maternal sensitivity moderates the relation between negative discipline and aggression in early childhood. *Social Development, 18*, 99–120.

Annan, J., Blattman, C., & Horton, R. (2006). *The state of youth and youth protection in Northern Uganda: Findings from the Survey of War Affected Youth* (pp. 1–89). Uganda: UNICEF.

Appleyard, K., Egeland, B., van Dulmen, M. H., & Sroufe, L. A. (2005). When more is not better: The role of cumulative risk in child behavior outcomes. *Journal of Child Psychology and Psychiatry, 46*, 235–245.

Bacchini, D., Miranda, M. C., & Affuso, G. (2011). Effects of parental monitoring and exposure to community violence on antisocial behavior and anxiety/depression among adolescents. *Journal of Interpersonal Violence, 26*, 269–292.

Banks, D. M., & Weems, C. F. (2014). Family and peer social support and their links to psychological distress among hurricane-exposed minority youth. *American Journal of Orthopsychiatry, 84*, 341.

Barber, B. K. (2001). Political violence, social integration, and youth functioning: Palestinian youth from the Intifada. *Journal of Community Psychology, 29*, 259–280.

Betancourt, T. S., Borisova, I. I., Williams, T. P., Brennan, R. T., Whitfield, T. H., De La Soudiere, M., . . . Gilman, S. E. (2010). Sierra Leone's former child soldiers: A follow-up study of psychosocial adjustment and community reintegration. *Child Development, 81*, 1077–1095.

Bokszczanin, A. (2008). Parental support, family conflict, and overprotectiveness: Predicting PTSD symptom levels of adolescents 28 months after a natural disaster. *Anxiety Stress and Coping, 21*, 325–335.

Bowlby, J. (1969/1982). *Attachment and loss: Vol. 1. Attachment*. New York, NY: Basic Books.

Brookmeyer, K. A., Henrich, C. C., & Schwab-Stone, M. (2005). Adolescents who witness community violence: Can parent support and prosocial cognitions protect them from committing violence? *Child Development, 76*, 917–929.

CDC. (2016a). *Towards a violence-free generation: Using science to fuel action and end violence against children*. Atlanta, GA. Retrieved from https://www.compassion.com/multimedia/violence-against-children.pdf

CDC. (2016b). Child abuse and neglect prevention. Atlanta, GA. Retrieved from https://www.cdc.gov/violenceprevention/childmaltreatment/index.html

CDC. (2016c). Youth violence. Atlanta, GA. Retrieved from https://www.cdc.gov/violenceprevention/youthviolence/index.html

Cicchetti, D. (2010). Resilience under conditions of extreme stress: A multilevel perspective. *World Psychiatry, 9*, 145–154.

Collishaw, S., Pickles, A., Messer, J., Rutter, M., Shearer, C., & Maughan, B. (2007). Resilience to adult psychopathology following childhood maltreatment: Evidence from a community sample. *Child Abuse and Neglect, 31*, 211–229.

DeBoard-Lucas, R. L., Fosco, G. M., Raynor, S. R., & Grych, J. H. (2010). Interparental conflict in context: Exploring relations between parenting processes and children's conflict appraisals. *Journal of Clinical Child and Adolescent Psychology, 39*, 163–175.

Dozier, M., Peloso, E., Lewis, E., Laurenceau, J. P., & Levine, S. (2008). Effects of an attachment-based intervention on the cortisol production of infants and toddlers in foster care. *Development and Psychopathology, 20,* 845–859.

Dubow, E. F., Huesmann, L. R., Boxer, P., Landau, S., Dvir, S., Shikaki, K., & Ginges, J. (2012). Exposure to political conflict and violence and posttraumatic stress in Middle East youth: Protective factors. *Journal of Clinical Child & Adolescent Psychology, 41,* 402–416.

Duraković-Belko, E., Kulenović, A., & Dapić, R. (2003). Determinants of posttraumatic adjustment in adolescents from Sarajevo who experienced war. *Journal of Clinical Psychology, 59,* 27–40.

Dybdahl, R. (2001). Children and mothers in war: An outcome study of a psychosocial intervention program. *Child Development, 72,* 1214–1230.

Erickson, M. F., & Egeland, B. (2004). Linking theory and research to practice: The Minnesota Longitudinal Study of Parents and Children and the STEEP™ program. *Clinical Psychologist, 8,* 5–9.

Finkelhor, D., Turner, H., Ormrod, R., Hamby, S., & Kracke, K. (2009). *Children's exposure to intimate partner violence and other family violence: A comprehensive national survey.* OJJDP Juvenile Justice Bulletin—NCJ 227744, pp. 1–12. Washington, DC: U.S. Government Printing Office.

Fraiberg, S., Adelson, E., & Shapiro, V. (1975). Ghosts in the nursery: A psychoanalytic approach to the problem of impaired infant-mother relationships. *Journal of the American Academy of Child and Adolescent Psychiatry, 14,* 387–421.

Gewirtz, A., Forgatch, M., & Weiling, E. (2008). Parenting practices as potential mechanisms for child adjustment following mass trauma. *Journal of Marital and Family Therapy, 34,* 177–192.

Gil-Rivas, V., Holman, E. A., & Silver, R. C. (2004). Adolescent vulnerability following the September 11th terrorist attacks: A study of parents and their children. *Applied Developmental Science, 8,* 130–142.

Gil-Rivas, V., Silver, R. C., Holman, E. A., McIntosh, D. N., & Poulin, M. (2007). Parental response and adolescent adjustment to the September 11, 2001 terrorist attacks. *Journal of Traumatic Stress, 20,* 1063–1068.

Gorman-Smith, D., Henry, D. B., & Tolan, P. H. (2004). Exposure to community violence and violence perpetration: The protective effects of family functioning. *Journal of Clinical Child and Adolescent Psychology, 33,* 439–449.

Grych, J. H., Raynor, S. R., & Fosco, G. M. (2004). Family processes that shape the impact of interparental conflict on adolescents. *Development and Psychopathology, 16,* 649–665.

Hamby, S. L., Finkelhor, D., Turner, H., & Ormrod, R. (2011). *Children's exposure to intimate partner violence and other forms of family violence: Nationally representative rates among US youth.* OJJDP Juvenile Justice Bulletin—NCJ 232272, pp. 1–12. Washington, DC: U.S. Government Printing Office.

Hoven, C.W., Duarte, C.S., Lucas, C.P., Wu, P., Mandell, D.J., Goodwin, R.D., . . . Susser, E. (2005). Psychopathology among New York City public school children 6 months after September 11. *Archives of General Psychiatry, 62*, 545–552.

Howell, K.H. (2011). Resilience and psychopathology in children exposed to family violence. *Aggression and Violent Behavior, 16*, 562–569.

Howell, K.H., Graham-Bermann, S.A., Czyz, E., & Lilly, M. (2010). Assessing resilience in preschool children exposed to intimate partner violence. *Violence and Victims, 25*, 150–164.

Jain, S., Buka, S.L., Subramanian, S.V., & Molnar, B.E. (2012). Protective factors for youth exposed to violence: Role of developmental assets in building emotional resilience. *Youth Violence and Juvenile Justice, 10*, 107–129.

Katz, L.F., & Gottman, J.M. (1997). Buffering children from marital conflict and dissolution. *Journal of Clinical Child Psychology, 26*, 157–171.

Khamis, V. (2005). Post-traumatic stress disorder among school age Palestinian children. *Child Abuse and Neglect, 29*, 81–95.

Kliewer, W., Cunningham, J.N., Diehl, R., Parrish, K.A., Walker, J.M., Atiyeh, C., . . . Mejia, R. (2004). Violence exposure and adjustment in inner-city youth: Child and caregiver emotion regulation skill, caregiver–child relationship quality, and neighborhood cohesion as protective factor. *Journal of Clinical Child and Adolescent Psychology, 33*, 477–487.

Labella, M.H., & Masten, A.S. (2017). Family influences on aggression. In B. Bushman (Ed.), *Social psychology of aggression and violence: Frontiers of social psychology* (pp. 74–89). New York, NY: Taylor & Francis.

Lansford, J.E., Sharma, C., Malone, P.S., Woodlief, D., Dodge, K.A., Oburu, P., . . . Tirado, L.M.U. (2014). Corporal punishment, maternal warmth, and child adjustment: A longitudinal study in eight countries. *Journal of Clinical Child & Adolescent Psychology, 43*, 670–685.

Levendosky, A.A., Huth-Bocks, A.C., Shapiro, D.L., & Semel, M.A. (2003). The impact of domestic violence on the maternal-child relationship and preschool-age children's functioning. *Journal of Family Psychology, 17*, 275–287.

Lieberman, A.F., Díaz, M.A., & Van Horn, P. (2009, May). Safer beginnings: Perinatal Child-Parent Psychotherapy for newborns and mothers exposed to domestic violence. *Zero to Three, 29*, 17–22.

Lieberman, A.F., Ghosh Ippen, G., & Van Horn, P. (2006). Child-Parent Psychotherapy: 6-month follow-up of a randomized controlled trial. *Journal of the American Academy of Child & Adolescent Psychiatry, 45*, 913–918.

Lieberman, A.F., Padrón, E., Van Horn, P., & Harris, W.W. (2005a). Angels in the Nursery: The intergenerational transmission of benevolent parental influences. *Infant Mental Health Journal, 26*, 504–520.

Lieberman, A.F., Van Horn, P., & Ozer, E.J. (2005b). Preschooler witnesses of marital violence: Predictors and mediators of child behavior problems. *Development and Psychopathology, 17*, 385–396.

Luthar, S.S., Cicchetti, D., & Becker, B. (2000). The construct of resilience: A critical evaluation and guidelines for future work. *Child Development, 71*, 543–562.

Luthar, S.S., Crossman, E.J., & Small, P.J. (2015). Resilience and adversity. In R.M. Lerner and M.E. Lamb (Eds.), *Handbook of child psychology and developmental science* (7th ed., Vol. III, pp. 247–286). New York, NY: Wiley.

Martinez-Torteya, C., Anne Bogat, G., Von Eye, A., & Levendosky, A.A. (2009). Resilience among children exposed to domestic violence: The role of risk and protective factors. *Child Development, 80*, 562–577.

Masten, A.S. (2001). Ordinary magic: Resilience processes in development. *American Psychologist, 56*, 227–238.

Masten, A.S. (2014a). *Ordinary magic: Resilience in development.* New York, NY: Guilford.

Masten, A.S. (2014b). Global perspectives on resilience in children and youth. *Child Development, 85*, 6–20.

Masten, A.S., Best, K.M., & Garmezy, N. (1990). Resilience and development: Contributions from the study of children who overcome adversity. *Development and Psychopathology*, 2, 425–444.

Masten, A.S., & Cicchetti, D. (2016). Resilience in development: Progress and transformation. In D. Cicchetti (Ed.), *Developmental psychopathology, Vol. 4: Risk, resilience, and intervention* (3rd ed., pp. 271–333). New York, NY: Wiley.

Masten, A. S., & Narayan, A. J. (2012). Child development in the context of disaster, war, and terrorism: Pathways of risk and resilience. *Annual Review of Psychology, 63*, 227–57. https://doi.org/10.1146/annurev-psych-120710-100356

Masten, A.S., Narayan, A.J., Silverman, W.K., & Osofsky, J.D. (2015). Children in war and disaster. In R.M. Lerner (Ed.), M.H. Bornstein and T. Leventhal (Vol. Eds.), *Handbook of child psychology and developmental science. Vol. 4. Ecological settings and processes in developmental systems* (7th ed., pp. 704–745). New York, NY: Wiley.

McKee, L., Roland, E., Coffelt, N., Olson, A.L., Forehand, R., Massari, C., . . . Zens, M.S. (2007). Harsh discipline and child problem behaviors: The roles of positive parenting and gender. *Journal of Family Violence, 22*, 187–196.

Narayan, A.J. (2015). Personal, dyadic, and contextual resilience in parents experiencing homelessness. *Clinical Psychology Review, 36*, 56–69.

Narayan, A. J., Ippen, C. G., Harris, W. W., & Lieberman, A. F. (2017). Assessing angels in the nursery: A pilot study of childhood memories of benevolent caregiving as protective influences. *Infant Mental Health Journal, 38*(4), 461–474.

Narayan, A.J., & Masten, A.S. (2012). Children and adolescents in disasters, war, and terrorism: Developmental pathways to psychopathology and resilience. In C. Widom (Ed.), *Trauma, psychopathology, and violence* (pp. 131–158). New York, NY: Oxford University Press.

Narayan, A. J., Oliver Bucio, G., Rivera, L. M., & Lieberman, A. F. (2016). Making sense of the past creates space for the baby: Perinatal Child-Parent Psychotherapy for pregnant women with childhood trauma. *Zero to Three Journal, 36*, 22–28.

Narayan, A. J., Rivera, L. M., Bernstein, R. E., Castro, G., Gantt, T., Thomas, M., . . ., Lieberman, A. F. (2017). Between pregnancy and motherhood: Identifying unmet mental health needs in pregnant women with lifetime adversity. *Zero to Three Journal, 37*, 4–13.

Narayan, A. J., Rivera, L. M., Bernstein, R. E., Harris, W. W., & Lieberman, A. F. (2018). Positive childhood experiences predict less psychopathology and stress in pregnant women with childhood adversity: A pilot study of the benevolent childhood experiences (BCEs) scale. *Child Abuse and Neglect, 78*, 19–30.

Narayan, A. J., Sapienza, J. K., Monn, A. R., Lingras, K. A., & Masten, A. S. (2015). Risk, vulnerability, and protective processes of parental expressed emotion for children's peer relations in contexts of parental violence. *Journal of Clinical Child and Adolescent Psychology, 44*, 676–688.

Otto, M. W., Henin, A., Hirshfeld-Becker, D. R., Pollack, M. H., Biederman, J., & Rosenbaum, J. (2007). Posttraumatic stress disorder symptoms following media exposure to tragic events: Impact of 9/11 on children at risk for anxiety disorders. *Journal of Anxiety Disorders, 21*, 888–902.

Papadatou, D., Giannopoulou, I., Bitsakou, P., Bellali, T., Talias, M. A., & Tselepi, K. (2012). Adolescents' reactions after a wildfire disaster in Greece. *Journal of Traumatic Stress, 25*, 57–63.

Proctor, L. J., Fauchier, A., Oliver, P. H., Ramos, M. C., Rios, M. A., & Margolin, G. (2007). Family context and young children's responses to earthquake. *Journal of Child Psychology and Psychiatry, 48*, 941–949.

Punamäki, R. L., Qouta, S., & El Sarraj, E. (1997). Models of traumatic experiences and children's psychological adjustment: The roles of perceived parenting and the children's own resources and activity. *Child Development, 68*, 718–728.

Rutter, M. (1987). Psychosocial resilience and protective mechanisms. *American Journal of Orthopsychiatry, 57*, 316–331.

Sameroff, A. J. (2000). Developmental systems and psychopathology. *Development and Psychopathology, 12*, 297–312.

Skopp, N. A., McDonald, R., Jouriles, E. N., & Rosenfield, D. (2007). Partner aggression and children's externalizing problems: Maternal and partner warmth as protective factors. *Journal of Family Psychology, 21*, 459.

Sroufe, L. A., Egeland, B., Carlson, E. A., & Collins, W. A. (2005). *The development of the person*. New York, NY: Guilford Press.

Thabet, A. A., Ibraheem, A. N., Shivram, R., Winter, E. A., & Vostanis, P. (2009). Parenting support and PTSD in children of a war zone. *International Journal of Social Psychiatry, 55*, 226–237.

Toth, S. L., Maughan, A., Manly, J. T., Spagnola, M., & Cicchetti, D. (2002). The relative efficacy of two interventions in altering maltreated preschool children's representational models: Implications for attachment theory. *Development and Psychopathology*, *14*(4), 877–908.

UNICEF. (2011a). Young people launch "Children's Charter to be Safe from Disasters." Geneva, Switzerland. Retrieved from https://www.unicef.org/esaro/children_youth_Global_platform_for_disaster_reduction.html

UNICEF. (2011b). Children and disasters. Building resilience through education. Geneva, Switzerland. Retrieved from https://www.unisdr.org/we/inform/publications/24583

UNICEF. (2013). Fact sheet: Children associated with armed groups and forces Central Africa. Geneva, Switzerland. Retrieved from https://www.unicef.org/wcaro/FactSheet100601Final_E_100603_.pdf

UNICEF. (2015). UNICEF 2015 Report: Millions of children caught in the middle of conflict. Geneva, Switzerland. Retrieved from http://www.dw.com/en/unicef-2015-report-millions-of-children-caught-in-the-middle-of-conflict/a-18554668

UNICEF. (2016). Press release: Nearly a quarter of the world's children live in conflict or disaster-stricken countries: UNICEF. Geneva, Switzerland. Retrieved from https://www.unicef.org/media/media_93863.html

United Nations. (2014). Guiding principles on young people's participation in peacebuilding. Retrieved from http://www.un.org/youthenvoy/armed-conflict/

Van Horn, P., Lieberman, A. F., & Harris, W. W. (2008). The Angels in the Nursery Interview. Department of Psychiatry, University of California, San Francisco.

Wickrama, K. A. S., & Kaspar, V. (2007). Family context of mental health risk in tsunami-exposed adolescents: Findings from a pilot study in Sri Lanka. *Social Science and Medicine*, *64*, 713–723.

Wright, M. O., Masten, A. S., & Narayan, A. J. (2013). Resilience processes in development: Four waves of research on positive adaptation in the context of adversity. In S. Goldstein & R. B. Brooks (Eds.), *Handbook of resilience in children* (2nd ed., pp. 15–37). New York, NY: Kluwer Academic/Plenum.

Zahr, L. K. (1996). Effects of war on the behavior of Lebanese preschool children: Influence of home environment and family functioning. *American Journal of Orthopsychiatry*, *66*, 401–408.

CHAPTER 4

Posttraumatic Growth and Resilience

Laura Marie Armstrong, Cecily Basquin, and Richard Tedeschi

Children can be quite extraordinary in their ability to manage stressful life events. In this chapter, we consider one of the most remarkable ways they may respond: an apparent transformation of core beliefs about their world, themselves, and their futures called *posttraumatic growth* (PTG).

Jackie was 12 years old when her mother became disabled in the aftermath of an auto accident that left her with chronic pain, unable to walk, and with moderate cognitive impairment. At that time, Jackie's sister, Connie, and her twin brother, Raymond, were 5 years old. Their mother had been the lynchpin of the household as their father had a drinking problem and sometimes left the family for days at a time. He became even more unreliable after his wife suffered her disability. The children were confronted with a move from their house to a rather cramped apartment as the disability payments their mother received did not allow for their previous standard of living. Their mother was coping with her injuries and taking medication that sapped her strength, energy, and concentration. From these circumstances, Jackie and Raymond became responsible for much of the running of the household.

Jackie had been a good student, quiet and unassuming in school, attracting little attention from her teachers, since she was not outstanding but no trouble to them either. Raymond was outgoing and very popular, especially because he was a gifted athlete. In the aftermath of their mother's disability, and in father's absence, Jackie and Raymond determined they needed to work together to help their mother raise Connie and make the household a place where their mother would be comfortable and would not have to worry, as they feared that stress and anxiety would worsen her condition. It soon became obvious, however, that Jackie was the leader in these efforts. Raymond had trouble sustaining his commitments as he was continuing to be interested in his athletics and his mother did not wish to discourage this. Jackie also knew this was important to Raymond and decided she could do most of what was necessary in the household. She took on the usual household tasks, including cooking, and enlisted the help of neighbors in making sure that when her mother was unable to go for groceries, the neighbors would do this for them. She learned how to check the mail for bills and make sure they got paid, as she made out the checks and sent them out. She made sure Connie was dressed and ready for her school in the morning and went to bed at the proper time at night. She also developed a greater sense of urgency in her schoolwork as she came to think that excelling there would mean she could do better in life and be in a position to help her family. However, she also came to see many of her peers as being preoccupied with things that seemed to be of little importance to her, so she did not have close friends. This is how Jackie described her experience after she came to college and looked back on the intervening years.

> It may look to the outsider that I sacrificed my adolescence in taking care of my family. There is truth to that, but I don't see the sacrifice as that great compared to what I gained after having handled all this responsibility. My mom and I developed a very close relationship and I could tell she was grateful and proud of me. This gave me a great deal of pride in myself. I felt I made the decisions for myself about this, and mom never pushed me into it. I also think I am really close to Connie and Raymond. I was like a second mother to Connie and Raymond has been grateful to me; he was not selfish about doing his sports things in school. My father is a different story and that is something I don't know what I can do anything about. But you know, his failures also allowed me to be a more mature person now. I feel like adulthood is not a major challenge like it seems to be for a lot of my peers in school. I think I understand life in a way they don't. And I like that. A lot of people haven't developed the pride that comes from handling things, coping with stuff, taking on challenges. I have, and I know what is important, and I know how to have real relationships with people, rather than superficial ones. This was tough, but good. Now, I am preparing to do something in the medical field, and I understand why this

> is important—it is so obvious. But I am ready and serious about it. I regret that my mom has had to deal with her seizures and the after-effects; that is the only real bad part. But for us kids, we are a strong bunch for having to deal with this.

Jackie's story is a powerful example of PTG, the positive psychological change experienced because of the emotional and cognitive struggle with trauma (Kilmer & Gil-Rivas, 2010; Little, Akin-Little, & Somerville, 2011). There are many factors that might contribute to Jackie's capacity not only to persevere but also to develop personal strength and perspective in the aftermath of this family trauma. Stories such as Jackie's raise questions about how we can account for these positive changes, including factors such as emotion regulation and coping, cognitive processing, and supportive and significant relationships with adults.

Although Tedeschi and Calhoun (1995) delineated their model of PTG more than 20 years ago, human interest in growth in the face of hardship can be traced back to ancient literature and philosophy (Meyerson, Grant, Carter, & Kilmer, 2011). A wealth of empirical evidence supports the model of PTG put forth by Calhoun and Tedeschi (2006) among adults and adolescents, but there are fewer investigations exploring the nature of this process with children. This is surprising given the significant body of work related to childhood trauma, stress, and resilience. The exploration of PTG among children may provide useful information for families and health providers working with children who have experienced trauma. The aims of this chapter are to (a) provide an overview of PTG and evidence of its applicability to children, (b) consider developmental competencies that likely support PTG among children, and (c) discuss ways that clinicians and parents can foster PTG in children.

An Overview of PTG

When individuals experience traumatic events, it can shatter assumptions about the self, others, and one's expected life course, which in turn may spur efforts to cope and ultimately lead to a transformation in one's goals, core beliefs, and worldview (Kilmer, 2006; Kilmer et al., 2014). According to PTG theory, the type of trauma is less important than the internal struggle that occurs in its aftermath. It is this struggle that leads to a fundamental shift in how the individual views the world. Individuals who have experienced trauma often report feeling greater vulnerability and distress, indicating that they continue to endure pain, and at the same time many report improvements across a variety of domains. As illustrated by Jackie's story, after experiencing trauma many report a greater personal strength and a heightened appreciation for their ability to survive and endure whatever comes their way. They also report a new perspective on relationships, often developing a more realistic and complex picture of the positive and negative attributes of others, as well as gaining a better sense of who their true friends are and to whom they can turn amid life's joys and sorrows. As part of the coping process, individuals may find comfort and validation by talking with others who have experienced similar circumstances and in turn develop greater empathy for others facing life's challenges.

Trauma can also raise existential questions about one's identity and purpose. To address these questions, many report deepening their spiritual, religious, and existential practice in an effort to answer these fundamental questions about life. In addition, individuals often report a shift in priorities and values as well as greater appreciation for life and its possibilities. For example, trauma survivors often report that spending time with family and friends is more important than before and more valued than the daily demands of work and chores (Calhoun & Tedeschi, 2006; Little et al., 2011; Meyerson et al., 2011). To demonstrate growth across these multiple domains, PTG theory and research suggest that one's post-trauma experience will likely include emotional distress, rumination, and eventually a change in one's schema, beliefs, and worldview (Taku, Cann, Calhoun, & Tedeschi, 2008; Tedeschi & Calhoun, 1996).

Differentiating PTG from Resilience

At first glance it might seem that resilience and PTG reflect the same construct, yet they are actually distinct experiences. The overlapping aspects of resilience and PTG stem from the concept of multifinality or the idea that there are many possible outcomes after experiencing a trauma, one of which is personal growth. However, resilience is considered a *dynamic developmental process* that reflects positive or successful adaptation to difficulties that threaten one's functioning (Masten, 2016). PTG, on the other hand, is a *transformative process*, in which individuals show qualitative change from pretrauma levels of adaptation. Positive adjustment is not necessary for PTG, and in fact PTG and mental health problems often co-occur. Therefore, another distinction between resilience and PTG is the way that distress is viewed. Emotional distress is thought to be a necessary component of the PTG process as the individual deals with and tries to create meaning from the traumatic events that have occurred (Kilmer et al., 2014; Tedeschi & Calhoun, 1995). Consistent with this perspective, many trauma survivors who experience PTG also continue to report posttraumatic stress symptoms (Kilmer et al., 2009) as well as suffering and pain resulting from the long-ranging consequences of trauma and coping with one's new reality. However, this does not fit with the concept of resilience, where ongoing distress may be considered an indicator of poorer coping and adaptation. In fact, those experiencing PTG may report more distress and lower levels of emotional well-being than those exhibiting resilience (Calhoun & Tedeschi, 2006; Cryder, Kilmer, Tedeschi, & Calhoun, 2006).

Another important distinction between resilience and PTG is that the area of resilience has a long history of including child populations and drawing from bioecological and family systems frameworks. Developmental processes and contextual factors are inextricably linked to the conceptualization and study of resilience in children. In contrast, PTG among children is an emerging area of study, and recent efforts aim to demonstrate that PTG is possible for children, can be reliably assessed, and can contribute to our understanding of how to foster transformative growth among children who have faced trauma (Kilmer et al., 2014). There is still much to learn regarding the developmental and contextual processes that impact the nature and trajectory of children's growth in the aftermath of trauma. As efforts to understand childhood PTG increase, additional similarities to and distinctions from resilience will likely arise.

Evidence That Children Experience PTG

Research examining connections among childhood PTG and aspects of the trauma, the child, and the family has yielded mixed results. Most studies include samples of children that span multiple developmental periods (i.e., ages 7–18), and therefore the term "youth" will be used when findings refer to both children and adolescents. PTG can be seen among children who have experienced a variety of traumas (Cryder et al., 2006; Kilmer & Gil-Rivas, 2010). This is consistent with research on adults, demonstrating that it is not the type of trauma faced by the individual but rather one's struggle to cope and adjust afterward that matters for PTG. Some studies suggest that youth who experience more severe trauma (as measured by self-report) are more likely to experience PTG (Barakat, Alderfer, & Kazak, 2006; Taku, Kilmer, Cann, Tedeschi, & Calhoun, 2012). However, other research has not found a relation between trauma severity and PTG (Cryder et al., 2006; Milam, Ritt-Olson, Tan, Unger, & Nezami, 2005). Interestingly, Laufer and Solomon (2006) found that adolescents who reported moderate levels (rather than high or low levels) of trauma severity evidenced the most PTG. With respect to the timing of the traumatic event, some work has shown that as more time passes, PTG is less likely to occur (Phipps, Long, & Ogden, 2007; Wolchik, Coxe, Tein, Sandler, & Ayers, 2009), but other work has found no association between timing and PTG (Alisic, van der Schoot, van Ginkel, & Kleber, 2008; Currier, Hermes, & Phipps, 2009; Milam, Ritt-Olson, & Unger, 2004). In summary, youth may be more likely to experience PTG when faced with moderate levels of trauma in the recent past. Perhaps traumatic events that are of moderate severity are less likely to overwhelm children's emotional resources compared to more severe trauma, therefore making it easier to cope and make meaning of the experience. Moreover, if the trauma occurred recently, the child's support system may be marshalled to help the child cope in the immediate aftermath, but over time this support may decrease.

Several studies have examined associations between youth characteristics and PTG. Some work has shown that adolescents are more likely to experience PTG than school-aged children (Barakat et al., 2006; Currier et al., 2009; Milam et al., 2004; Phipps et al., 2007), but other work finds no age effects (Cryder et al., 2006; Hafstad, Gil-Rivas, Kilmer, & Raeder, 2010; Hafstad, Kilmer, & Gil-Rivas, 2011; Kilmer et al., 2009; Kilmer & Gil-Rivas, 2010). Boys and girls are equally likely to show signs of PTG (Ickovics et al., 2006; Milam et al., 2004; Oltjenbruns, 1991), and the handful of studies examining ethnicity/race yield mixed results. This is in contrast to research on adults, which demonstrates that females and minorities report more growth after trauma than males and nonminorities (Helgeson, Reynolds, & Tomich, 2006).

The inconclusive nature of existing literature suggests that it will be important to move beyond demographics in order to understand the precise mechanisms that facilitate PTG among children. One line of research that has been particularly fruitful is the examination of the links between coping style and PTG among adolescents. Coping is a complex process whereby individuals use cognitive and behavioral strategies to manage the demands of stressful situations. Active coping (Aldridge and Roesch, 2008; Wolchik et al., 2009), positive reappraisal (Vaughn, Roesch, & Aldridge, 2009), and religious coping and involvement (Laufer, Raz-Hamama, Levine, & Solomon, 2009; Milam et al., 2005; Park & Helgeson, 2006; Vaughn et al., 2009) have emerged as strong predictors of PTG among adolescents. Other work has demonstrated that when youth report positively valanced emotions and perceptions about themselves, they are more likely to show signs of PTG, with research suggesting that positive affect (Currier et al., 2009), hope (Vaughn et al., 2009), self-esteem (Phipps et al., 2007), competency beliefs (Cryder et al., 2006), and optimism (Currier et al., 2009; Milam et al., 2005; Phipps et al., 2007) may be of relevance. In addition to coping style and self-perceptions, it will also be important to delineate how development across key domains, such as social-emotional functioning, cognition, and temperament, influences children's experiences of PTG.

Research on the association between family and contextual supports and PTG has been mixed. Some work has demonstrated that social support from parents and caregivers (Wolchik et al., 2009), the larger family unit (Kimhi, Eshel, Zysberg, & Hantman, 2009), peers (Yu et al., 2010), and teachers (Yaskowich & Stam, 2003; Yu et al., 2010) predicts PTG among adolescents; however, studies focused on children have found no association between caregiver support and PTG (Cryder et al., 2006; Kilmer & Gil-Rivas, 2010). When social support was examined separately from other types of parental influence, caregivers' coping advice and specifically advice about positive reframing were related to PTG (Kilmer & Gil-Rivas, 2010). A more fine-grained analysis of the support received from others may yield important insights about PTG among children.

Summarizing the above research, children and adolescents appear to exhibit signs of PTG across a multitude of traumatic experiences, with some evidence that recent trauma, perceived to be of moderate severity, is most likely to result in growth. Coping styles, positive emotions and self-perceptions, as well as caregiver support in the form of coping advice have the most robust associations with PTG in youth. Given that much of the research has yielded inconclusive findings, there is a clear need for prospective, longitudinal designs with a stronger integration of developmental and contextual frameworks.

Developmental Domains Relevant for PTG among Children

Children of different ages respond differently to trauma because of developmental stage, social-emotional abilities, and cognitive capacities (Kilmer & Gil-Rivas, 2010), and therefore, existing theories of PTG, developed in the context of adult reactions to trauma, are not well suited for children. Studying PTG in children is complicated by the fact that trauma can disrupt biological, psychological, and developmental milestones (McElheran et al., 2012). Moreover, it can be hard to disentangle whether children reporting PTG actually experience PTG or if they are simply experiencing natural maturation (Kilmer & Gil-Rivas, 2010). Finally, methodological issues come into play as PTG is typically assessed by parent or child report, which are necessarily limited by parents' awareness of children's internal processes, as well as children's ability to report on these processes.

The ability to experience PTG likely depends on the growth and integration of key developmental domains; however, these have not been clearly specified in the literature. The ability to "struggle with trauma" as a way toward experiencing positive change requires cognitive and emotional capacities that are still emerging in children. For this reason, Kilmer (2006) suggests that the minimum age for PTG in children may be seven years old.

Integration of Cognitive and Emotional Capacities

Drawing from a developmental framework, the adaptive integration of cognitive and emotional abilities is a hallmark of healthy functioning that emerges over the course of childhood and may set the foundation for PTG among children. PTG theory suggests that in order to undergo transformative growth in the aftermath of trauma, one must be able to feel, express, and manage a range of emotions, as well as marshal the cognitive resources to make sense of and cope with the traumatic experience. Although children have an active emotional life from birth, advances in cognitive skills over the course of childhood allow for increasing accuracy, sophistication, and complexity in their emotional capacities (Denham, 1998). By age six, children identify and label their own and other people's emotions (Bretherton, Fritz, Zahn-Waxler, & Ridgeway, 1986), understand the situations that elicit different emotions (Stegge & Terwogt, 2007), talk about the causes and consequences of emotions (Bretherton et al., 1986), have an awareness of effective and ineffective strategies for managing negative emotions (Dennis & Kelemen, 2009), and are developing a sense of efficacy in their ability to change emotional states. Taken together, these abilities should lay the groundwork for coping with trauma and exhibiting growth in its aftermath.

Trauma elicits an array of emotions that may be conflicting, confusing, and overwhelming for children, and PTG is thought to require that children express and understand both positive and negative reactions to trauma (Harter, 1986, 2006; Harter & Buddin, 1987; Kilmer, 2006). Although children as young as 3 years old have a basic understanding of the causes and consequences of emotions, it is not until children are about 10 years old that they understand the conditions that elicit complex or mixed emotions (Saarni, Campos, Camras, & Witherington, 2006). The ability to find benefits or feel positively about a traumatic experience is an advanced skill that likely requires abstract reasoning and an appreciation of both the gains and losses that have resulted from the trauma (Kilmer, 2006). In addition, children likely need to be skilled in regulating their distress in order for the traumatic event to spur adaptation, growth, and positive feelings in its aftermath. In fact, Kilmer et al. (2014) suggest that the ability to regulate trauma-related emotions and thoughts (Salmon & Bryant, 2002) is necessary for PTG. The beginnings of emotion regulation can be seen in infancy, and over time children become increasingly skilled at managing negative emotions independently. As children grow, their emotion regulation strategies shift from being primarily behavioral in nature (e.g., seeking support, distracting oneself by engaging in an alternative activity) to more cognitively oriented processes (e.g., reappraisal, distracting oneself by thinking about something else). Children as young as 8 years old can regulate their thinking about traumatic events, and over time children report greater use of cognitive strategies, such as generating pleasant thoughts, using reappraisal, and shifting one's attention (Eisenberg, Cumberland, & Spinrad, 1998; Thompson, 1994).

Parallels can be found between the emotion regulation literature and the work on stress and coping (Lazarus & Folkman, 1987), within which two broad types of coping have been identified: problem-focused and emotion-focused. When problem-focused coping is used, youth might seek information, problem solve to come up with potential solutions to their difficulties, or take actions to create change, whereas in the case of emotion-focused coping, children might use reappraisal techniques, paint a negative situation in a more positive light, or engage in cognitive distraction by pushing negative emotions out of mind, focusing on something other than the trauma experience (Compas, Connor-Smith, Saltzman, Thomsen, & Wadsworth, 2001). School-aged children (5–12 years old) generate problem-focused coping strategies to deal with challenging situations, whereas those who are closer to adolescence also mention emotion-focused coping (i.e., using internal or cognitively oriented strategies) for managing negative emotions that arise in response to stressful circumstances (Harris, Olthof, & Terwogt, 1981).

In addition to child age, the controllability of the problem is also relevant for children's selection of coping strategies. This is meaningful given that many of the traumas that children face are out of their own control. School-aged children are more likely to use problem-focused coping in situations perceived as controllable (e.g., peer problems, school failure) and to use emotion-focused coping in less controllable situations (e.g., traumatic events like medical emergencies, physical accidents, family conflict). Thus, children with realistic perceptions about the controllability of the trauma and those who use emotion-focused coping in its aftermath may be more likely to exhibit PTG (Compas et al., 2001; Salmon & Bryant, 2002).

In the case of Jackie, she used problem-focused coping by finding solutions to keep her family afloat and raise her younger sister. For example, she learned how to pay bills, manage her schoolwork, and ask for help from other supportive adults to make wise decisions instead of letting her emotions overwhelm her. Jackie also used emotion-focused coping by reappraising the hardship that befell her family as a challenge that she could conquer and use to guide her future experiences. These coping strategies helped Jackie to grow while she struggled through the experiences of helping her family after her mother became disabled.

The capacity to talk about one's emotional experience is another facet of PTG that develops over the course of childhood. Growth in language skills, and emotion language in particular, affords children the opportunity to talk about their trauma-related emotions with supportive adults and can provide another avenue for regulating their emotional experience (Cole, Armstrong, & Pemberton, 2010). In fact, simply labeling one's emotional experience is linked to decreases in negative emotionality (Moyal, Henik, & Anholt, 2014). Furthermore, children's discussion of negative experiences (compared to positive ones) includes more information about their thoughts and emotions and is recounted in a more coherent fashion (Fivush & Haden, 2003). Other work has shown that children who recalled more information and used more positive emotion terms to describe their experiences of Hurricane Andrew in the immediate aftermath had better psychological outcomes (i.e., less PTSD symptomatology) six years later (Sales, Fivush, Parker, & Bahrick, 2005). Therefore, the way that children discuss trauma-related emotions is tied to the ways that they create meaning and cope with the experience. This is likely why the trauma narrative, or describing one's personal experience of trauma in detail, is often a key component of treatment among children and adolescents who have faced traumatic experiences (Cohen, Deblinger, Mannarino, & Steer, 2004).

Rumination

Cognitive processing of the trauma through rumination is thought to be vital in facilitating PTG by helping one accept his or her new reality and its implications for one's future (Calhoun & Tedeschi, 2006; Kilmer et al., 2014). Ruminative thinking is defined as "recurrent event-related thoughts that help one understand, resolve, and make sense of trauma-related events" (Cryder et al., 2006, p. 67). The struggle with trauma through rumination realigns one's goals, beliefs, and worldview in a way that reconciles the trauma with understanding oneself, others, and the world (Kilmer et al., 2014; Meyerson et al., 2011). Two types of rumination have been implicated in PTG, intrusive and productive. Intrusive rumination is an automatic, involuntary cognitive process thought to maintain distress, motivating the individual to engage in coping efforts. Productive rumination, on the other hand, is thought to be a deliberate attempt to develop a narrative around the trauma that creates meaning from the event and integrates the traumatic experience into one's worldview (Calhoun & Tedeschi, 2006).

Although rumination is consistently associated with PTG in adults, the findings for children are less conclusive. Some studies find no association between ruminative thinking and PTG in children (Cryder et al., 2006; Wolchik et al., 2009). However, other studies have demonstrated that both intrusive and productive rumination are associated with PTG among children (Kilmer & Gil-Rivas, 2010; Taku et al., 2012). In addition, Cryder et al. (2006) found that rumination involving positive reappraisal was correlated with children's coping competency beliefs or children's confidence in their ability to handle problems, which is a prime correlate of PTG. The inconsistency in findings may be a function of how rumination was defined and assessed, as well as developmental variations in the process of rumination. For example, children may process trauma through rumination, as well as through creative activities, play, reexperiencing the event, daydreams, and nightmares. Future work is needed to examine how a child's developmental abilities impact rumination and whether the timing and nature of rumination matter for PTG.

Schemas about the Self

Kilmer (2006) argued that self-system schema or views and beliefs about oneself (e.g., perceptions of competence, self-efficacy, self-worth, future expectations) play a critical role in experiencing PTG. Beliefs about the self may influence how children perceive the traumatic event and their attempts to cope with the trauma afterward. In fact, positive views of the self and one's abilities are robust predictors of resilience in children (e.g., Cowan, Cowan, & Schulz, 1996; Luthar, Cicchetti, & Becker, 2000; Masten, 2001). Furthermore, adults who experience growth after trauma report a transformation in how they view themselves, others, and their future. In other words, they experience a qualitative shift in their schemas. However, this type of radical change becomes more complicated for children who are still in the process of developing their self-system schemas. According to Janoff-Bulman (1992), children's basic assumptions about themselves and the world are more malleable than adults, which can mean not only greater opportunities for positive change but also greater vulnerability in the face of trauma.

Children's basic assumptions about the self and the world are shaped throughout childhood and adolescence as youth incorporate new experiences into the construction of their mental representations. According to attachment theory (Bowlby, 1988), children's internal working models or mental representations for understanding the self, others, and the world emerge as a result of their everyday interactions with their primary caregivers (usually parents). During the first year of life, children develop expectations about the reliability and accessibility of their caregivers, as well as the level of safety and security that they provide; these internal working models become the framework for understanding themselves and others and guide children's interactions in future relationships. Children who develop a secure attachment to their primary caregivers come to view themselves as capable and worthy of love, and they perceive the world as safe and predictable. In contrast, children who are insecurely attached tend to view themselves as ineffective and unlovable, and they view others as unsupportive, unpredictable, and potentially threatening. Of potential relevance for PTG, children with a secure attachment are more effective at seeking support after a trauma compared to children with an insecure attachment (Cryder et al., 2006; Milam et al., 2005). Experiencing trauma has the potential to derail children's adaptive views of themselves and their sense of security or to affirm their unhealthy views of themselves and the dangerousness of the world. The earlier the children experience trauma, the greater the likelihood that it will disrupt their burgeoning sense of self and contribute to long-lasting and harmful developmental consequences (Lieberman & Van Horn, 2004). Therefore, PTG may depend on the extent to which children's basic assumptions about the self, others, and the world are firmly entrenched, as well as the availability of a warm and supportive caregiving environment that can help the child cope in the aftermath. Caregivers and other important adults likely play an essential role in helping the child make sense of the event and its relevance for the child's perceptions of oneself and others.

Among the studies that have examined links between PTG and children's self-system schemas, results have been mixed. Phipps et al. (2007) found that among pediatric cancer patients, those with higher self-esteem were able to find more benefits from having cancer (e.g., becoming a stronger person, learning who one's real friends are, dealing with problems better, discovering what is really important in life). Furthermore, children who report greater competency in their ability to cope with problems also endorse greater growth after a natural disaster (Cryder et al., 2006). In contrast, Kilmer and Gil-Rivas (2010), who studied children affected by Hurricane Katrina, did not find an association between PTG and coping competency or future expectations. In addition, a qualitative study of children between 8 and 12 years old demonstrated that posttrauma, children's outlook on the world changed, but their self-image was still intact (Alisic, Boeije, Jongmans, & Kleber, 2011). The authors concluded that as children cope with a traumatic event, their basic schemas may be retained, especially those that reflect core assumptions about the self.

Clinical Strategies for Promoting PTG in Children

Although clinical strategies for facilitating PTG in children have not yet been tested, an evidence-informed approach that builds upon core components of trauma-focused therapy interventions for children and practice parameters for fostering PTG in adults can be used to guide clinicians in promoting PTG among children who have experienced trauma. According to Calhoun, Cann, and Tedeschi (2010) and Calhoun and Tedeschi (2013), clinicians can foster PTG in adults by helping them (1) understand that negative aspects of the trauma experience lay the foundation for growth, (2) implement adaptive emotion regulation skills that manage distressing emotions and intrusive thoughts so that deliberate rumination and cognitive processing can occur, (3) engage in constructive self-disclosure as a means of accessing emotional support, developing a coherent trauma narrative, and finding models of healthy responses to trauma, (4) incorporate elements of PTG into the trauma narrative, and (5) develop ways of thinking and behaving that will enable them to express important truths about life, face future challenges, and be open to future opportunities. In adults, PTG is thought to largely involve unintentional change, and therapy is viewed as a way to enhance this growth (Zoellner & Maercker, 2006). However, children may need greater scaffolding to (a) process their traumatic experiences in ways that effectively manage emotional distress and allow for deliberate rumination, (b) construct a coherent trauma narrative, and (c) recognize the gains and strengths acquired in the aftermath of the trauma.

The majority of evidence-based trauma interventions for children begin with the initial step of creating a safe and accepting therapeutic environment to support relationship building between the child and the clinician. Another critical component of the early stages of therapy is helping the child and the larger family unit reestablish a sense of safety, structure, and normalcy (Kilmer et al., 2014). Additionally, educating children and parents about trauma and typical physiological and psychological reactions is important in the beginning stages of treatment to help children make sense of and normalize their responses, which can in turn rebuild or stabilize their core beliefs (Calhoun & Tedeschi, 2013; Kilmer et al., 2014).

Clinicians can also teach children how to manage their posttraumatic stress symptoms. In order to manage their thoughts and feelings effectively, children must be able to identify emotions, correctly label emotional experiences, express these emotions appropriately, and discriminate (and understand the connections) between thoughts and feelings. This should equip children with the foundational tools to handle the complex responses to trauma and begin to integrate their trauma experiences into their worldview. Clinicians should actively listen to the child's experience of trauma, their feelings associated with the trauma, and their feelings in the aftermath of trauma while providing support and showing empathy for the child's difficult situation (Kilmer et al., 2014). The clinician can support children's ability to manage their feelings by modeling, describing, and reinforcing adaptive coping strategies (Kilmer et al., 2014). Behavioral strategies, including progressive muscle relaxation and deep breathing, are often effective for helping children manage anxiety and physiological responses to trauma. In addition, cognitive strategies, like reappraisal, can be useful in helping children to deal with the dysregulated sympathetic nervous system responses and intrusive thinking common in trauma survivors (Calhoun & Tedeschi, 2013; Kilmer et al., 2014).

An essential component of many trauma-focused interventions, such as TF-CBT (trauma-focused cognitive behavioral therapy) is supporting children in the creation of a trauma narrative, which can be used to discuss the child's struggle in the aftermath of trauma, to identify and correct the child's cognitive distortions, and integrate this narrative into the child's worldview. When clinicians identify maladaptive thoughts, they can also encourage the child to reframe and replace them with positive, helpful thoughts, thereby restructuring the child's narrative (Yi & Kim, 2014). It is important to recognize and emphasize the child's strengths, and highlighting characteristics like optimism, self-efficacy, and adaptive coping skills can help children maintain a positive self-concept and encourage growth (Yi & Kim, 2014). Additionally, therapists can probe the child about instances of growth observed in the narrative. For example, "You told me that you feel closer to the people in your life since the trauma occurred, can you tell me more about that?" Recognizing these elements of PTG can reinforce and encourage children's integration of these themes into their trauma narrative (Kilmer et al., 2014).

Coping with trauma is difficult, and therefore the discussion of potential gains and benefits should not occur right away. Clinicians should be attentive to the speed with which they attempt to facilitate PTG and understand that some children may never accept the idea that trauma can bring about growth. Ultimately, children should not feel inadequate if they do not experience PTG, and children should not have the concept of PTG forced on them if they are not receptive to the possibility of its occurrence (Kilmer et al., 2014).

The Role of Parents and Other Adults in Promoting PTG in Children

Parents and other significant adults (hereafter referred to as caregivers) are critically important in promoting PTG in children. Treatment for childhood trauma that involves caregivers is more effective than treatment that does not include caregivers (Deblinger, Lippman, & Steer, 1996). However, the quality of the caregiving environment and caregiver–child relationship pretrauma will likely impact the nature and effectiveness of caregiver support posttrauma. Children must know that they have a safe and supportive environment to express themselves and to struggle with their experience. Joint therapy sessions with the child and caregivers, in which the therapist helps facilitate a discussion of the child's trauma narrative, can be beneficial for all involved (Kilmer et al., 2014). Techniques such as these can result in caregivers feeling more efficacious and at ease in supporting their child through trauma (Kilmer et al., 2014). Caregivers can provide nurturance and emotional support (Jieling & Xinchun, 2017), as well as model adaptive responses and coping strategies for the child (Kilmer et al., 2014). Perhaps, most important, caregivers can help children understand that they do not have to struggle with the trauma alone.

Another key role that caregivers can play in promoting PTG is guiding them toward interpreting and understanding what has taken place (Kilmer et al., 2014). In fact, ongoing dialogue between family members about the child's experiences and struggle with trauma can be vital in helping children reconstruct their narrative. Caregivers can help children label their feelings and provide a safe space to discuss and reflect on the trauma, which may prevent children from becoming overwhelmed or dysregulated by their internal experience. Participation in conversations about the traumatic experience should aid children in developing a vocabulary to describe their inner world, organizing their emotional experience, and in turn shaping their thoughts and feelings about the trauma and its aftermath, all of which should support deliberate rumination about the trauma, fostering schema change and growth. It can often be beneficial for parents to share their feelings and views on the trauma as well so that children can use these perspectives to help develop their new worldview (Yi & Kim, 2014).

Caregivers can also help children reconstruct their worldview by influencing children's contact with the external world (Kilmer et al., 2014). For instance, when caregivers give children the opportunity to attend memorial services or watch news coverage, it can prompt deliberate rumination and the recognition of losses and gains that come from traumatic experiences (Yoshida et al., 2016). In cases of death, it can be important to work with the child to find ways to honor the person who was lost. For example, a child who lost a friend to cancer might donate her hair to cancer survivors or shave her head as an act of solidarity (Kilmer et al., 2014).

Caregivers can also provide and encourage various means of creative expression (e.g., art, music, writing, play) and make an effort to understand what the child is expressing through each medium. As one example, the "after the storm, comes a rainbow" activity has been used to foster PTG in bereaved children. In this activity, children are given a drawing of a storm cloud and a rainbow. They are instructed to draw/write the hardest parts of their trauma experience in the storm cloud, the things that helped them get through the experience in the rainbow, and how they are now or hope they will be in the future at the bottom of the rainbow (Kilmer et al., 2014).

Conclusions and Recommendations for Future Research

Traumatic experiences are unfortunately common in childhood, and the successful navigation of these experiences is important for a child's lifelong success. The concept of PTG may explain how some children respond to trauma in remarkable ways, evidencing maturity and wisdom beyond their years. The existing literature suggests that children are quite capable of experiencing at least some aspects of PTG, but there is much that remains unknown regarding this process. Future research can play a critical role in delineating the nature and mechanisms by which children experience growth after trauma.

First, it will be important to integrate developmental and ecological frameworks into childhood PTG research. Future work would benefit from examining narrower age ranges to capture PTG processes among children in similar developmental periods. This way, conclusions can be drawn regarding the cognitive, linguistic and emotional competencies necessary for PTG and how they influence its emergence. In addition, closer attention to the ecology or contexts in which children are embedded could provide a more comprehensive understanding of how families, peers, schools, and communities (e.g., neighborhoods, as well as religious and cultural communities) support children's growth in the aftermath of trauma.

Second, prospective, longitudinal studies will be a crucial next step in understanding childhood trajectories after trauma and the extent to which PTG predicts healthy developmental outcomes over time. Longitudinal designs are also necessary to clarify the degree to which the nature, process, and presentation of PTG change as children get older (Kilmer et al., 2014). Furthermore, issues related to the role and timing of rumination and schema change within the growth process for children can be most effectively addressed by prospective, longitudinal work (Kilmer et al., 2014).

Third, it will be beneficial to explore the parenting and therapeutic practices that are most useful for promoting PTG in childhood. It will be important to go beyond broad concepts like social support and take a more fine-grained approach to understand precisely how and when parents, therapists, and important others can most effectively harness children's emerging skills in ways that support their capacity to cope.

Fourth, studies should utilize multimethod, multiinformant techniques to assess PTG and the developmental constructs thought to be relevant for PTG (e.g., child temperament, attachment, self-efficacy, emotion regulation, language skill). Expanding beyond self-report questionnaires will be vital in capturing the complexities of PTG among children. Additionally, use of mixed-method designs allows children and caregivers to describe their experiences in detail and discuss issues that are important to them, possibly leading to new avenues for research.

Children are quite capable of responding to adversity with increased maturity, the development of coping capabilities, and a more developed sense of themselves and the world. This process of PTG results from the struggle to understand a changed and challenging world, and a different future than was expected. This can be a naturally occurring process. Adults can facilitate it by encouraging exploration of how the child's world has changed and highlighting the ongoing changes in the child as they struggle with the new territory they confront. Although adults may sympathize with children in difficult circumstances, they can also acknowledge that children are capable of remarkable growth in the aftermath of trauma. With the proper support, adverse childhood events can become important turning points that children look back on with an appreciation for the growth and wisdom that ensued.

References

Aldridge, A. A., & Roesch, S. C. (2008). Developing coping typologies of minority adolescents: A latent profile analysis. *Journal of Adolescence, 31*(4), 499–517.

Alisic, E., Boeije, H. R., Jongmans, M. J., & Kleber, R. J. (2011). Children's perspectives on dealing with traumatic events. *Journal of Loss and Trauma, 16*(6), 477–496.

Alisic, E., van der Schoot, T. A., van Ginkel, J. R., & Kleber, R. J. (2008). Looking beyond posttraumatic stress disorder in children: Posttraumatic stress reactions, posttraumatic growth, and quality of life in a general population sample. *Journal of Clinical Psychiatry, 69*, 1455–1461.

Barakat, L. P., Alderfer, M. A., & Kazak, A. E. (2006). Posttraumatic growth in adolescent survivors of cancer and their mothers and fathers. *Journal of Pediatric Psychology, 31*(4), 413–419.

Bowlby, J. (1988). *A secure base: Parent-child attachment and healthy human development*. New York, NY: Basic Books.

Bretherton, I., Fritz, J., Zahn-Waxler, C., & Ridgeway, D. (1986). Learning to talk about emotions: A functionalist perspective. *Child Development, 57*, 529–548.

Calhoun, L. G., Cann, A., & Tedeschi, R. G. (2010). The posttraumatic growth model: Sociocultural considerations. In T. Weiss & R. Berger (Eds.), *Posttraumatic growth and culturally competent practice: Lessons learned from around the globe* (pp. 1–14). Hoboken, NJ: John Wiley & Sons.

Calhoun, L. G., & Tedeschi, R. G. (2006). *Handbook of posttraumatic growth: Research and practice*. Mahwah, NJ: Lawrence Erlbaum Associates.

Calhoun, L. G., & Tedeschi, R. G. (2013). *Posttraumatic growth in clinical practice*. New York, NY: Routledge.

Cohen, J. A., Deblinger, E., Mannarino, A. P., & Steer, R. A. (2004). A multisite, randomized controlled trial for children with sexual abuse-related PTSD symptoms. *Journal of the American Academy of Child and Adolescent Psychiatry, 43*, 393–402.

Cole, P. M., Armstrong, L. M., & Pemberton, C. K. (2010). The role of language in the development of emotion regulation. In S. D. Calkins & M. A. Bell (Eds.), *Child development at the intersection of emotion and cognition* (pp. 59–77). Washington, DC: American Psychological Association.

Compas, B. E., Connor-Smith, J. K., Saltzman, H., Thomsen, A. H., & Wadsworth, M. E. (2001). Coping with stress during childhood and adolescence: Problems, progress, and potential in theory and research. *Psychological Bulletin, 127*(1), 87–127.

Cowan, P. A., Cowan, C. P. & Schulz, M. S. (1996). Thinking about risk and resilience in families. In E. M. Hetherington & E. A. Blechman (Eds.), *Stress, coping, and resiliency in children and families* (pp.1–38). Hillsdale, NJ: Lawrence Erlbaum Associates.

Cryder, C. H., Kilmer, R. P., Tedeschi, R. G., & Calhoun, L. G. (2006). An exploratory study of posttraumatic growth in children following a natural disaster. *American Journal of Orthopsychiatry, 76*(1), 65–69. doi:10.1037/0002-9432.76.1.65

Currier, J. M., Hermes, S., & Phipps, S. (2009). Children's response to serious illness: Perceptions of benefit and burden in a pediatric cancer population. *Journal of Pediatric Psychology, 34*(10), 1129–1134.

Deblinger, E., Lippmann, J., & Steer, R. (1996). Sexually abused children suffering posttraumatic stress symptoms: Initial treatment outcome findings. *Child Maltreatment, 1*(4), 310–321.

Denham, S. A. (1998). *Emotional development in young children*. New York, NY: Guilford Press.

Dennis, T. A., & Kelemen, D. A. (2009). Preschool children's views on emotion regulation: Functional associations and implications for social-emotional adjustment. *International Journal of Behavioral Development, 33*(3), 243–252.

Eisenberg, N., Cumberland, A., & Spinrad, T. L. (1998). Parental socialization of emotion. *Psychological Inquiry, 9*(4), 241–273.

Fivush, R., & Haden, C. A. (Eds.). (2003). *Autobiographical memory and the construction of a narrative self: Developmental and cultural perspectives*. Mahwah, NJ: Lawrence Erlbaum Associates.

Hafstad, G. S., Gil-Rivas, V., Kilmer, R. P., & Raeder, S. (2010). Parental adjustment, family functioning, and posttraumatic growth among Norwegian children and adolescents following a natural disaster. *American Journal of Orthopsychiatry, 80*(2), 248–257.

Hafstad, G. S., Kilmer, R. P., & Gil-Rivas, V. (2011). Posttraumatic growth among Norwegian children and adolescents exposed to the 2004 tsunami. *Psychological Trauma: Theory, Research, Practice, and Policy, 3*(2), 130–138.

Harris, P. L., Olthof, T., & Terwogt, M. M. (1981). Children's knowledge of emotion. *Journal of Child Psychology and Psychiatry, 22*(3), 247–261.

Harter, S. (1986). Cognitive-developmental processes in the integration of concepts about emotions and the self. *Social Cognition, 4*(2), 119–151.

Harter, S. (2006). The self. In W. Damon & R. M. Lerner (Series Eds.) & N. Eisenberg (Vol. Ed.), *Handbook of child psychology: Vol. 3 Social, emotional, and personality development* (6th ed., pp. 505–570). Hoboken, NJ: Wiley.

Harter, S., & Buddin, B. J. (1987). Children's understanding of the simultaneity of two emotions: A five-stage developmental acquisition sequence. *Developmental Psychology, 23*(3), 388–399.

Helgeson, V. S., Reynolds, K. A., & Tomich, P. L. (2006). A meta-analytic review of benefit finding and growth. *Journal of Consulting and Clinical Psychology, 74*(5), 797–816.

Ickovics, J. R., Meade, C. S., Kershaw, T. S., Milan, S., Lewis, J. B., & Ethier, K. A. (2006). Urban teens: Trauma, posttraumatic growth, and emotional distress among female adolescents. *Journal of Consulting and Clinical Psychology*, *74*(5), 841–850.

Janoff-Bulman, R. (1992). *Shattered assumptions: Towards a new psychology of trauma*. New York, NY: Free Press.

Jieling, C., & Xinchun, W. (2017). Post-traumatic stress symptoms and post-traumatic growth among children and adolescents following an earthquake: A latent profile analysis. *Child and Adolescent Mental Health*, *22*(1), 23–29. doi:10.1111/camh.12175

Kilmer, R. P. (2006). Resilience and posttraumatic growth in children. In L. G. Calhoun & R. G. Tedeschi (Eds.), *Handbook of posttraumatic growth: Research and practice* (pp. 264–288). Mahwah, NJ: Lawrence Erlbaum Associates.

Kilmer, R. P., & Gil-Rivas, V. (2010). Exploring posttraumatic growth in children impacted by Hurricane Katrina: Correlates of the phenomenon and developmental considerations. *Child Development*, *81*(4), 1211–1227. doi:10.1111/j.1467–8624.2010.01463.x

Kilmer, R. P., Gil-Rivas, V., Griese, B., Hardy, S. J., Hafstad, G. S., & Alisic, E. (2014). Posttraumatic growth in children and youth: Clinical implications of an emerging research literature. *American Journal of Orthopsychiatry*, *84*(5), 506–518.

Kilmer, R. P., Gil-Rivas, V., Tedeschi, R. G., Cann, A., Calhoun, L. G., Buchanan, T., & Taku, K. (2009). Use of the revised Posttraumatic Growth Inventory for Children. *Journal of Traumatic Stress*, *22*(3), 248–253. doi:10.1002/jts.20410

Kimhi, S., Eshel, Y., Zysberg, L., & Hantman, S. (2009). Getting a life: Gender differences in postwar recovery. *Sex Roles*, *61*(7–8), 554–565.

Laufer, A., Raz-Hamama, Y., Levine, S. Z., & Solomon, Z. (2009). Posttraumatic growth in adolescence: The role of religiosity, distress, and forgiveness. *Journal of Social and Clinical Psychology*, *28*(7), 862–880.

Laufer, A., & Solomon, Z. (2006). Posttraumatic symptoms and posttraumatic growth among Israeli youth exposed to terror incidents. *Journal of Social and Clinical Psychology*, *25*(4), 429–447.

Lazarus, R. S., & Folkman, S. (1987). Transactional theory and research on emotions and coping. *European Journal of Personality*, *1*(3), 141–169.

Lieberman, A. F., & Van Horn, P. (2004). Assessment and treatment of young children exposed to traumatic events. In J. D. Osofsky (Ed.), *Young children and trauma: Intervention and treatment* (pp. 111–138). New York, NY: Guilford Press.

Little, S. G., Akin-Little, A., & Somerville, M. P. (2011). Response to trauma in children: An examination of effective intervention and post-traumatic growth. *School Psychology International*, *32*(5), 448–463. doi:10.1177/0143034311402916

Luthar, S.S., Cicchetti, D., & Becker, B. (2000). The construct of resilience: A critical evaluation and guidelines for future work. *Child Development, 71*(3), 543–562.

Masten, A.S. (2001). Ordinary magic: Resilience processes in development. *American Psychologist, 56*(3), 227–238.

Masten, A.S. (2016). Resilience in developing systems: The promise of integrated approaches. *European Journal of Developmental Psychology, 13*(3), 297–312.

McElheran, M., Briscoe-Smith, A., Khaylis, A., Westrup, D., Hayward, C., & Gore-Felton, C. (2012). A conceptual model of post-traumatic growth among children and adolescents in the aftermath of sexual abuse. *Counselling Psychology Quarterly, 25*(1), 73–82.

Meyerson, D.A., Grant, K.E., Carter, J.S., & Kilmer, R.P. (2011). Posttraumatic growth among children and adolescents: A systematic review. *Clinical Psychology Review, 31*(6), 949–964. doi:10.1016/j.cpr.2011.06.003

Milam, J., Ritt-Olson, A., Tan, S., Unger, J., & Nezami, E. (2005). The September 11th 2001 terrorist attacks and reports of posttraumatic growth among a multi-ethnic sample of adolescents. *Traumatology, 11*(4), 233–246.

Milam, J.E., Ritt-Olson, A., & Unger, J.B. (2004). Posttraumatic growth among adolescents. *Journal of Adolescent Research, 19*(2), 192–204.

Moyal, N., Henik, A., & Anholt, G.E. (2014). Cognitive strategies to regulate emotions-current evidence and future directions. *Frontiers in Psychology, 4*, 1019.

Oltjenbruns, K.A. (1991). Positive outcomes of adolescents' experience with grief. *Journal of Adolescent Research, 6*(1), 43–53.

Park, C.L., & Helgeson, V.S. (2006). Introduction to the special section: Growth following highly stressful life events—current status and future directions. *Journal of Consulting and Clinical Psychology, 74*(5), 791–796.

Phipps, S., Long, A.M., & Ogden, J. (2007). Benefit finding scale for children: Preliminary findings from a childhood cancer population. *Journal of Pediatric Psychology, 32*(10), 1264–1271.

Saarni, C., Campos, J.J., Camras, L.A., & Witherington, D. (2006). Emotional development: Action, communication, and understanding. In W. Damon & R.M. Lerner (Series Eds.) & N. Eisenberg (Vol. Ed.), *Handbook of child psychology: Vol. 3 Social, emotional, and personality development* (6th ed., pp. 226–299). Hoboken, NJ: Wiley.

Sales, J.M., Fivush, R., Parker, J., & Bahrick, L. (2005). Stressing memory: Long-term relations among children's stress, recall and psychological outcome following Hurricane Andrew. *Journal of Cognition and Development, 6*(4), 529–545.

Salmon, K., & Bryant, R.A. (2002). Posttraumatic stress disorder in children: The influence of developmental factors. *Clinical Psychology Review, 22*(2), 163–188.

Stegge, H., & Terwogt, M.M. (2007). Awareness and regulation of emotion in typical and atypical development. In J.J. Gross (Ed.), *Handbook of emotion regulation* (pp. 269–286). New York, NY: Guilford Press.

Taku, K., Cann, A., Calhoun, L. G., & Tedeschi, R. G. (2008). The factor structure of the Posttraumatic Growth Inventory: A comparison of five models using confirmatory factor analysis. *Journal of Traumatic Stress, 21*(2), 158–164.

Taku, K., Kilmer, R. P., Cann, A., Tedeschi, R. G., & Calhoun, L. G. (2012). Exploring posttraumatic growth in Japanese youth. *Psychological Trauma: Theory, Research, Practice, and Policy, 4*, 411–419.

Tedeschi, R. G., & Calhoun, L. G. (1995). *Trauma & transformation: Growing in the aftermath of suffering*. Thousand Oaks, CA: Sage Publications.

Tedeschi, R. G., & Calhoun, L. G. (1996). The Posttraumatic Growth Inventory: Measuring the positive legacy of trauma. *Journal of Traumatic Stress, 9*(3), 455–471.

Thompson, R. A. (1994). Emotion regulation: A theme in search of definition. *Monographs of the Society for Research in Child Development, 59*(2–3), 25–52.

Vaughn, A. A., Roesch, S. C., & Aldridge, A. A. (2009). Stress-related growth in racial/ethnic minority adolescents: Measurement structure and validity. *Educational and Psychological Measurement, 69*(1), 131–145.

Wolchik, S. A., Coxe, S., Tein, J. Y., Sandler, I. N., & Ayers, T. S. (2009). Six-year longitudinal predictors of posttraumatic growth in parentally bereaved adolescents and young adults. *OMEGA-Journal of Death and Dying, 58*(2), 107–128.

Yaskowich, K. M., & Stam, H. J. (2003). Cancer narratives and the cancer support group. *Journal of Health Psychology, 8*(6), 720–737.

Yi, J., & Kim, M. A. (2014). Postcancer experiences of childhood cancer survivors: How is posttraumatic stress related to posttraumatic growth? *Journal of Traumatic Stress, 27*(4), 461–467.

Yoshida, H., Kobayashi, N., Honda, N., Matsuoka, H., Yamaguchi, T., Homma, H., & Tomita, H. (2016). Post-traumatic growth of children affected by the Great East Japan earthquake and their attitudes to memorial services and media coverage. *Psychiatry and Clinical Neurosciences, 70*, 193–201. doi:10.1111/pcn.12379

Yu, X. N., Lau, J. T., Zhang, J., Mak, W. W., Choi, K. C., Lui, W. W., & Chan, E. Y. (2010). Posttraumatic growth and reduced suicidal ideation among adolescents at month 1 after the Sichuan earthquake. *Journal of Affective Disorders, 123*(1), 327–331.

Zoellner, T., & Maercker, A. (2006). Posttraumatic growth and psychotherapy. In L. G. Calhoun & R. G. Tedeschi (Eds.), *Handbook of posttraumatic growth: Research and practice* (pp. 334–354). Mahwah, NJ: Erlbaum.

CHAPTER 5

Trauma-Informed Care in the Pediatric Primary Care Setting

Larry Wissow and Betsy McAlister Groves

Other chapters in this volume address the definitions and ubiquity of trauma, its potential long-term impact, and ways in which traumatic stress may be prevented and treated. This chapter addresses how health-care systems in general, and children's health care in particular, can play a role in identifying, preventing, and treating trauma in children and adolescents. In the United States, children's visits to their pediatrician's office are frequent in the early years of life and continue on at least a yearly basis through adolescence. These visits provide numerous opportunities to ask about traumatic experiences and to provide general education about the impact of ongoing stress or trauma in the lives of children and families. The term "traumatic stress" refers to both chronic or ongoing trauma and single-incident traumatic events. Chronic traumatic exposure can include child abuse, exposure to domestic violence, exposure to community violence, and multiple painful medical procedures or treatments. It can also include the constant threats to stable nutritional, housing, and interpersonal resources experienced by families living in poverty. Single-incident traumas include sudden loss of a family member or close friend, serious accidents, natural disasters, residential fires, dog bites, and motor vehicle accidents. Given the wide range of potential traumatic stressors, virtually all pediatric practices see children and families who are impacted by trauma (Gillespie et al., 2009).

When families have adequate health insurance or if they are lucky enough to live where there are good free facilities, parents and children receive what is known as primary care—regular visits with either the same clinician or to a group of clinicians who share the same medical records, and visits that focus on prevention and health monitoring as well as sudden or chronic health problems. Despite the increased availability of health insurance, many families remain without insurance or are forced to change providers frequently for economic or social reasons, limiting their ability to form trusting relationships with a primary provider. These families often also struggle with poverty, which may be caused or compounded by trauma, and emergency facilities are likely to be their predominant source of medical care (Gindi, Cohen, & Kirzinger, 2012). Thus, although much of what is discussed in this chapter relates to the primary care system, the principles covered are even more important in emergency or urgent care facilities and health-care programs for the homeless.

When families receive primary care, they have an opportunity to get to know and hopefully come to trust the clinicians and other staff members caring for them. They feel more comfortable bringing up sensitive topics and are more likely to positively consider clinicians' advice. In turn, the clinicians and staff come to know the families, remembering issues from visit to visit, putting new problems in context, and noticing changes even when families don't immediately voice new concerns (Wissow et al., 2002). Primary care clinicians organize their prevention and health monitoring around recommendations from professional groups (the American Academy of Pediatrics, the American Academy of Family Physicians) and the U.S. Preventive Services Task Force or its equivalent in other countries. These recommendations cover a wide range of physical, developmental, mental health, and social problems that can be threats to health. Being aware of trauma, and being responsive to the needs of traumatized families, is increasingly included in these recommendations (Committee on Psychosocial Aspects of Child and Family Health, 2012).

At its best, primary care offers what has been called a "medical home"—a place where families feel comfortable, welcomed, and can count on having their needs met and coordinated (Asarnow, Kolko, Miranda, & Kazak, 2017). However, this ideal can be challenged even if families have adequate means and an identified primary care clinician. For its part, the primary care site may be busy beyond its true capabilities or staffed in a way that favors attending to physical health problems but no other issues. Preventive and monitoring visits may seem rushed given the volume of recommended checks and counseling the staff tries to include, leaving parents and children confused or without the opportunity to bring up other concerns. Families may not know that their clinician would welcome a discussion of fears, depression, stress, or other concerns not always associated with a "doctor visit." Families may also worry that bringing up these topics may make them appear badly in the eyes of the staff, or that saying the wrong thing could trigger reports to police or social service agencies (Polk et al., 2017). Much of what is discussed in this chapter is designed first and foremost to avoid these challenges to primary care and then to build upon a well-functioning primary care system to provide special resources that address trauma prevention and treatment. In a well-functioning system that recognizes the frequency with which trauma occurs, we want to:

- reduce or eliminate barriers to obtaining mental health or medical care for families who have experienced trauma;
- assure that health-care systems do not retraumatize individuals or contribute to stigma or any other adverse consequences of trauma;
- help clinicians recognize, and make it possible for individuals to safely disclose, traumatic experiences; and
- help families decide if trauma plays a role in any particular problem they seek care for, and, if they want, access trauma-related services when and how they would find them most useful.

Additional Definitions

In this chapter, we use the term "clinician" to refer to doctors, nurses, nurse practitioners, physician's assistants, social workers, psychologists, counselors, and community health workers; the term "staff" is used broadly to include all those with whom families may come in contact, especially individuals involved in reception, scheduling, referrals, and security. But it may be even more inclusive—even administrative staff members with no patient contact have a role in creating the culture of clinical care.

"Integrated care" refers to health care that brings together all the services that a patient (or ideally a family) requires in a coordinated fashion. When care is integrated, clinicians and staff communicate regularly, and together they act in a way that is responsive to a patient's unique needs and preferences (Singer et al., 2011). This chapter will focus on integration of mental health and primary care, though for many families integration must encompass mental health, primary care, developmental, medical, and social services.

"Trauma-informed care" recognizes the ubiquitous nature of trauma, its many manifestations, and the need to provide a safe place for recovery and growth. Trauma-informed integrated care takes special notice of the need to coordinate a multitude of services while helping families maintain a feeling of control and security.

A Framework for Strengthening the Role of Primary Care for Families with Children Who Experience Traumatic Stress

In 2012, with funding from the Substance Abuse and Mental Health Services Administration (SAMHSA) and its National Child Traumatic Stress Network, the Center for Mental Health Services in Pediatric Primary Care at Johns Hopkins University launched the Pediatric Integrated Care Collaborative, a multiyear project to increase the quality of child trauma services by integrating behavioral and physical health services, targeting traumatic stress exposure and recovery. This project brings together teams of pediatric clinicians, mental health providers, and family and community partners from around the country to participate in 18-month learning collaboratives. The broad goals of the learning collaboratives are to allow teams to develop plans for their practices to sustainably integrate trauma-informed behavioral health services with primary care. To date, 45 teams have participated in the collaboratives. They use a common framework of change to guide their work, using self-assessments to determine which components to prioritize for their individual practices. The components of the framework include:

1. **Creating a trauma-informed office**: Creating a warm and pleasant office environment communicates important messages to families, helping them to feel safe, improving communication and trust.
2. **Involving families in program development, implementation, and evaluation**: Family input into policy and practice decisions can improve the quality of care and communicates a sense of partnership between families and their primary care providers.
3. **Collaboration and coordination with mental health and community services**: Developing partnerships with community agencies to better meet the needs of families in areas such as housing, food and income security, and education; improving communication and coordination with clinicians who provide trauma-focused counseling services.
4. **Promoting resilience—Primary prevention of trauma and stress**: Providing guidance and education about the impact of stress on children;

assessing for exposure to potential traumatic experiences, supporting resilience and health coping strategies.

5. **Assessing trauma-related mental health and somatic issues**: Developing guidelines or protocols for systematically inquiring about trauma and stress.
6. **Addressing trauma-related mental health and somatic issues**: Providing brief services during the visit; referring for mental health services within or outside the practice.

These components of practice provide a framework for primary care practices, addressing the broader office culture and ensuring family input (see the Integrated Care Toolkit in Resources at the end of the chapter). The remainder of this chapter will explore these components in more depth.

Organizational Culture and Climate

Psychologists in industry and business have long paid attention to how the atmosphere in a factory or office plays a role in productivity and the quality of work. Efforts to improve the quality of health care have brought such studies to medical offices and hospitals, with similar findings. When medical staff members feel that they are respected and can trust each other, when they are open to new ideas and can be flexible in response to colleagues and patients' needs, the health of their patients is better (Becker & Roblin, 2008). Staff members are also more satisfied with their jobs and stay in them longer, which means that patients can interact with staff who know them better and who are more experienced (Brazil, Wakefield, Cloutier, Tennen, & Hall, 2010).

In contrast, when staff members feel burdened by their work, perceiving it as inappropriate for their expectations or overly stressful, patient care suffers. Primary care offices, not to mention emergency or urgent care sites, can be very busy places seeking to meet a wide range of needs often with minimal staff and resources. In addition, providing even routine care can be stressful for clinicians and staff members. While prevention and monitoring visits may bring opportunities to interact with healthy, happy families, other visits may involve families caring for seriously ill children or adults, or grieving for recent losses. For all of us, functioning on a day-to-day basis requires an optimism that good things will happen and bad things will not. Being a medical provider or working in a medical setting may challenge that optimism. Providers are faced with concentrated reminders of the misfortunes that can happen. Talking about traumatic experiences with families can be a particularly potent reminder that life can be difficult. Staff members can find themselves feeling angry and depressed, and becoming irritable or even punishing with colleagues and patients.

Building the capacity for health-care systems to play a role in trauma prevention and care thus involves creating and maintaining a culture that supports staff and makes it possible for them to offer the flexible, compassionate care that all families require. Health-care systems and offices can start by focusing on their environment (Mohr, Benzer, & Young, 2013). There are various tools to assess office climate. One, the "Friends and Family" method, simply asks staff members (and patients) if they would refer a friend or family member to get care at the site where they work (National Health Service, 2014). It has been used as part of systematic efforts to promote equitable high quality care. More elaborate questionnaires ask about opportunities for input into important decisions, feelings of control over day-to-day tasks, or a sense of respect for personal strengths and challenges (AHRQ, 2013; Jaén & Palmer, 2012). Sites can take stock of whether they have routines in place to uncover and solve system problems or to "huddle" and plan the care of families with more complicated needs. The best sites find ways to promote staff wellness on a daily basis and provide pathways for staff members to grow in their jobs through acquiring new skills or advancing to new positions. Sites that offer the best care also have clearly stated values that apply to both patients and staff—a commitment to listening, empathy, being of service, and working constantly to step back from the stresses of the moment and refocus on important human connections.

Trauma-Specific Knowledge

Child/adolescent victimization and exposure to traumatic experiences are common and can negatively impact physical and emotional health (Heleniak, Jenness, Vander Stoep, McCauley, & McLaughlin, 2016). As such, the identification of trauma belongs in the purview of the pediatrician and pediatric staff, in the same way that identifying child allergies or developmental problems is the clinicians' responsibility. However, clinicians and their staff may not feel that they are trained for or prepared to respond to trauma in their patients. Even when clinicians agree that trauma falls within their scope of practice, nurses, social workers, physicians, counselors, and administrators may have different skills and styles in responding. Their terminology may be different, and they may have conflicting approaches to care. Staff members who come from the community the site serves may have a very different view of the adversities faced by families compared to staff members who know little of their patients' lives outside the site's building.

Thus, a foundation of trauma readiness involves training and the exchange of experience and information among staff members (see listings at the end of this chapter for training resources). This process should be carefully planned so that the motivation and goals are clear: the recognition of trauma addresses problems that are lurking in plain sight, complicating existing care and reducing its effectiveness. Trauma is often a difficult subject to discuss and treat. The goal of training is to improve the situation for staff and patients—to potentially make work easier rather than harder by making it possible to talk about what is often the "elephant in the room" while other problems are being discussed. As with any training, the information must come from trusted sources and be delivered in a safe environment. Trauma touches nearly everyone, including staff members, so training requires recognition of the commonalities between client and staff experiences, and the possibility that staff members will want to talk openly or in private about their own experiences.

Core components of trauma training include a shared definition of trauma and data about why it is an important health issue psychologically and physiologically (National Child Traumatic Stress Network Core Curriculum on Childhood Trauma Task Force, 2012). Staff should develop a common understanding of the sources of trauma, the common responses of children and other family members to traumatic experiences, and the role of parents in supporting and buffering children from the intensity of the experience. There should be discussion and consensus on how those who experience trauma can be helped. In particular, staff should learn that trauma must be approached in an empathetic, nonjudgmental way, with a presumption that recovery is possible, and that perhaps the most important first step in working with those who have experienced trauma is to help restore their sense of control and mastery over their lives. With these principles in mind, learning about the communities from which families come can take place. What are the conditions of housing, transportation, schools, and recreational facilities, and how do they facilitate or limit a family's possibilities? To what kinds of violence might families be exposed—whether that is physical or emotional—because of where they live or where they are not able to live? What are the costs to families of seeking care—lost time, lost income, risks of disclosure? Some of this information is readily obtained from local governments or advocacy groups—much of it is best heard from the point of view of family members themselves who are invited to participate in the training and in planning the site's overall response to community needs.

Many health-care sites offer training in what is called "patient-centered" communication—ways of interacting that demonstrate respect and foster sharing of information and shared decision making (see resources following this chapter). However, trauma can challenge even experienced and well-trained clinicians, because individuals who have experienced trauma can have stronger emotional responses to routine care, be ambivalent or dismissive when given advice, or be demoralized to the point of invoking similar feelings of helplessness in clinicians. Training can provide additional skills that help clinicians navigate these situations: focusing on partnership, emphasizing choice, creating a sense of safety and time, and contributing to the sense that the medical site is a place where even very difficult matters can be aired and eventually dealt with.

Trauma-related knowledge and a comfort level with talking about trauma to families are not achieved in a single lecture or online module or from a single source. As with any other complex matter, successful learning and practice lead to a sense of mastery and to additional questions and a desire for more learning. The culture of a site prepared to prevent and treat trauma not only supports but also insists on ongoing learning both formally and informally. A set of topics may be planned for staff meetings or skills-based trainings, and supervisors or colleagues should voice their openness to talk about experiences as new knowledge is put to use.

Trauma-Aware Practices

In clinic settings where parents and children interact with multiple staff members, it is often someone other than a family's doctor—the person at the check-in desk, the medical assistant, the lab technician, the billing office staff—who encounters families when they are most stressed. Sometimes parents informally share information with office staff. The family may have had a difficult journey to the clinic; they may be late for reasons that they cannot control; they may have long waits in the waiting area with ill, tired, or frightened children. Front-desk staff can be trained (and supported) in ways to respond to stressed or angry parents (Christensen, Brown, Wissow, & Cook, 2016). Policies can assure that no one is turned away for being late without some discussion of the causes, current needs, and the burdens of trying to return at another time. Registration areas can afford a modicum of comfort and privacy, and waiting areas can be furnished in a way that allows for adult comfort and some degree of child freedom and entertainment. In particularly stressed communities, waiting areas by design are used as places of respite, education, and connection to resources. Assistants who help to collect previsit information (height, weight, main concerns) can be trained to elicit concerns that might not be immediately divulged and recognize when families seem to be distressed out of proportion to the situations that they say they are seeking help for.

How Is Trauma Recognized in Primary Care?

The majority of individuals—both children and adults—who have experienced a traumatic event may display few or no "symptoms," even to a trained observer. Sometimes this is because the individuals have been able to cope well and, at least for the present, have not experienced trauma-related distress. Individuals respond in different ways, some showing more symptoms than others. For children, the variance may be related to age, the severity of the traumatic stressor, the child's proximity to the event, whether the event involved a parent or someone known to the child, and the chronicity of the traumatic stressor. Many children and adolescents can adapt and regain equilibrium after a traumatic experience. This ability to adapt to stress and continue to function well or quickly return to healthy functioning is often referred to as resiliency (Ungar, 2015).

In contrast, some children who experience trauma find that the experience initially or for a longer term exceeds their ability to cope; they have difficulties in social and emotional functioning and may have problems with sleep, appetite, or pain. Immediately after trauma these difficulties may be obvious; children can be angry, fearful, "shut down," or agitated. The longer-term impact of trauma can be harder to detect. Children can appear to be "normal," but many have come to see the world in a different way than their peers. They may be more pessimistic, less trusting, or have a more negative view of themselves—or they find themselves reacting strongly to situations that remind them even obliquely of traumatic events. A minority of those who have experienced trauma will have chronic difficulties regulating their feelings and behavior in any situation in which they feel that their safety or autonomy are threatened.

Experts remain divided on how primary care sites can best recognize trauma, and whether attempts at recognition should focus on traumatic events themselves or on individuals or families' reactions to them. For example, some experts have suggested that families be asked if they have experienced certain stresses or traumatic events, regardless of whether they are reporting any sort of distress. Other experts suggest focusing questions on the distress itself—for example, sudden changes in behavior, increased fear, or avoidance of certain people or situations. There are several pathways for identifying potentially traumatic experiences in children or families. Parents may directly disclose a traumatic experience that the child or family has experienced: a death in the family, an automobile accident, a shooting in the neighborhood. Another pathway is offered when parents describe changes in a child's behavior and/or symptoms that are commonly associated with childhood trauma: sleep difficulties, changes in behavior, new fears or anxieties, school avoidance. A parent's concern about these changes provides an opportunity for the clinician to ask about stressful or potentially traumatic experiences that might have occurred. A third option is to provide systematic inquiry about traumatic stress to all families seen in the practice. Primary care sites have long incorporated checklists and questionnaires as part of their preventive care, notably for monitoring children's development. In recent years, this practice has expanded to include use of questionnaires about child and adolescent mental health and substance abuse, depression among mothers of young children, social stressors including hunger and housing problems, and exposure to domestic violence. However, validated tools for screening for exposure to traumatic events in primary care have not yet been established (see resources at the end of this chapter).

The routine use of questionnaires has several advantages. The topics the questionnaires cover are announced to families as something important to discuss and within the scope of care at the site. Questionnaires—and the answers to them—can be counted, enabling clinicians to track whether care is being delivered as planned and to systematically learn about the needs of those coming to the site. However, questionnaires also pose risks and challenges (Wissow et al., 2013). It takes time and infrastructure to assure that everyone who is supposed to respond to a questionnaire not only does so but also understands why the questions are being asked and what will happen to the answers. Families may need time and privacy to give their answers and may want to ask questions about items they have trouble understanding. There is the risk that families will run out of time, not complete the questionnaire, or tire of the process. Clinicians must review the questionnaire answers and discuss them with families. This is especially important because the answers that families give can be very subjective and variable. Answers—positive or negative—are a starting point for discussion rather than an expression of a medical certainty. Assuring that this review happens may add a new component to the already-packed visit. In addition, clinicians may have to change established routines or alter the topics they normally cover.

These issues are particularly important for questionnaires that ask about trauma. There are a growing number of trauma-focused questionnaires in use or under development (see resources at end of chapter). However, there is as yet no agreement on a standard approach. It is unlikely that one approach will prove useful and acceptable across the range of practice settings and with families who might be asked about trauma. Facilities can consider incorporating questions about trauma into previsit questionnaires or questions during a visit, but only after exploring acceptable ways of doing this in the populations served. This is an important opportunity to seek direct input from parents about which questions are suitable and how to frame the questions. Questionnaires that focus only on negative or traumatic experiences, not inquiring about strengths or resilience in children, may be more difficult for families. Two questionnaires in particular, the SWYC (Strengths and Weaknesses in Young Children; Sheldrick & Perrin, 2013) and the SEEK, ask a range of questions that explore both potential strengths as well as vulnerabilities (Feigelman, Dubowitz, Lane, Grube, & Kim, 2011). Protocols for following up on both positive and negative responses are also essential.

When a Traumatic Event Is Disclosed—First Steps in Primary Care

The primary health-care clinic can be an essential source of support and information to help a family weather trauma with minimal impact. Pediatric clinicians and staff are among the first people that parents turn to when they are concerned about their children. Clinicians can help by responding with empathy, respect, and assurance of support. No matter how dangerous or disruptive the family's life may be, the clinic can be a place of emotional and physical safety. Depending on the clinic staff roles and responsibilities, the pediatric clinician may be the provider who talks with parents about their child's traumatic experience, or in many integrated practices, the behavioral health clinician is available to meet with the family for a more extensive discussion of the trauma and the family's needs. In many clinics, other staff members including nurses, medical assistants, and even front-desk or security staff may have established trusting relationships with families over time and can serve as essential members of a team that offers support and understands the family's needs.

People who have experienced trauma may feel ashamed or fear the consequences of disclosure. As the sociologist David Finkelhor noted, people often experience trauma at the hands of those whom they otherwise would trust the most, making it difficult to risk new, confiding relationships (Finkelhor & Browne, 1985). Trauma can harm the fragile sense that people have of being able to control what happens to them, including confidence in the ability to control their own emotions and reactions. Confronted by reminders of trauma or day-to-day difficulties, people who have experienced trauma can have intense feelings of worry, anger, or an intense desire to flee.

For these reasons, the first step in responding to a child or parent's disclosure of trauma is establishing or reinforcing an atmosphere of privacy, respect, and safety. Clinicians may start by asking permission to explore or bring up subjects related to trauma and take time to explain why they want to have the conversation. They can check on how their patient is experiencing the conversation, asking if it would help to take a break. The clinician might provide reassurance that there is no right or wrong amount of disclosure about what has happened in the past; for now the main concern is what can be done to help those involved.

The next step is to assess if there are ongoing threats to the family's safety or to their basic needs. If there are, a plan must be developed to address these essential needs. Sometimes, one or more family members are in immediate danger, perhaps from an abusive partner or because they have become homeless. Parents or children may report that they feel so desperate or hopeless in the face of what has happened that they have thought about killing themselves. Just as medical care sites are prepared for medical emergencies, they should also be prepared for psychosocial emergencies, rehearsing their responses and having personnel, supplies, and referral resources at hand. If possible, having access to food, diapers or other supplies, in a quiet place while families wait for information or transportation, can help them maintain their dignity and make the best decisions on their own behalf. Being able to offer to monitor children while parents make telephone calls or talk to police or other services is also a much-valued service.

After the basic needs are addressed, the clinician may provide information and education (see resources at end of chapter) about trauma: what it can do to the body, the common symptoms or behaviors associated with trauma, and information about how best to support the child. This guidance and education can be a powerful intervention. Parents are reassured that the behaviors they see in their children are "normal" responses to abnormal events. It reassures them that others have experienced the same situation and found ways to cope. They have concrete information from a respected professional about how to support their child. If the clinician is able to reassure the parent and reduce his/her anxiety, this will also benefit the child. It also helps parents feel confident that clinicians are knowledgeable and competent about trauma. Topics covered might include:

- Typical reactions that children or other family members might have (or not have) and how to interpret them
- Stress-related physical symptoms like headaches, stomach aches, or vomiting
- Healing from trauma—supports and treatments that can help, what families may expect over time
- The importance of predictability and routines for the child: regular daily schedules, meals, bedtimes, and parent–child activities
- For traumas that are reported in the media as news, guidelines for parents on how they can regulate children's exposure to reports and talk with them about the events in an age-appropriate way
- Techniques to promote relaxation and a sense of well-being—deep breathing, progressive relaxation, trying to resume some previously enjoyed activities
- Talking with children about the traumatic experience—being open to children's concerns; thinking about ways to respond with small active steps that demonstrate the possibility of retaking some control over life
- Helping parents seek support for themselves—recognition of parent stress, self-care, access to mental health or other support services if requested or needed

Despite the complexity of trauma, many important strategies for help are within the toolbox of primary care providers—making sure that medical issues are taken care of, that basic needs are being met, and that parents feel capable of responding to their children's emotional, behavioral, and educational needs.

Supporting Child–Parent Relationships

Within families, many of the manifestations of trauma play out as difficulties with parent–child interactions. It is not unusual to see families in which a parent has a history of trauma or has been exposed to the same trauma as the child. This is often the case in working with families affected by domestic violence. In these cases, both the parent and the child may be impacted by trauma. For children, this often results in dysregulated sleep and behavior. For stressed parents, their patience and their resources for coping with challenging behavior in children may be limited. Primary care clinicians are usually good sources of brief advice and trouble-shooting on parent–child interactions.

Several programs have been developed—some of which can be made available directly in health-care offices—that offer more intensive help for parents of children of various ages (Barlow, Bergman, Kornør, Wei, & Bennett, 2016; Furlong et al., 2013). These programs improve parents' ability to help children of all ages regulate their behavior and emotions and form strong, trusting bonds with family members (see resources at end of chapter). They teach parents about the usual range of children's behavior, provide support for the difficulties of parenting, and advice about activities that promote both parent and child wellness. Though programs come in virtually every form imaginable—group or individual, self-instructional via books or electronically—the most effective seem to be ones in which parents have a chance to practice and get feedback from instructors or fellow parents. Many programs find benefits for parents as well as for children—the child's behavior improves and so does parents' mood and sense of well-being. Studies show that a strong child–parent relationship is an essential tool in helping children cope with stress—from moderate stress to overwhelming stress (Child Welfare Information Gateway, 2014).

Preventing or reducing the impact of trauma overlaps with another goal of children's primary care, which is to promote cognitive development. Being ready to start school, and later on succeeding in school's academic and social demands, is one of the best predictors of children's long-term developmental success and a powerful factor in their ability to cope with trauma. School success gives children a strong sense of satisfaction and the ability to connect with helping adults and peers outside of their family (Ungar, 2015).

One of the most widely disseminated programs promoting parent–child interaction, school readiness, and literacy is the American Academy of Pediatrics' "Reach Out and Read" (Thakur, Sudhanthar, Sigal & Mattarella, 2016). The program provides free books—selected for their popularity with parents and children and matched to age groups from toddlers to high school—that can be given out at medical visits with the suggestion that parents read them to younger children or have parents and children read separately and discuss for older children. The program's goal is to promote early literacy as well as the intimacy and interpretive abilities afforded by sharing a book and talking about its contents.

Talking about reading also offers the opportunity to discuss other topics with parents that can contribute to trauma awareness or prevention. One of the ways that families help children learn how to regulate behavior and emotion, including regulating sleep and eating, is by having routines on which children can depend. Asking about when parents and children might read together makes for a natural way to discuss routines and their benefits.

In recent years, pediatric primary care sites have taken on responsibility for identifying parents who may be challenged by depression, alcohol or drug problems, or abusive partners (Earls & Committee on Psychosocial Aspects of Child and Family Health, 2010). Parents affected by these problems deserve help in their own right. All are threats to parents' ability to provide the kinds of interactions and support that promote healthy child development, and in some cases they have a direct relationship to children's exposure to trauma. When children are cared for by family physicians or nurse practitioners, detection and discussion of these parental problems may be routine and relatively simple, especially if parents get their care at the same medical site. However, in pediatric primary care settings, this task is more difficult. Pediatric practitioners may not feel competent or supported to assess and provide care for adults. In pediatric clinics parents are not the formal patient, and pediatric providers may hesitate to write about parent problems in a child's medical record. Pediatric providers, however, frequently give parents advice about breastfeeding, self-care, and other issues related to health in the first weeks of a child's life. Pediatricians may offer parents suggestions about managing their own eating habits in the context of counseling about a child's diet, or about smoking cessation in the context of raising a child with asthma (Farber, Walley, Groner, & Nelson, 2015). Advisory bodies recommend that clinicians, regardless of specialty, look routinely for depression among the parents of young children. Asking about abuse in the home and assisting parents to find services for intimate partner violence or alcohol and drug abuse, has long been a recognized responsibility in pediatric primary care practices, though sites vary in their knowledge of these services and of the extent to which they can help affected parents. Parents may not have their own health insurance, or they do not consider it necessary to have a regular, trusted source of care. Women experiencing interpersonal violence may not be free to seek care for themselves but can safely attend medical visits for their children. Thus, children's services may be a critical gateway to help for parents as well as for children.

Links to Community and Other Mental Health Services

In a "medical home," a member of the care team may assume responsibility for providing links to additional services, if needed. The family and the primary clinician decide who should be involved, what the other services will be, and how important information will be shared.

When the word "referral" is used with families, some may interpret the suggestion in a negative way: their case is beyond the scope of a regular doctor and only a specialist offers any hope; their story is so awful that it has repulsed the referring clinician, who cannot tolerate working with them; the referral is just one more instance in which someone who might have been trusted has abandoned them. The families may dread having to tell their story again, worry that they will not be understood, or that in another setting their confidence will be betrayed. Worst of all, they fear that in some new setting they will lose control of the process and find themselves feeling coerced into treatment or action that is at best uncomfortable and at worst causes additional trauma. With these thoughts in mind, clinicians should discuss referrals carefully and transparently.

Many mental health and community service agencies require that families call to initiate services as a test of their motivation to follow through with appointments. Research in children's mental health services has shown that these sorts of policies serve as a barrier to care rather than an incentive. The term "warm handoff" has become popular in medical circles. It implies that when referrals are initiated, they happen in the context of a personal introduction from someone on the team to the new referral source or provider. Ideally, the present team member knows the new person and can give an endorsement, a summary of what to expect, and plan for how the new and existing team members will communicate and share information (if the family consents). Personal interaction or relationships between collaborating providers may make it easier to secure services for patients and improve the outcomes. To accomplish the goal of the "warm handoff," primary care clinicians should develop relationships with specialty and community services. They must also understand the forms of treatment those services provide, what it is like to receive the treatment, and what outcomes can be expected.

Increasingly, medical care sites are employing community health workers or case managers who can either make arrangements for families or accompany them to initial visits (Moffett, Kaufman, & Bazemore, 2017). In some settings, these types of staff members are recruited from the community where patients live and play an essential role as language or cultural translators for families that do not speak English or who are unfamiliar with the health-care system.

Conclusions

Research has clearly shown the link between child exposure to trauma or ongoing significant stress and long-term adverse physical and mental health impacts. Pediatric primary care systems have unique opportunities for identifying and responding to child traumatic stress. Virtually all children are seen in the pediatric health system at some point. There are well-established protocols for routine well-child visits with a pediatrician, beginning at the two-week postpartum visit, and going through adolescence, providing ongoing opportunities for inquiry, guidance, and preventive education. The "medical home" and its team of clinicians and staff can provide education about the impact of stress on children and families, inquire about stressors in families' lives, and connect families with needed services.

A trauma-informed health practice infuses awareness about the pervasiveness of trauma into all aspects of its services. It provides a safe, trusted environment. Using a strength-based approach, clinicians routinely ask about trauma and stress while supporting the child and families' resilience. In short, the trauma-informed practice assures families of ongoing support and assistance, helping them to reestablish a sense of control over their lives.

Resources

Organizational culture

- The National Coalition for Dialogue and Deliberation provides materials for a wide range of participatory approaches to building consensus and promoting change. www.ncdd.org
- The COMPASS-Primary Health and Behavioral Health questionnaire is a self-assessment tool designed to facilitate group discussions about behavioral health-related culture in primary care. http://www.integration.samhsa.gov/operations-administration/assessment-tools

Trauma-prepared pediatric primary care

- The integrated care "Toolkit" from the National Child Traumatic Stress Network's Pediatric Integrated Care Collaborative includes a trauma-specific readiness assessment and links to other tools related to providers' trauma-related stress and resilience. http://web.jhu.edu/pedmentalhealth/PICC.html
- Substance Abuse and Mental Health Services Administration. Trauma-Informed Care in Behavioral Health Services. Treatment Improvement Protocol (TIP) Series 57. HHS Publication No. (SMA) 13–4801. Rockville, MD: Substance Abuse and Mental Health Services Administration, 2014.

Core clinician skills and knowledge for trauma-related care

- Patient-centered care training: listing of training opportunities from the Patient-Centered Primary Care Collaborative. https://www.pcpcc.org/training-programs/list
- National Center on Domestic Violence, Trauma, and Mental Health. Exercises for grounding, emotional regulation and relaxation for children and

their parents, 2014. http://www.nationalcenterdvtraumamh.org/wp-content/uploads/2012/01/Exercises-for-Grounding-Emotional-Regulation-Relaxation-Final.pdf

- Academy on Violence and Abuse. "Best Practices" for adverse childhood experiences. http://www.avahealth.org/resources/aces_best_practices/aces-best-practices.html

Prevention

- Center for the Study of Social Policy—Strengthening Families. http://www.cssp.org/reform/strengtheningfamilies
- The Centers for Disease Control's newly enhanced website targeted directly to families with downloadable materials for children of all ages and videos about parenting young children. http://www.cdc.gov/parents/
- Essentials for Childhood Framework: Steps to Create Safe, Stable, Nurturing Relationships and Environments for All Children. https://www.cdc.gov/violenceprevention/childmaltreatment/essentials.html
- Fussy Baby Network. The Facilitating Attuned Interactions (FAN) approach. http://www.erikson.edu/fussybaby/national-network/
- American Academy of Pediatrics. Center on Healthy Resilient Children. https://www.aap.org/en-us/advocacy-and-policy/aap-health-initiatives/CHRC/Pages/Default.aspx

Screening

- Compendium of tools asking about exposure to adverse childhood experiences (ACEs). http://www.acesconnection.com/g/resource-center/blog/resource-list-extended-aces-surveys
- Safe Environment for Every Kid (SEEK) screening tool and training. http://umm.edu/programs/childrens/services/child-protection/seek-project
- Survey of Well-being of Young Children (SWYC). www.theswyc.org

Evidence-based practice

- Blueprints for Health Youth Development. http://www.blueprintsprograms.com/
- National Child Traumatic Stress Network—Treatments That Work. http://www.nctsn.org/resources/topics/treatments-that-work/promising-practices#q4

Community collaboration

- http://tamarackcci.ca/blogs/liz-weaver/turf-trust-and-collaboration-spectrum

References

Agency for Healthcare Research and Quality (AHRQ). (2013). *Team-based primary care measures database*. Retrieved from https://primarycaremeasures.ahrq.gov/team-based-care/

Asarnow, J.R., Kolko, D.J., Miranda, J., & Kazak, A.E. (2017). The pediatric patient-centered medical home: Innovative models for improving behavioral health. *American Psychologist, 72*(1), 13–27.

Barlow, J., Bergman, H., Kornør, H., Wei, Y., & Bennett, C. (2016). Group-based parent training programmes for improving emotional and behavioural adjustment in young children. *The Cochrane Database of Systematic Reviews, 8*, CD003680.

Becker, E.R., & Roblin, D.W. (2008). Translating primary care practice climate into patient activation: The role of patient trust in physician. *Medical Care, 46*(8), 795–805.

Brazil, K., Wakefield, D.B., Cloutier, M.M., Tennen, H., & Hall, C.B. (2010). Organizational culture predicts job satisfaction and perceived effectiveness in pediatric primary care practices. *Health Care Management Review, 35*, 365–371.

Child Welfare Information Gateway. (2014). *Parenting a child who has experienced trauma*. Washington, DC: U.S. Department of Health and Human Services, Children's Bureau.

Christensen, A.L., Brown, J.D., Wissow, L.S., & Cook, B. (2016). Spillover of ratings of patient-and family-centered care. *The Journal of Ambulatory Care Management, 39*(4), 308–315.

Committee on Psychosocial Aspects of Child and Family Health (COPACFH). (2012). Early childhood adversity, toxic stress, and the role of the pediatrician: Translating developmental science into lifelong health. *Pediatrics, 129*(1), e224–e231. doi:10.1542/peds.2011–2662

Earls, M.F., & Committee on Psychosocial Aspects of Child and Family Health. (2010). Incorporating recognition and management of perinatal and postpartum depression into pediatric practice. *Pediatrics, 126*(5), 1032–1039.

Farber, H.J., Walley, S.C., Groner, J.A., & Nelson, K.E. (2015). Clinical practice policy to protect children from tobacco, nicotine, and tobacco smoke. *Pediatrics, 136*(5), 1008–1017.

Feigelman, S., Dubowitz, H., Lane, W., Grube, L., & Kim, J. (2011). Training pediatric residents in a primary care clinic to help address psychosocial problems and prevent child maltreatment. *Academic Pediatrics, 11*(6), 474–480.

Finkelhor, D., & Browne, A. (1985). The traumatic impact of child sexual abuse: A conceptualization. *American Journal of Orthopsychiatry, 55*(4), 530–541.

Furlong, M., McGilloway, S., Bywater, T., Hutchings, J., Smith, S.M., & Donnelly, M. (2013). Cochrane review: Behavioural and cognitive-behavioural group-based parenting programmes for early-onset conduct problems in children aged 3 to 12 years. *Evidence-Based Child Health: A Cochrane Review Journal, 8*(2), 318–692.

Gillespie, C. F., Bradley, B., Mercer, K., Smith, A. K., Conneely, K., Gapen, M., . . . Ressler, K. J. (2009). Trauma exposure and stress-related disorders in inner city primary care patients. *General Hospital Psychiatry, 31*(6), 505–514.

Gindi, R. M., Cohen, R. A., & Kirzinger, W. K. (2012). Emergency room use among adults aged 18–64: Early release of estimates from the National Health Interview Survey, January—June 2011. *National Center for Health Statistics*. Retrieved from http://www.cdc.gov/nchs/nhis/releases.htm

Heleniak, C., Jenness, J. L., Vander Stoep, A., McCauley, E., & McLaughlin, K. A. (2016). Childhood maltreatment exposure and disruptions in emotion regulation: A transdiagnostic pathway to adolescent internalizing and externalizing psychopathology. *Cognitive Therapy and Research, 40*(3), 394–415.

Jaén, C. R., & Palmer, R. F. (2012). Shorter adaptive reserve measures. *The Annals of Family Medicine, 8*(Suppl 1), 1–2.

Moffett, M. L., Kaufman, A., & Bazemore, A. (2017). Community health workers bring cost savings to patient-centered medical homes. *Journal of Community Health*, 1–3. doi:10.1007/s10900–017–0403-y

Mohr, D. C., Benzer, J. K., & Young, G. J. (2013). Provider workload and quality of care in primary care settings: Moderating role of relational climate. *Medical Care, 51*(1), 108–114.

National Child Traumatic Stress Network Core Curriculum on Childhood Trauma Task Force. (2012). *The 12 core concepts: Concepts for understanding traumatic stress responses in children and families*. Retrieved from http://www.nctsn.org/resources/audiences/parents-caregivers/what-is-cts/12-core-concepts

National Health Service. (2014). *The NHS Friends and Family Test (FFT)*. Retrieved from https://www.nhs.uk/NHSEngland/AboutNHSservices/Pages/nhs-friends-and-family-test.aspx

Polk, S., Horwitz, R., Longway, S., Bonilla, A., Fothergill, K., Karver, M., . . . Wissow, L. (2017). Surveillance or engagement: Children's conflicts during health maintenance Visits. *Academic Pediatrics, 7*, 739–746.

Sheldrick, R. C., & Perrin, E. C. (2013) Evidence-based milestones for surveillance of cognitive, language and motor development. *Academic Pediatrics, 13*(6), 577–586. doi:10.1016/j.acap.2013.07.001

Singer, S. J., Burgers, J., Friedberg, M., Rosenthal, M. B., Leape, L., & Schneider, E. (2011). Defining and measuring integrated patient care: Promoting the next frontier in health care delivery. *Medical Care Research and Review, 68*, 112–127.

Thakur, K., Sudhanthar, S., Sigal, Y., & Mattarella, N. (2016). Improving early childhood literacy and school readiness through Reach Out and Read (ROR) program. *BMJ Quality Improvement Reports, 5*(1), u209772–w4137.

Ungar, M. (2015). Practitioner review: Diagnosing childhood resilience—a systemic approach to the diagnosis of adaptation in adverse social and physical ecologies. *Journal of Child Psychology and Psychiatry, 56*(1), 4–17.

Wissow, L. S., Brown, J., Fothergill, K. E., Gadomski, A., Hacker, K., Salmon, P., & Zelkowitz, R. (2013). Universal mental health screening in pediatric primary care: A systematic review. *Journal of the American Academy of Child & Adolescent Psychiatry, 52*(11), 1134–1147.

Wissow, L. S., Roter, D., Larson, S. M., Wang, M. C., Hwang, W. T., Johnson, R., & Luo, X. (2002). Mechanisms behind the failure of residents' longitudinal primary care to promote disclosure and discussion of psychosocial issues. *Archives of Pediatrics & Adolescent Medicine, 156*(7), 685–692.

CHAPTER 6

Trauma-Informed Schools and a Framework for Action

Christopher Blodgett

As research has informed our understanding of the short- and long-term consequences of trauma on children and adolescents, there has been strong interest in translating the science of child traumatic stress into actionable interventions. Not surprisingly, schools have become a major focus for these efforts. In 2005, the publication *Helping Traumatized Children Learn* (Cole et al., 2005) proposed a flexible framework of interventions that focused on whole-school change. Since then, there have been numerous articles and publications written on the topic, and in 2015, the release of a documentary that chronicled the efforts of a high school in Washington, *Paper Tigers* (Pritzker & Redford, 2015), helped make accessible to a broad audience the scope of the problem and the power of sensitive intervention from adults in the school.

This awareness has not only changed policy in many schools but also changed national policy and state/municipal laws. A first-of-its-kind lawsuit (Watanabe, 2015) asserts that failure to address trauma in students is a failure to provide educational access. Further, the federal Every Student Succeeds Act (ESSA), enacted in 2015 as the replacement for the No Child Left Behind Act, defines the obligation of schools to address trauma to improve student supports. The ESSA directs state and local educational authorities to provide professional development in assessment of the effects of trauma in students, identification and referral for trauma-related needs, and knowledge of trauma-informed educational practices. The ESSA guidance is broad, and the manner in which educational systems interpret these new directives will evolve over time. Despite the explosive rise in interest and efforts in many parts of the country, knowledge of effective school-based trauma-informed interventions is in its infancy, and there have been few, if any, systematic evaluations of such interventions.

This chapter will focus on the following areas: (1) a brief review of the relevant research that supports the framework for trauma-informed school practices; (2) research on resilience, building child resilience in school settings, and the uses of strength-based approaches; (3) the range of strategies that fall under the definition of trauma-informed school-based interventions; and (4) how trauma-informed practices align with other significant educational improvement practices.

Research Supporting Trauma-Informed School Practices

Two bodies of research on child and adolescent trauma have particular relevance for designing school-based interventions: the findings from the Adverse Childhood Experiences Study (ACES) and research on complex trauma (see Chapters 3 and 14 in Volume I for detailed discussions of both topics). Children and adolescents may be exposed to a wide range of traumatic experiences, including natural disaster, war, terrorism, medical trauma, and accidents. The research on ACES and complex trauma focuses on chronic interpersonal trauma, including physical and sexual abuse, domestic violence, and other familial stressors. In school-age children, national surveys estimate that annually more than 60 percent of children are either directly or indirectly exposed to violence (Finkelhor, Turner, Ormrod, Hamby, & Kracke, 2009; Finkelhor, Turner, Shattuck, & Hamby, 2015). Traumatic events can be life altering particularly because of the power of tragedies such as sexual assault, terrorism, and community or school violence. However, traumatizing events for most individuals do not result in long-term developmental and adjustment struggles. For example, lifetime prevalence rates for PTSD are estimated at 6.8 percent in the general adult population (Kessler et al., 2005) and 5 percent in adolescents (Merikangas et al., 2010).

Distinguishing acute traumatic events from a child's chronic experiences of trauma helps to define a school's response. The focus of intervention and skills required in schools to address single or acute traumatic events versus chronic experiences are distinct even while they incorporate common support goals. Traumatic events such as school shootings, hurricanes, or a sudden death of a member of the school community are acute crises—sometimes preventable but always unpredictable. These crises require immediate actions to protect and address the acute struggles of adjusting to tragedy. An example of a crisis response protocol that is trauma informed, psychological first aid (PFA; Brymer et al., 2006), is a widely employed evidence-informed set of recommendations that addresses the acute crisis response with the goal of minimizing the risk of persisting adaptive struggles. A school specific version of PFA is available at http://www.nctsn.org/content/psychological-first-aid-schoolspfa.

By contrast, the developmental struggles associated with adverse childhood experiences (ACEs) are chronic processes contributing to persistent difficulties in school. While ACEs can occur at any time during childhood or adolescence, these disruptions typically are established early in life when the child is least capable of exercising control over the environment and lacks the language to create meaning from tragedy. For instance, 28 percent of child maltreatment victims are identified before the age of three (U.S. Department of Health and Human Services, 2015).

Until recently, little has been known about the scope of ACEs in childhood and the effects of ACEs exposure on concurrent child development. Using data from the National Survey of Children's Health, Bethell, Newacheck, Hawes, and Halfon (2014) reported that 23 percent of children ages 0–17 and 31 percent of children ages 12–17 experienced two or more ACEs with most exposure initiated before the age of 11. Blodgett (2014) found that among children (N = 1,066) enrolled in an urban Head Start program, 55 percent of children had experienced two or more ACEs and 25 percent had experienced four or more ACEs. Blodgett and Lanigan (2016) used school personnel's knowledge as the mechanism to assess ACEs exposure and found in a random sample of 2,101 elementary-aged children that 22 percent of children had two or more known ACEs and 11 percent had three or more known ACEs. Burke, Hellman, Scott, Weems, and Carrion (2011) found that 36 percent of children ages 0–20 in a high-risk pediatric practice experienced at least two ACEs. The emerging research on ACEs in childhood confirms the significant exposure in the general population, its emergence through preschool and the elementary years, and the disproportionate levels of exposure in disadvantaged communities.

ACEs in childhood are associated with significant direct impacts on child well-being and academic success. Bethell et al. (2014) found that when children with no reported ACEs were compared to children with two or more ACEs, the children with two or more ACEs were 2.7 times more likely to repeat a grade in school, demonstrated lower school engagement, and were significantly more likely to be identified with special health-care needs (32% vs. 15%). Burke et al. (2011) reported that children with four or more ACEs compared to children with no ACEs were at significantly greater risk for learning and school behavior problems (51% of children with four or more ACEs compared to 3% of children with no ACEs) and were more likely to be obese. In an urban Head Start program, Blodgett (2014) associated childhood ACEs with teachers' independent ratings of child development. Children with four or more ACEs were rated as significantly delayed on multiple cognitive and social emotional development indicators at enrollment, and this developmental gap persisted one year after enrollment. Blodgett and Lanigan (2016) found a linear relationship between known ACE exposure and academic failure such that the 11 percent of children with three or more known ACEs compared to children with no known ACEs were respectively three times more likely to be academically failing in elementary school, five times more likely to experience chronic attendance problems, and six time more likely to be identified with significant school behavior concerns. While more research is needed, ACEs in children appear to have a significant contributing role in academic success and the quality of individual student and whole-school educational experiences.

Child exposure to multiple ACEs typically results in severe, persisting disruptions to caregiver–child relationships and threats to basic emotional and physical safety. Brain development is placed at risk because of disruption in key developmental resources due to disrupted caregiving and hypersensitization to potential threats. Trauma resulting from ACEs is expressed through a variety of biological, affective, behavioral, and cognitive adaptations referred to in mental health disciplines as *complex trauma* (Spinazzola et al., 2005). Complex trauma includes both exposure to multiple ACEs early in life and the process of adaptation when a child is exposed to disrupted caregiving, violence, and/or child maltreatment. In more impacted children, when daily function is significantly compromised, complex trauma is also referred to as complex posttraumatic stress disorder or developmental trauma disorder.

Complex trauma disrupts the capacity of the young child to develop the skills to manage or regulate emotions, an essential developmental skill. Courtois (2004) and Cook, Blaustein, Spinazzola, and van der Kolk (2003) describe complex trauma as expressed through alterations in attention and consciousness, including dissociative experiences that interfere with full awareness of immediate circumstances; hypervigilance and heightened reactivity to environmental changes; irritability; distorted self-perception, including a persistent sense of shame and lack of worth;

sensory–motor development and sensory integration difficulties that result in disruptive sensitivity to environmental stimuli; somatization of stress and a sense of poor well-being; struggles with intimacy, fear of rejection, and poor skills in managing conflict; and impulsivity, lack of planning, and coping strategies that are self-defeating and disturbing to others. Each of these characteristics of complex trauma can interfere with learning and school adjustment.

The aforementioned expressions of complex trauma are familiar to most educators as common behavior problems in the classroom. The challenge for educators is to move from awareness of trauma and its effects to the capacity to recognize and respond effectively to complex trauma's expression. This shift in practice involves a range of skills that both draw upon and challenge existing educator practices. Adopting a complex trauma framework provides a focus to understanding both *why* a child is behaving as he or she is and *how* to invest efforts to mitigate the developmental disruptions that result from ACEs.

Multiple mental health interventions for complex trauma share a common core of recommendations for effective treatment (adapted from Courtois & Ford, 2009):

- Interrupting continuing traumatic experiences for children and their caregivers
- Creating supportive relationships for the child and the child's caregivers
- Maintaining high quality and continuing relationships as the foundation of care
- Building affect recognition and self-regulations skills to address common skills deficits
- Support for the anticipatory management of new developmental challenges and crises

The Attachment, Self-Regulation, and Competence (ARC) Framework (Blaustein & Kinniburgh, 2010) is a widely used framework for educators. Rather than a highly prescriptive and structured intervention, ARC is an adaptive framework to guide response to trauma in support of both caregivers and children. Reflecting the consensus recommendations for addressing complex trauma (Cook et al., 2003), the ARC Framework addresses complex trauma as biological adaptations largely outside of intentional control that address two interwoven needs: securing safety and having core needs met. Safety needs arise principally because highly unpredictable and inconsistent caregiving early in life disrupts secure relationships critical to learning that the world can be a stable and reasonable safe place. Without this essential foundation of security, seeking safety becomes a dominating concern for trauma-affected individuals. Blaustein and Kinniburgh further argue that trauma disrupts the protective function of the caregiver–child relationship. In the absence of consistent modeling of effective and socially appropriate means to getting needs met for human connection, sense of mastery, and basic physical needs, the child will develop his or her own strategies to get needs met.

In summary, two conceptual contributions from understanding ACEs and complex trauma provide distinctive tools for schools. The first contribution is that the behaviors that are characterized as trauma-related often evolved as strategies that were at one time adaptive in the face of overwhelming stress. What was adaptive for the child in the past does not work in school settings, where persistence and self-regulation skills are essential. Trauma recovery can thus be approached through a skills development framework, which is well aligned with schools' educational mission. Addressing the graded impact of trauma in the lives of children aligns well with the adoption in education of a multi-tiered system of support (MTSS; e.g., Sulkowski & Michael, 2014) with its emphasis on integration of academic and social emotional learning.

The second contribution of the ACEs and complex trauma research is the concept of the continuum of severity of a child's adaptation to trauma. Many children who struggle with complex trauma will not meet standards for a formal mental health diagnosis; however, they still struggle profoundly with school and other developmental tasks essential to lifelong success. The struggles include impulsivity, noncompliance, and problems with attention, leading to disciplinary consequences, social isolation, and poor academic performance issues. Adversity exposure in childhood is an active process, and developmental deficits may only become apparent with increasing developmental demands as the child ages. The graded effect of trauma and the scope of exposure to ACEs underscore the importance of addressing the developmental needs of all children and not restricting our attention to the most vulnerable and most challenging.

Thirty years of evolving mental health treatment for children affected by trauma yields several lessons that can be translated into educational practice. The core question for addressing a traumatized child's distressing behavior is, *what is the need that is being served?* This focus on understanding the function of behavior is a fundamental shift in practice for educators who have been trained to focus on the behavior itself and the antecedents and consequences that frame the behavior. Adopting the view that trauma behavior is driven by safety-seeking and fulfillment of needs challenges the practices of many educators. Preservice teacher preparation rarely includes significant education in child development, and only a few universities include courses addressing adversity and trauma. Therefore, there are systematic gaps in the preparation of many educators and school practices to address trauma.

At its core, the shift to trauma-informed practice moves our attention from the functional analysis of behavior to the functional analysis of need. The goals in addressing complex trauma include (1) skills to recognize the need being served by students' behaviors, (2) creation and maintenance of high-quality relationships, (3) age-appropriate regulation of emotions, (4) skills training to replace adaptive strategies no longer suited to the setting, and (5) progressive mastery of age-appropriate developmental skills. The foundation for this shift is the student–teacher relationship. This relationship can have powerful effects on student achievement, and it has the power to mitigate the disruptions in primary caregiver relationships (Bergin & Bergin, 2009; Verschueren & Koomen, 2012).

Resilience as the Strength-Based Complement to Addressing Trauma

Resilience is broadly defined as the ability to grow and thrive despite prolonged adversity (Luthar et al., 2000). Even in the face of significant cumulative adversity, children can have experiences that build resilience. We are both the things taken from us and the gifts we have received. Under optimal conditions, resilience develops within the family and in natural communities such as schools. Schools can be a critical resource in offering opportunities to children to succeed and to enhance their resilience. This is important for all children and essential for children who have histories of trauma.

Michael Rutter, an early pioneer in the study of child resilience (1987), proposed that changing the trajectory of risk from adversity requires several mutually supportive strategies, beginning with efforts to address basic safety or survival needs. This is familiar territory in any school. Staff may identify child maltreatment, homelessness, food insecurity, or other risks. Coordination of referrals to needed services as well as food and clothing banks in schools are existing practices in many schools. Second, students need targeted education in effective relationships and self-management strategies to replace the trauma responses that were effective in surviving adversity but now are mismatches to conditions in the school. Addressing trauma must be complemented with new opportunities for students' growth that is built through persistent and meaningful effort. Rutter argues this is accomplished by creating experiences with students that (1) support a reality-based and earned sense of self-esteem and self-efficacy and (2) create opportunities for students to have restorative experiences by accomplishing real and meaningful contributions through work and relationships that promote genuine personal mastery. It is this focus on building a trajectory of growth out of trauma that is at the heart of adopting resilience as a core component of trauma-informed school practice.

Ginsberg (2011) identified seven "Cs" to define the goals of resilience work: competence, confidence, character, connection, contribution, coping, and control. Three of these goals—competence, confidence, and contribution—require opportunities for students to try with real opportunities to fail. Resilience-building work in trauma-informed schools require a school culture for the systematic scaffolding of the conditions for real work calibrated to the current capacity of the student. Schools offer many opportunities for such experiences to be embedded in the school routine through academics, athletics, the arts, and the school as a community. These kinds of opportunities provide important support for all students in building resilience and a sense of mastery or competence.

Addressing the Family and Community Context in Which Schools Operate

Implementing effective school trauma responses requires an understanding of the familial and community context in which schools operate. The core social resources (caregiver capacity, social connections, and material resources) are essential for recovery from complex trauma. While schools can be sanctuaries and critical settings for mitigating the effects of complex trauma, school responses will be most effective when supported by family and community engagement efforts. Parents both serve as first teachers and have a critical role throughout a student's educational experience (Henderson & Mapp, 2002). The capacity for parent–school alliances is influenced by the parents' own experience with education and by the quality of their attachment to their children (Bergin & Bergin, 2009). Consequently, a parent's own trauma history has the potential for intergenerational continuation of trauma (McDonnell & Valentino, 2016; Schofield, Lee, & Merrick, 2013; Thornberry & Henry, 2013; Thornberry, Knight, & Lovegrove, 2012) and the potential to significantly impact the developmental and academic success of his or her own children (Bifulco et al., 2002). There is hope that intergenerational continuation of adversity can be interrupted when parents have a positive approach (growth mind-set; e.g., Haimovitz & Dweck, 2016) to challenges and authoritative rather than authoritarian parenting skills (Jeon & Neppl, 2016; Narayan et al., 2017; Schofield et al., 2013). Alliance building with parents and supporting the essential roles they play in the lives of their children are an important element of a trauma-informed school. Creating partnerships with community agencies and programs helps to address the concrete needs that many students and their families face.

Strategies for Creating Trauma-Informed Schools

While there is general agreement about the core components of a trauma-informed school, there is no consensus on the best approach for creating such a school. Efforts to create and evaluate a systemic implementation approach are in their infancy, with recognition of a variety of potential strategies. School approaches to trauma-informed practice can be organized along three continua:

- **Locally initiated versus formal structured model programs intended for replication.** Locally initiated programs may take a decentralized, "bottom-up" approach, with staff using a flexible approach to training and implementation. The more structured approaches are carefully sequenced, often using a more centralized approach to implementation.
- **Mental health focused and trauma-specific versus population health–focused and trauma-informed.** Trauma-specific refers to focused efforts to address specific trauma symptoms through formal treatment while trauma-informed and population-focused usually indicate a greater emphasis on recognizing the broad effects of adversity and trauma. Population-focused places an emphasis on overall ACEs' risk and the graded impact of trauma while mental health-focused addresses the most vulnerable students
- **Student-centered versus system-centered.** Student-centered prioritizes response to individual students while system-centered refers to efforts that include student supports but emphasizes how overall policies and school climate need to be trauma informed.

Despite a lack of consensus on implementation, a range of strategies are being used. These include:

- **Structured, mental health–focused, student-centered, and trauma-specific** strategies exemplified by school-based mental health services and targeted trauma response interventions such as Cognitive Behavioral Interventions for Trauma in Schools (CBITS; Stein et al., 2003). CBITS is a structured brief group intervention, supported by individual child and caregiver sessions, to address skills for recovery following an acute traumatic event.

- **Locally initiated, trauma-informed, population-focused, and system-centered** strategies represented by several school specific efforts:
    - San Diego, California: Cherokee Point Elementary School
    - Walla Walla, Washington: Lincoln High School
    - Massachusetts Advocates for Children Trauma and Learning Policy Initiative (TLPI; Cole, Eisner, Gregory, & Ristuccia, 2013; Cole et al., 2005). https://traumasensitiveschools.org/
    - Compassionate Schools (e.g., Washington State Office of the Superintendent of Public Instruction, Washington Department of Education). http://www.k12.wa.us/compassionateschools/pubdocs/TheHeartofLearningandTeaching.pdf
- **Structured, population-focused, trauma-informed, and system-centered models** reflected in programs such as:
    - The Sanctuary Model (Bloom & Farragher, 2013)
    - Collaborative Learning for Educational Achievement and Resilience (CLEAR; http://ext100.wsu.edu/clear/about/)
    - Healthy Environments and Response to Trauma in Schools (HEARTS; Dorado, Martinez, McArthur, & Leibovitz, 2016). http://coe.ucsf.edu/coe/spotlight/ucsf_hearts.html
    - The Neurosequential Model in Education (http://childtrauma.org/nme/)
    - Turnaround for Children (https://www.turnaroundusa.org/)

Locally initiated trauma-informed school efforts dominate the national landscape of trauma-informed school practice, although the spread of these efforts is difficult to measure because there is no central repository for these efforts. This reflects the strong national interest in adversity and trauma, as well as the tradition in American education that supports significant local control of educational practices. The appeal of frameworks such as the Massachusetts Advocates for Children's TLPI is that they provide a flexible design approach and targets for change, allowing for schools to assess their individual strengths and needs and design interventions accordingly. However, the decentralized nature of these efforts makes drawing generalization about implementation and impact difficult.

Structured, mental health–focused, trauma-specific strategies, such as CBITS, are valued as specific evidence-based resources for students who have trauma histories. These services may exist in integrated mental health services in schools where services can be coordinated with educational goals for affected children or colocated in schools without extensive coordination. These school–mental health partnerships reduce barriers to accessing care. These services are intended to address acute traumatic crises and treatment for formal mental health disorders. While there are efforts to align trauma-informed mental health services in an MTSS strategy that aligns treatment with health promotion and school climate initiatives, the success in integration is variable (Adelman & Taylor, 2008; Weist et al., 2014).

The third strategy for trauma-informed school response includes formal intervention models that address schoolwide system change to become trauma-informed organizations. Models such as the Sanctuary Model, mentioned previously, provide formal education and skills-building strategies to shift adult practices on behalf of children. Like locally initiated trauma-informed school efforts, these structured interventions reflect MTSS practices including formal treatment services. They are explicit about change strategies with common targets but varying strategies to reach intended changes in practice. These models share broad strategies including formal professional development, coaching to support adoption of new practices, and formally sequenced implementation of strategies over extended time periods. While only preliminary outcome evidence is available for these formal models given their relatively recent development, a principal advantage of this approach, in contrast to locally initiated efforts and similar to mental health treatment strategies, is that the nature of the intervention and their theories of change can be specified in detail as a core condition for outcomes research.

Alignment of Educational Improvement Practices and Trauma-Informed Care

Initiative overload is common in schools, and both initiative fatigue and cynicism about poorly executed or unsustainable innovations in the schools create barriers to implementing new initiatives. There are two common initial responses among most educators when the concept of trauma-informed practices is introduced. First, they comment on the scope of ACEs and how trauma is reflected in the day-to-day challenges they address in their classrooms. The second response is typically, "How can I add one more thing to my plate"? Aligning trauma-informed practices with existing school initiatives and providing hope that good practice can be enhanced with new skills to reach children helps mobilize educators and open the opportunity for this work. The pervasiveness of adversity and resulting trauma helps educators see this opportunity as a unique approach to multiple barriers to school success. As one educator said, "You're not telling me that trauma response is one more thing on my plate. You're telling me it's the plate." While not a panacea, trauma-informed practices hold the promise of reducing disciplinary struggles, low school commitment, poor school climate, and classroom management struggles while offering effective strategies for individualization of instruction for the highest need students.

Educators are also curious about the value added above the current best practices and how can trauma-informed practices align with current efforts to reduce burden on educators due to increasing rules and performance standards. The question is addressed initially by presenting the evidence that trauma has complex negative impacts in ways that can be understood and addressed. Ultimately, the question will be answered by measurable improvements in educators' work performance, work satisfaction, quality of school climate, and the ability to raise the collective success of the whole school.

The alignment discussion is addressed by explicitly demonstrating how trauma-informed practice extends rather than competes with existing educational practices. In the education improvement practice literature, significant alignment exists between trauma-informed whole-school strategies and two education practices: social emotional learning (SEL) as a universal education practice and the shift in school climates from punitive disciplinary practices to restorative or other alternative disciplinary practices and the adoption of authoritative school leadership practices.

SEL practices, which have been extensively adopted across the United States, include a variety of curricula, skills building interventions, school policy, and climate strategies to support social emotional competence in all students. Social emotional competence is characterized by the consistency with which one regulates emotional arousal, forms mutually supportive relationships with others, copes with reasonable levels of change, exercises empathy and social awareness in decisions, and persists in the face of frustration (Eisenberg & Fabes, 1992). Multiple meta-reviews have demonstrated that social emotional competence is a primary predictor of academic success and life-span social and health adjustment (Durlak, Weissberg, Dymnicki, Taylor, & Schellinger, 2011; Elias, Parker, Kash, & Dunkeblau, 2007; Suido & Shaffer, 2008). High quality SEL school programs have also been demonstrated to increase competence and produce improved academic success (Durlak et al., 2011). The promise of SEL practice for schools is, however, dependent on the quality of implementation (Social and Character Development Research Consortium, 2010) and effectiveness in managing how complex systems such as schools introduce and sustain innovations in practice (Evans, Murphy, & Scourfield, 2015).

Effective SEL practice addresses the core elements of self-regulation, persistence, and capacity to form high-quality interpersonal relationships that are central to resilience and most likely to be disrupted by trauma. When addressing whole-school improvement goals, schoolwide SEL practices are trauma-informed practices. The universal shifts in school community expectations and skills building benefit all students by creating more respectful, predictable, and consistent environments. These shifts in the schools' social environment have the potential to be particularly beneficial to students with significant trauma exposure. However, high-quality SEL practices are the necessary but may not be the sufficient conditions to address trauma's impact on individual students and the school community. As an example, the use of positive reinforcement for practice of SEL principles is a universal characteristic of SEL programs. But positive attention for some individuals with trauma histories is a triggering event and can lead to counterintuitive reactions that can be disruptive to educator–student relationships. Given the scope of trauma risk in the general population, enhancing SEL practices with skills to recognize and respond to trauma responses can support both educators and students through complementary practices rather than competitive strategies.

In the past 25 years, school disciplinary practices have moved toward the adoption of zero tolerance policies and the related use of punitive disciplinary practices (suspensions, expulsions, pushing out to alternative education programs). This strategy has proven to be a failed experiment. The evidence demonstrates that these practices have not contributed to safety and have been significant contributors to educational access disparities for disadvantaged and vulnerable students, particularly students of color (Mallett, 2016). In a review of the literature, Skiba, Arredondo, and Williams (2014) concluded that "above and beyond individual, family, and community risk factors, exclusionary school discipline makes a significant contribution in and of itself to a range of negative developmental outcomes" (p. 556).

In the pursuit of alternative approaches, accountability strategies that minimize punishment and increase the overall quality of the school's climate have been principle innovations in recent years. Accountability strategies involve consistent rules with consistent consequences that are applied without the use of guilt or shame. The focus of accountability is on restoration, not retribution. In schools, the rise of restorative practices (e.g., Gregory, Cornell, & Fan, 2011), which emphasizes understanding, repair in relationships, and restitution when required, has been associated with improved attendance, lower referrals for disruptive behaviors, and increased likelihood of being on track for graduation or improved academic progress. Fully implemented, restorative practices are whole-school strategies to reduce and resolve conflict and are intended to create respectful and supportive school climates. Closely aligned in values if not specific methods, authoritative school climate theory (Gregory et al., 2010) asserts that high-quality school environments producing better student outcomes are defined by a balanced use of clear rules, high expectations, and support to students and staff defined by warmth and emotional responsiveness. Authoritative school practices contribute to reduced student risk behaviors (Cornell & Huang, 2016), reduced peer victimization (Gregory et al., 2010), as well as teachers experiencing reduced aggression from students and reduced work stress (Berg & Cornell, 2016). Both the practices of restorative justice and authoritative school climate align with SEL practices and are aligned with core trauma-informed care principles of building human connections, allowing for failure and repair, and supporting resilience through efforts to grow past disruption and loss. However, the success of these strategies for trauma-affected students and staff depends on the level of individual self-regulation, particularly under stress, that allows them to be fully engaged participants in these community building and conflict resolution efforts. As with SEL practice, understanding how trauma affects students is likely to increase the consistency and effectiveness of these strategies to the benefit of the individual and the school community.

The Challenges That Lie Ahead

The need for adopting trauma-informed school practices is unambiguous, and the cost of not doing so is clear. Research has shown that early indicators of education failure—attendance problems, low academic achievement, grade retention, and school behavior problems—are directly linked to ACEs' history and resulting trauma adaptations. These indicators have direct impact on graduation rates, which are one of the strongest predictors of life-span health and social success (Freudenberg & Ruglis, 2007). The impact of trauma on a child's early school success is not only an individual matter, but it also contributes to the quality of schools as communities.

However, our knowledge of what works in schools is limited. With the exception of trauma-informed mental health services that ideally are part of a school's continuum of trauma-informed practices, the outcome evidence for trauma-informed school practices is largely anecdotal or from small-scale studies. Reductions in disciplinary referrals, improved attendance, and improved staff satisfaction are common indicators in the limited evaluations of trauma-informed practices. There is a critical need for better evaluation and controlled studies.

Fortunately, much has been learned about the spread of evidence-based practices (EBPs) in medicine, social services, and education that can provide a guide. The acknowledged challenge for EBPs is that despite their strong initial evidence for effectiveness, the nature of organizational resources, process, and management support routinely compromises successful adoption of specific EBPs. These costly and common failures in scaling up EBPs have led to specific recommendations under the umbrella of "implementation science" (Fixsen, Naoom, Blase, Friedman, & Wallace, 2005). Implementation science is now a well-established research-to-practice improvement effort that pairs innovative practices with guidelines for installation and support of sustainable practices.

Kitson, Harvey, and McCormack (1998) proposed that implementation requires management of three processes to support innovation success, "the level and nature of the evidence, the context or environment into which the research is to be placed, and the method or way in which the process is facilitated." (p. 149). The quality of the evidence to address ACEs, trauma, and resilience is extensive, and the credibility of the evidence drives the need to act. Context refers to leadership practices, access to supervision, quality of training in new practices, preparedness of staff, the scope of internal and external demands on the organization, and the culture of the organization regarding risk-taking and rewards. Facilitative conditions refer to the organization's capacity and resources to ease change. Critically, facilitative success is a leadership function with qualities of authoritative leadership (openness, reliability, skill in role) being critical conditions for success.

Fixsen and colleagues have extended this work with both assessment and support strategies to address the "drivers" of successful implementation. Implementation drivers include competency in staff, supervisors, and management; organizational capacity to support practice and use data to guide implementation; and leadership capacity to both inspire and facilitate effective practices. In their approach, implementation progresses in predictable stages that need to be navigated successfully. These stages include exploration regarding practices to be adopted, instillation of the new practices through training and systems development, initial implementation including management of challenges, full implementation, and finally transition to sustainable practice. When the persistent management of the stages of implementation and building of capacity in each the three implementation drivers is incomplete, innovation fails. In this period of experimentation in trauma-informed school practices, the challenges are considerable.

Despite these challenges, there is reason for hope. The necessary steps to help children replace trauma behaviors and to build resilience are within reach of any adult who cares for children. Children and their caregivers are easily engaged and validated by first understanding how adaptation to adversity can change them and also how to learn and incorporate new behaviors. The concepts of ACEs normalize the experience of trauma for professionals, students, and families, so the conversations about how to move forward and thrive are possible. The experience of ACEs and potential resulting trauma is more about how we are the same than how we are different or broken. For educators, trauma-informed practice is not one more thing but the heart of the work that they do on behalf of children.

References

Adelman, H. S., & Taylor, L. (2008). School-wide approaches to addressing barriers to learning and teaching. In B. Doll & J. Cummings (Eds.), *Transforming school mental health services: Population-based approaches to promoting the competency and wellness of children*. Thousand Oaks, CA: Corwin Press.

Berg, J., & Cornell, D. (2016). Authoritative school climate, aggression toward teachers, and teacher distress in middle school. *School Psychology Quarterly, 31*(1), 122–139.

Bergin, C., & Bergin, D. (2009). Attachment in the classroom. *Educational Psychology Review, 21*(2), 141–170.

Bethell, C. D., Newacheck, P., Hawes, E., & Halfon, N. (2014). Changing epidemiology of children's health. Adverse childhood experiences: Assessing the impact on health and school engagement and the mitigating role of resilience. *Health Affairs, 33*(12), 2106–2115.

Bifulco, A., Moran, P. M., Ball, C., Jacobs, C., Baines, R., Bunn, A., & Cavagin, J. (2002). Childhood adversity, parental vulnerability and disorder: Examining inter-generational transmission of risk. *Journal of Child Psychology and Psychiatry, 43*(8), 1075–1086.

Blaustein, M., & Kinniburgh, K. (2010). *Treating traumatic stress in children and adolescents: How to foster resilience through Attachment, Self-Regulation, and Competency*. New York, NY: The Guilford Press.

Blodgett, C. (2014). ACEs in Head Start children and impact on development. Manuscript submitted for publication.

Blodgett, C., & Lanigan, J. (2016). The association between adverse childhood experience and academic risk in elementary school children. Manuscript submitted for publication.

Bloom, S. L., & Farragher, B. (2013). *Restoring sanctuary: A new operating system for trauma informed organizations*. New York, NY: Oxford University Press.

Brymer, M., Jacobs, A., Layne, C., Pynoos, R., Ruzek, J., Steinberg, A., Vernberg, E., & Watson P. (National Child Traumatic Stress Network and National Center for PTSD). (2006, July). *Psychological first aid: Field operations guide* (2nd ed.). Retrieved from www.nctsn.org and www.ncptsd.va.gov

Burke, N.J., Hellman, J.L., Scott, B.G., Weems, C.F., & Carrion, V.G. (2011). The impact of adverse childhood experiences on an urban pediatric population. *Child Abuse & Neglect, 35*(6), 408–413.

Cole, S.F., Eisner, A., Gregory, M., & Ristuccia, J. (2013). *Helping traumatized children learn: Creating and advocating for trauma-sensitive schools.* Boston, MA: Massachusetts Advocates for Children.

Cole, S.F., O'Brien, J.G., Gadd, M.G., Ristuccia, J., Wallace, D.L., & Gregory, M. (2005). *Helping traumatized children learn: Supportive school environments for children traumatized by family violence.* Boston, MA: Massachusetts Advocates for Children.

Cook, A., Blaustein, M., Spinazzola, J., & van der Kolk, B. (Eds.). (2003). Complex trauma in children and adolescents. National Child Traumatic Stress Network. Retrieved from http://www.NCTSNet.org

Cornell, D., & Huang, F. (2016). Authoritative school climate and high school student risk behavior: A cross-sectional multi-level analysis of student self-reports. *Journal of Youth and Adolescence, 45*(11), 2246–2259.

Courtois, C. A. (2004). Complex trauma, complex reactions: Assessment and treatment. *Psychotherapy, 41*(4), 412–425. https://doi.org/10.1037/0033-3204.41.4.412

Courtois, C. A., & Ford, J. D. (2009). *Treating complex traumatic stress disorders: an evidence-based guide.* New York, NY: Guilford Press.

Dorado, J.S., Martinez, M., McArthur, L.E., & Leibovitz, T. (2016). Healthy environments and response to trauma in schools (hearts): A whole-school, multi-level, prevention and intervention program for creating trauma-informed, safe and supportive schools. *School Mental Health, 8*(1), 163–176.

Durlak, J.A., Weissberg, R.P., Dymnicki, A.B., Taylor, R.D., & Schellinger, K.B. (2011). The impact of enhancing students' social and emotional learning: A meta-analysis of school-based universal interventions. *Child Development, 82*(1), 405–432.

Eisenberg, N., & Fabes, R.A. (1992). Emotion, regulation, and the development of social competence. In Margaret S. Clark (Ed.), *Emotion and social behavior. Review of personality and social psychology* (Vol. 14, pp. 119–150). Thousand Oaks, CA: Sage Publications, Inc.

Elias, M.J., Parker, S.J., Kash, V.M., & Dunkeblau, E. (2007). Social-emotional learning and character and moral education in children: Synergy or fundamental divergence in our schools? *Journal of Research in Character Education, 5*(2), 167–181.

Evans, R., Murphy, S., & Scourfield, J. (2015). Implementation of a school-based social and emotional learning intervention: Understanding diffusion processes within complex systems. *Prevention Science, 16*, 754–764.

Finkelhor, D., Turner, H., Ormrod, R., Hamby, S., & Kracke, S. (2009). Children's exposure to violence: A comprehensive national survey. *Juvenile Justice Bulletin, October*, 1–11.

Finkelhor, D., Turner, H., Shattuck, A., & Hamby, S. (2015). Prevalence of childhood exposure to violence, crime, and abuse: Results from the national survey of children's exposure to violence, *JAMA Pediatrics, 169*(8), 746–754.

Fixsen, D.L., Naoom, S.F., Blase, K.A., Friedman, R.M., & Wallace, F. (2005). *Implementation research: A synthesis of the literature* (FMHI Publication #231).

Freudenberg, N, & Ruglis, J. (2007). Reframing school dropout as a public health issue. *Prevention of Chronic Disease, 4*(4), 1–11.

Ginsberg, K. (2011). *A parent's guide to building resilience in children and teens: Giving your child roots and wings*. Elk Grove, IL: American Academy of Pediatrics.

Gregory, A., Cornell, D., & Fan, X. (2011). The relationship of school structure and support to suspension rates for black and white high school students. *American Educational Research Journal, 48*(4), 904–934.

Gregory, A., Cornell, D., Fan, X., Sheras, P., Shih, T., & Huang, F. (2010). Authoritative school discipline: High school practices associated with lower bullying and victimization. *Journal of Educational Psychology, 102*(2), 483–496.

Haimovitz, K., & Dweck, C.S. (2016). What predicts children's fixed and growth intelligence mind- sets? Not their parents' views of intelligence but their parents' views of failure. *Psychological Science, 27*, 859–869.

Henderson, A.T., & Mapp, K.L. (2002). *A new wave of evidence: The impact of school, family, and community connections on student achievement*. Austin, TX: Southwest Educational Development Laboratory.

Jeon, S., & Neppl, T.K. (2016). Intergenerational continuity in economic hardship, parental positivity, and positive parenting: The association with child behavior. *Journal of Family Psychology, 30*(1), 22–32.

Kessler, R.C., Berglund, P., Delmer, O., Jin, R., Merikangas, K.R., & Walters, E.E. (2005). Lifetime prevalence and age-of-onset distributions of DSM-IV disorders in the National Comorbidity Survey Replication. *Archives of General Psychiatry, 62*(6), 593–602.

Kitson, A., Harvey, G., & McCormack, B. (1998). Enabling the implementation of evidence based practice: A conceptual framework. *Qualitative Health Care, 7*(3), 149–158.

Luthar, S.S., & Cicchetti, D. (2000). The construct of resilience: Implications for intervention and social policy. *Development and Psychopathology, 12*, 857–885.

Luthar, S. S., Cicchetti, D., & Becker, B. (2000). The construct of resilience: A critical evaluation and guidelines for future work. *Child Development, 71*(3), 543–62. Retrieved from http://www.ncbi.nlm.nih.gov/pubmed/10953923

Mallett, C. A. (2016). The school-to-prison pipeline: A critical review of the punitive paradigm shift. *Child & Adolescent Social Work Journal, 33*(1), 15–24.
Merikangas, K. R., He, J., Burstein, M., Swanson, S. A., Avenevoli, S., Cui, L., Benjet, C., Georgiades, K., & Swendsen, J. (2010). Lifetime prevalence of mental disorders in U.S. adolescents: Results from the national comorbidity survey replication-adolescent supplement (NCS-A). *Journal of the American Academy of Child & Adolescent Psychiatry, 49*(10), 980–989.
McDonnell, C. G., & Valentino, K. (2016). Intergenerational effects of childhood trauma: Evaluating pathways among maternal ACEs, perinatal depressive symptoms, and infant outcomes. *Child Maltreatment, 21*(4), 317–326.
Narayan, A. J., Kalstabakken, A. W., Labella, M. H., Nerenberg, L. S., Monn, A. R., & Masten, A. S. (2017). Intergenerational continuity of adverse childhood experiences in homeless families: Unpacking exposure to maltreatment versus family dysfunction. *American Journal of Orthopsychiatry, 87*(1), 3–14.
Pritzker, K. (Producer), & Redford, J. (Director). (2015). *Paper tigers*. United States: KPJR Films.
Rutter, M. (1987). Psychosocial mechanisms and protective mechanisms. *American Journal of Orthopsychiatry, 57*(3), 316–331.
Schofield, T. J., Lee, R. D., & Merrick, M. T. (2013). Safe, stable, nurturing relationships as a moderator of intergenerational continuity of child maltreatment: A meta-analysis. *Journal of Adolescent Health, 53*(4), S32–S38.
Skiba, R. J., Arredondo, M., & Williams, N. T. (2014). More than a metaphor: The contribution of exclusionary discipline to a school-to-prison pipeline. *Equity & Excellence in Education, 47*(4), 546–564.
Social and Character Development Research Consortium. (2010). *Efficacy of schoolwide programs to promote social and character development and reduce problem behavior in elementary school children* (NCER 2011–2001). Washington, DC: National Center for Education Research, Institute of Education Sciences, U.S. Department of Education.
Spinazzola, J., Ford, J., Zucker, M., van der Kolk, B., Silva, S., Smith, S., & Blaustein, M. (2005). Survey evaluates complex trauma exposure, outcome, and intervention among children and adolescents. *Psychiatric Annals, 35*(5), 433–439.
Stein, B. D., Jaycox, L. H., Kataoka, S., Wong, M., Tu, W., Elliott, M. N., & Fink, A. (2003). A mental health intervention for school children exposed to violence: A randomized controlled trial. *Journal of the American Medical Association, 290*(5), 603–611.
Suido, S. M., & Shaffer, E. J. (2008). Looking beyond psychopathology: The dual-factor model of mental health in youth. *School Psychology Review, 37*, 52–68.
Sulkowski, M. L., & Michael, K. (2014). Meeting the mental health needs of homeless students in schools: A Multi-Tiered System of Support framework. *Children and Youth Services Review, 44*, 145–151. https://doi.org/10.1016/j.childyouth.2014.06.014

Thornberry, T.P., & Henry, K.L. (2013). Intergenerational continuity in maltreatment. *Journal of Abnormal Child Psychology, 41*(4), 555–569.

Thornberry, T.P., Knight, K.E., & Lovegrove, P.J. (2012). Does maltreatment beget maltreatment? A systematic review of the intergenerational literature. *Trauma, Violence, & Abuse, 13*(3), 135–152.

U.S. Department of Health & Human Services. (2015). Child Maltreatment 2015. https://doi.org/10.1177/1077559505283548

Verschueren, K., & Koomen, H.M.Y. (2012). Teacher–child relationships from an attachment perspective. *Attachment & Human Development, 14*(3), 205–211.

Watanabe, T. (2015, May 18). Compton Unified sued for allegedly failing to address trauma-affected students. *Los Angeles Times*. Retrieved from http://www.latimes.com/local/lanow/la-me-ln-trauma-school-lawsuit-20150518-story.html

Weist, M. D., Youngstrom, E. A., Stephan, S., Lever, N., Fowler, J., Taylor, L., . . . Hoagwood, K. (2014). Challenges and ideas from a research program on high-quality, evidence-based practice in school mental health. *Journal of Clinical Child & Adolescent Psychology, 43*(2), 244–255. https://doi.org/10.1080/15374416.2013.833097

CHAPTER 7

Addressing Child Trauma within the Child Welfare System

Prevention and Intervention Approaches

Brenda Jones Harden and Aimee Drouin Duncan

Children in the child welfare system are arguably exposed to the most pernicious form of trauma during childhood—complex trauma. Complex trauma is chronic, invasive, and perpetrated in the context of the caregiving system (Lieberman, Chu, Van Horn, & Harris, 2011; National Child Traumatic Stress Network, 2013). Child maltreatment is the most common form of complex trauma, affecting over 700,000 children in the United States, across class, racial/ethnic group, and geographical location (U.S. Department of Health and Human Services, 2016). Because maltreatment results in a broad range of deleterious outcomes for children, it is critical that human service policies and practices be leveraged to prevent child maltreatment, and to intervene with children and their families who have experienced this form of trauma exposure.

Most maltreated children are served by the public child welfare system, as well as a network of private and community-based organizations that target these very vulnerable children and families. The child welfare system is one of the most beleaguered human service delivery systems, criticized by child advocates, policymakers, and the media in its efforts to protect and care for the more than 3 million children who enter this service sector annually (U.S. Department of Health and Human Services, 2016; Wulczyn, Barth, Yuan, Jones Harden, & Landsverk, 2007). Unfortunately, child welfare system efforts aimed at preventing maltreatment and intervening with maltreating families and children have not met with great success, although there are pockets of highly effective child welfare service delivery. Effective child welfare systems capitalize on the many prevention and intervention programs that have been found to reduce maltreatment and promote the well-being of maltreated children and their families.

The aim of this chapter is to explore effective prevention and intervention strategies for children exposed to maltreatment, which could be implemented on a larger scale in the American child welfare system. Because adolescent maltreatment tends to have distinct etiology, epidemiology, and experiences for children, we focus on interventions for children from birth through age 12. We begin by examining the epidemiology of child maltreatment, followed by a brief conceptual and developmental discussion of child maltreatment. Then much of the chapter addresses prevention and intervention programs for children and families affected by child maltreatment, with a focus on trauma-informed and developmentally sensitive approaches to service delivery. Finally, we provide a case vignette to illustrate how such an approach can benefit children who are at risk for or are victimized by maltreatment, as well as their families who experience the child welfare system.

Epidemiological Background

American children are exposed to multiple forms of trauma at high rates. More often than not, the trauma that young children experience occurs within the home. Recent data from the National Child Abuse and Neglect Data System (NCANDS) indicate that 78.1 percent of all traumatized children in the child welfare data system were abused or neglected by one or both of their parents (U.S. Department of Health and Human Services, 2016). For 2014, the maltreatment victimization rate was 9.4 victims per 1,000 children in the population (U.S. Department of Health and Human Services, 2016). NCANDS documents that three-quarters (75.0%) of victims were neglected, 17.0 percent were physically abused, and 8.3 percent were sexually abused (U.S. Department of Health and Human Services, 2016).

There is a strong relation between age of victim and rate of maltreatment. Data from NCANDS document that the largest proportion of maltreated children is younger than age 3 (27.4%). Infants in their first year of life had the highest rate of victimization (24.4 per 1,000 children) compared to rates of 12.3, 11.6, and 11.0 out of 1,000 children for ages 1, 2, and 3, respectively (U.S. Department of Health and Human Services, 2016). The victimization rate for children 6–10 years of age is 9.0 per 1,000 children and 6.3 for children 11–17 years. A national study of childhood violence, abuse, and crime exposure confirms this relation between age and maltreatment prevalence (Finkelhor, Turner, Ormrod, & Hamby, 2009). In this study, mothers reported that 2.2 percent of infants (0–1 year), 8.1 percent of young children (2–5 years), 7.8 percent of 6–9-year olds, and 12.0 percent of 10–13-year-olds had experienced maltreatment. Overall, 1 in 10 (10.2%) children had experienced some form of maltreatment.

National estimates indicate that 1,580 children died of abuse and neglect in 2014, which represents a rate of 2.13 per 100,000 children in the national population. Consistent with the general maltreatment data, the rate of fatalities was highest in babies; 81 percent of child fatalities due to abuse and neglect occurred in the population of children who are zero to three years of age (U.S. Department of Health and Human Services, 2016). Even higher rates are reported for infants younger than one (18.09 per 100,000 babies) as compared to other age groups.

Trauma exposure extends beyond the direct victimization that occurs via maltreatment. Other common types of exposure are witnessing community violence, the physical abuse of other children, and/or witnessing domestic violence (Lipschitz, Winegar, Hartnick, Foote, & Southwick, 1999; Rivard et al., 2003). There is evidence that young children living in high-poverty communities are even more susceptible to these kinds of trauma exposure than their low-poverty counterparts (Bosquet Enlow, Blood, & Egeland, 2013; Ghosh Ippen, Harris, Van Horn, & Lieberman, 2011). For example, a recent study of young children documented that one-quarter of children under the age of 4 has experienced or witnessed a traumatic event (Briggs-Gowan, Carter, & Ford, 2012). Osofsky, Wewers, Hann, & Fick (1993) found 91 percent of elementary age youth witnessed life-threatening violence. Finkelhor et al. (2009) documented that one in four (24.6%) children had witnessed violence or experienced indirect victimization in the last year. Examining these data by age, these researchers found that 10.5 percent of 0–1-year-olds, 13.8 percent of 2–5-year-olds, 13.7 percent of 6–9-year-olds, and 33.0 percent of 10–13-year-olds had witnessed violence in the last year. Additionally,

9.8 percent of children in this study (Finkelhor et al., 2009) had witnessed assaults among family members, and almost half (46.3%) had experienced a physical assault.

Recent research has pointed to a strong association between child maltreatment and intimate partner violence. According to NCANDS, approximately one-quarter (27.4%) of maltreatment victims of all ages were exposed to intimate partner violence. In a study of children in the child welfare system in Los Angeles, California, 87 percent of children reported being a witness to or victim of assaultive, criminal, or weapon-related violence during their lifetime (Stein et al., 2001). In addition, almost one-fourth of the sample reported the violence they witnessed involved members of their household (Stein et al., 2001). The National Survey of Child and Adolescent Well-Being II (NSCAW II) documented that a quarter of parents whose children remained at home following a maltreatment report experienced physical domestic violence during the previous 12 months (Casanueva, Ringeisen, Smith, & Dolan, 2013). Further, 12.1 percent of children reported ever having witnessed an adult shoving another person, 11.9 percent reported ever having witnessed an adult slapping another person, and 11.5 percent reported ever having witnessed an adult throwing something at another person (Casanueva, Smith, Dolan, & Ringeisen, 2011).

Children and youth in foster care are more likely than the general population to have directly experienced traumatic violent events across their childhoods (Burns et al., 2004; Dorsey, Burns, Southerland, Cox, Wagner, & Farmer, 2012), with some evidence suggesting that exposure rates approach 90 percent (Stein et al., 2001). Hussey and Guo (2005) found almost half of 119 youth in treatment-level foster care programs in Ohio had experienced neglect, one-fifth had experienced physical abuse, and nearly 2.5 percent had experienced sexual abuse. In a second study that included 183 youth in treatment-level foster care in North Carolina, Farmer, Murray, Dorsey, and Burns (2005) found 85 percent of the children and adolescents reported being exposed to trauma.

There is a clear need for more research that examines the frequency with which these children are experiencing traumatic events inside and outside the home. Specifically, studies should address trauma exposure of very young children who are unable to communicate such information, and past experiences that are not revealed at the time the child enters the child welfare system, but are still a part of the child's individual experience of trauma during their lifetime. The high rates of child exposure to trauma highlight the need for programs both to prevent maltreatment and trauma exposure and to provide interventions for children in the child welfare system who have already experienced maltreatment and other forms of trauma.

Conceptual and Developmental Foundations

Two established conceptualizations of child maltreatment guide our considerations of prevention and intervention approaches in this chapter. First, Toth and Cicchetti (2013) argue for the use of a developmental psychopathology framework to address child maltreatment. This framework employs a developmental perspective to understand children's adaptation and maladaptation in the face of risks, such as maltreatment, and encourages the examination of core developmental processes in maltreated children. It also emphasizes the dynamic nature of children's adaptation and the multiple possible outcomes that emanate from the experience of maltreatment, including the presence and absence of psychopathology. Importantly, this framework highlights that positive outcomes for maltreated children can be fostered by prevention and targeted intervention programs that attenuate risks for maltreatment and promote resilience in maltreated children.

A second perspective emanates from Shonkoff's (2010) biodevelopmental framework. Building on this framework, maltreatment can be understood as an experience of *toxic stress*, defined as "strong, frequent, and/or prolonged activation of the body's stress-response system in the absence of stable adult support" (Shonkoff, 2010, p. 360). Shonkoff, Boyce, and McEwen (2009) assert that toxic stress is associated with "adverse childhood events" such as exposure to poverty, parental mental illness, parental alcohol or substance use, intimate partner violence, and child maltreatment. Toxic stress can disrupt brain architecture, compromise physiological and psychological responses to future stressors, limit cognitive development, and increase lifelong vulnerability to stress-related illnesses. This conceptualization underscores that such stressors can lead to adverse outcomes for affected children but that they may be mitigated by stable, nurturing caregiving. Thus, prevention and intervention programs that promote positive caregiving may buffer children against the consequences of exposure to toxic stress, such as child maltreatment.

As is emphasized by both these conceptualizations, trauma is best understood and addressed from a developmental perspective. Trauma, specifically maltreatment, impacts children across all domains of development and functioning. There is a wealth of research documenting compromised brain development, physical health, cognitive and language skills, social emotional functioning, and mental health among trauma-exposed children. This research is briefly presented in Table 7.1, which summarizes the evidence on maltreatment sequelae, according to developmental domain. More information on the developmental sequelae of specific aspects of maltreatment and trauma is included in Chapters 2 and 3 of Volume 1. The robust evidence regarding the adverse outcomes associated with trauma exposure argues for the design and delivery of prevention and intervention programs that could potentially alter the developmental trajectories of affected children and their families.

Other scholars (Wulczyn et al., 2007) have asserted that child welfare services, programs, and interventions should be designed using a developmental perspective. They have cautioned against a "one-size-fits-all" approach to service delivery, arguing for a developmental approach to linking families with appropriate programs in the child welfare system. Thus, preventive interventions should employ strategies that are aligned with the age of the target child. Additionally, programs could directly focus on core developmental processes (e.g., language, self-regulation) in maltreated children, skills that are critical for many areas of functioning, such as academic success and mental health. Further, programs can address facets of children's family experiences that have the potential to promote positive outcomes in specific developmental domains. In the following section, we describe exemplars of programs that achieve these developmental goals while preventing maltreatment and/or intervening with children and families who have experienced this multifaceted form of trauma.

Prevention and Intervention for Trauma-Affected Children and Families

Recently, scholars have advocated for child welfare service delivery that capitalizes on the substantial theoretical and empirical work emanating from public health and child development fields on prevention programs (e.g., Wulczyn et al., 2007). For example, the Institute of Medicine (2009, 2014) has issued two important reports on prevention, which build on earlier recommendations to employ a three-tiered approach to the prevention of mental, emotional, and behavioral disorders in children. Primary, or universal, prevention programs target entire populations or vulnerable subgroups of a population (e.g., impoverished families) with a goal of preventing the onset of a problem. For example, there is evidence that early childhood programs (e.g., home visitation, Early Head Start), which typically encompass universal prevention strategies, can improve parenting and child outcomes. Thus, primary prevention programs ameliorate the causes of child maltreatment, such as poverty and violence in communities (Geeraert, Van den Noortgate, Grietens, & Onghena, 2004).

Table 7.1 Developmental Sequelae of Maltreatment

Developmental Domain	Developmental Outcomes	Citation
Brain development	Altered brain size/volume and functioning a. Prefrontal cortex: implicated in abstract thinking, planning, executive functioning, behavioral regulation b. Occipital areas: utilized for visual processing c. Changes in amygdala and hippocampus: implicated in memory, decision-making, and emotion processing, particularly regarding the detection of environmental threat	[a,b]Anderson et al., 2008; Chugani et al., 2001; De Brito et al., 2013; Kelly et al., 2013; Sheridan & Nelson, 2009; Perry, 2008 [c]Hanson et al., 2014; 2015; Mehta et al., 2009; Ledoux, 2000; Tottenham et al., 2010
Health and physical outcomes	a. Physical injuries: Shaken Baby syndrome; retinal hemorrhaging, blindness, skull fractures, hearing loss, impaired motor skills, and/or seizures b. Growth delays: failure to thrive c. Chronic and heightened response to stressors: cardiovascular disease and asthma d. Compromised cortisol production: display dysregulated and atypical responses	[a]Chevignard & Lind, 2014; Narang & Clarke, 2014; Sieswerda-Hoogendoorn et al., 2012 [b]Block, Krebs, et al., 2005 [c]Miller & Chen, 2010; Slopen et al., 2013; Miller et al., 2011; Casanueva et al., 2012 [d]Bernard et al., 2010; Bernard, Dozier et al., 2015; Cicchetti et al., 2011; Dozier et al., 2006; Ivars et al., 2015
Cognitive, language, and academic skills	a. Developmental delays: delays in mental development and language skills b. Compromised cognitive functioning: Lower levels of intellectual functioning c. Compromised executive functioning: related to attention, memory, goal-direction, and self-monitoring d. Academic challenges	[a]U.S. Department of Health and Human Services, 2005; Casanueva et al., 2012 [b]Nelson et al., 2007; Chugani et al., 2001 [c]Crozier & Barth, 2005; Stahmer et al., 2009

(continued)

Table 7.1 *(continued)*

Developmental Domain	Developmental Outcomes	Citation
Social-emotional development and mental health	a. Disorganized attachment b. PTSD and dissociative symptoms c. More attuned to the expression of negative emotions; less able to discern distinct emotions; compromised goal-directed emotion regulation d. Compromised relational skills; problems in interpersonal relationships e. Hyperarousal, disturbed sleep, increased irritability, aggression and alertness, temper tantrums, and startled and extreme responses to stimuli f. Depression and anxiety g. Conduct and behavior problems	[a]Bernard et al., 2012; Cyr et al., 2010; Hesse & Main, 2006 [b]Kim-Spoon et al., 2013; Maughan, & Cicchetti, 2002; Robinson et al., 2009 [c]Kim & Cicchetti, 2009; Daignault & Hébert, 2009 [d]De Young et al., 2011; Scheeringa, Myers et al., 2015 [e]Casanueva et al., Hagan et al., 2015; Kaplow, & Widom, 2007; De Young et al., 2011; Scheeringa et al., 2015; Yoches et al., 2011; Briggs-Gowan et al., 2010; Hébert et al., 2006; Landsverk et al., 2002; Taussig, 2002

Developmental domain indicates the area of development affected by maltreatment. *Developmental outcomes* indicates the consequences within the domain of exposure to maltreatment.

Secondary, or selective, prevention strategies are designed to benefit individuals who display risk for the development of a particular problem. Risks for maltreatment include compromised parenting and impaired parent–child interaction, parental physical and mental illness, inadequate knowledge and skills about typical child development and caregiving, social isolation of parents, as well as parental concrete needs (Geeraert et al., 2004; Institute of Medicine, 2012). Interventions in the secondary tier have been documented to improve parental psychological functioning, enhance parenting skills, and thus reduce the risk for maltreatment.

Finally, tertiary, or indicated (i.e., when a problem such as child abuse and neglect has occurred) prevention programs have a goal of preventing the recurrence of a problem and adverse outcomes that emanate from the experience of a particular phenomenon. Tertiary programs target individuals who have already experienced a particular problem and address individual-level challenges and sequelae. These interventions have been found to reduce maltreatment recurrence and modulate children's adverse reactions to maltreatment experiences (e.g., mental health and behavior problems; Geeraert et al., 2004). Treatment interventions, which have a goal of enhancing children's functioning in the context of trauma, may also be included in the tertiary prevention level (Weisz, Sandler, Durlak, & Anton, 2005). There has been a recent proliferation of prevention programs at all three prevention tiers designed to address trauma in children, adults, and families. However, as many scholars assert, child welfare practice has not kept pace with the corpus of research on maltreatment prevention and intervention (Institute of Medicine, 2012). Although there is growing evidence for a range of universal, selective, and indicated prevention programs documented to attenuate the effects of maltreatment on children, they have not been widely disseminated to and evaluated in community-based settings, such as child welfare (Institute of Medicine, 2009, 2012, 2014). Scholars and practitioners alike have advocated for the integration of these evidence-based programs into the child welfare service delivery system.

In Tables 7.2–7.4, we delineate evidence-based programs in each of these three prevention tiers, including a brief description of the intervention, the age of child and type of risk targeted, and the outcomes achieved with respect to maltreatment, trauma, and associated risks. We have included prevention and intervention programs that have been evaluated with high-risk families (i.e., families who have similar characteristics to those in the child welfare system). Because of our focus on maltreatment and complex trauma, programs that are designed to address acute trauma or community violence are not examined. For the most part, we have only

Table 7.2 Primary Prevention Programs

Program Name	Target Population	Program Description	Program Outcomes	Citation
Durham Connects	New mothers and fathers recruited from birthing hospital; children 3–12 weeks of age	Nurse home visiting program implemented at population level; 1–3 home visits to evaluate families and connect them to appropriate resources	Improve parenting behaviors; enhance home environment; facilitate connections with community service providers; reduce incidence of emergency room visits	Dodge et al., 2014
Early Head Start (EHS)	Low-income families from prenatal period to child's 3rd birthday	Federal two-generation early childhood program delivered through center-based, home-based, and other models	[1]Enhance parent–child relationship; reduce incidence of spanking and substance abuse [2]Less frequent reports to Child Protection Service for physical and sexual abuse; lower likelihood of substantiation between 5–9 years	[1]Vogel et al., 2013; Love et al., 2005 [2]Green et al., 2014
Family Check-up (FCU)	Low-income families with children ages 2–4 years of age	Three home visits delivered annually, which include observation of parent–child interaction, intake session addressing family functioning, and individualized feedback session (referral to parenting management intervention)	Duration of positive engagement between caregivers and children led to decreases in child neglect; most beneficial for families with higher levels of adversity	Dishion et al., 2015

Healthy Families America (HFA)	Mothers at risk for child maltreatment; children from birth to 5th birthday	Population-based risk screening at birthing hospitals; voluntary, intensive home visits to promote positive parenting and reduce trauma-related, adverse public health outcomes	[1]Modest decrease in childhood neglect and parental threats of physical discipline [2]Lower likelihood of employing mild levels of physical discipline [3]Lower likelihood of seriously abusing children and higher frequency of employing nonviolent discipline strategies [4]Lower rates of Child Protection Service reports	[1]Duggan et al., 2007 [2]Dugggan et al., 2007 [3]Dumont et al., 2008 [4]Dumont et al., 2010
Nurse Family Partnership (NFP)	First-time mothers who are teenaged, single or of low socioeconomic status; child age—prenatal to two years of age	Intensive prenatal and postnatal home visits by a registered nurse	[1]Lower rates of infant death and childhood injury [2]Decrease reports to Child Protective Services [3]Decrease intimate partner violence	[1]Kitzman et al., 1997; Olds et al., 2014; Miller, 2015 [2]Olds et al., 1997; Mejdoubi et al., 2015 [3]Olds et al., 1997
Positive Parenting Program (Triple P)	Parents of varying needs with children from infancy through adolescence	Multilevel approach to reduce incidence of child maltreatment: universal media campaign with positive parenting information; brief individual consultation and group parenting seminars; home visits for parents needing intensive support	Lower rates of Child Protection System reports, out-of-home foster care placements, and abuse/neglect related medical injuries	Prinz et al., 2009

(continued)

Table 7.2 *(continued)*

Program Name	Target Population	Program Description	Program Outcomes	Citation
Strong Communities for Children	Children from birth through adolescence	Comprehensive community mobilization initiative to prevent child maltreatment by connecting families to communities, implementing activities to enhance social support networks, and providing direct support for families with needs	Improved social support, collective efficacy, child safety, observed and self-reported parenting practices, parental efficacy; reduced parental stress, substantiated child maltreatment rates, rates of child injuries related to maltreatment	McDonnell et al., 2015
Trauma-Adapted Family Connections	Families at risk for neglect with children from 6–12 years	Six-month, in-home prevention program to decrease trauma-related risk factors: trauma-informed engagement; family psychoeducation; family shared meaning of trauma	Reductions in caregiver and child post-traumatic stress symptomatology; improvements in caregiver, child, and family well-being and safety	Collins et al., 2015

Primary programs entire populations or vulnerable subgroups of a population with a goal of preventing the onset of a problem. Programs listed are evidence-based.

Table 7.3 Secondary Prevention Programs

Program Name	Target Population	Program Description	Program Outcomes	Citation
Attachment and Bio-behavioral Catch-up (ABC)	Mothers at risk of maltreating their children 0–24 months of age (toddler version is in development)	Ten-week home-based intervention focusing on providing nurturance, following child's lead, and avoiding frightening behaviors; uses experiential coaching and video feedback during parent–child interaction	[1]Children living with foster families: higher rates of secure attachment, fewer behavior problems, greater cognitive flexibility and theory of mind, more typical cortisol production [2]Children living with birth families: higher rates of secure attachment, less negative affect in problem-solving task, more typical cortisol production	[1]Dozier et al., 2009; Dozier et al., 2006; Lewis-Morrarty et al., 2012; Dozier et al., 2006; Dozier et al., 2008 [2]Bernard et al., 2012; Lind et al., 2014; Bernard et al., 2015
Circle of Security (COS)	High-risk caregivers and children ages 0–5 years	Group- or home-based intervention with direct focus on caregivers (~20 weeks); parents provided with visual aids and educational tools to learn about attachment, reading and responding to children's cues, developing empathy for children; view video-recorded parent–child interactions to reflect on parent and child behaviors	[1]Higher levels of secure attachment and lower levels of disorganized attachment [2]Increased maternal sensitivity	[1]Cassidy et al., 2010; Hoffman et al., 2006 [2]Cassidy et al., 2010

(continued)

Table 7.3 *(continued)*

Program Name	Target Population	Program Description	Program Outcomes	Citation
Incredible Years (IY)	High-risk families with children from age 2 to 12 years	Group-based intervention designed to promote positive parenting; review video samples and role-play to improve parenting, and to promote children's emotion regulation, academic success, social interactions and behaviors	[1]Improvement in parenting and support of children's autonomy in mothers of maltreated children [2] Improvements in parenting capabilities of biological and foster parents of neglected children [3] Fewer child externalizing behavior problems [4]Improvements in parents' nurturance and positive affect in Head Start families with history of maltreatment	[1]Hughes & Gottlieb, 2004 [2,3]Linares et al., 2006 [4]Hurlburt et al., 2013 [5]Webster-Stratton & Reid, 2010
Moving Beyond Depression (MBD)	Depressed mothers of children 0–5 years	Fifteen-week integration of cognitive-behavioral therapy into home visiting programs to treat maternal depression; therapy supplement to home visiting services; provided by therapist who collaborates with visitor	Lower likelihood of diagnosis of major depressive disorder, increased social support, decreased psychological distress, improved coping, fewer relationship difficulties; parents recovered from depression: improved coping, increased nurturing and stimulation	Ammerman et al., 2013

Promoting First Relationships (PFR)	Caregivers and children 0–3 years old (originally designed for homeless mothers)	Ten home visits with the aim of promoting positive parent–child relationships; uses videotapes of mother–child interactions to identify parent strengths and interpret children's cues	[1]Improvements in caregiver sensitivity and understanding of child social-emotional needs [2]Increased stability and permanency for children l iving with foster and kin caregivers [3]Birth parents: increased understanding of toddler social-emotional needs and observed sensitivity; Children: lower atypical communication and lower likelihood of foster care placement	[1]Spieker et al., 2012 [2]Spieker et al., 2014 [3]Oxford et al., 2016

Secondary prevention programs are designed to benefit individuals who display risk for the development of a particular problem. Programs listed are evidence-based.

Table 7.4 Tertiary Prevention Programs

Program Name	Target Population	Program Description	Program Outcomes	Citation
Attachment, Self-Regulation, and Competencies (ARC) Model	Children and adolescents who have experienced complex trauma (e.g., maltreatment	Four components: caregiver attachment; child's self-regulation; child's competency; and trauma experience integration; flexible to meet children's and families' needs; ranges from 12 to 52 sessions; various treatment modalities (groups, family therapy, home visits, and parent workshops)	Reduction in behavior problems for children who completed treatment	Arvidson et al., 2011
Child-Parent Psychotherapy	Families with a history of child maltreatment or intimate partner violence and traumatized children ages 0–5	Nondirective, non-didactic therapeutic intervention to enhance relationship between parents and traumatized children; weekly home visits for one year to increase parents' responsiveness, sensitivity and attunement to children and to promote secure parent–child attachment	[1]Increase in secure attachment and decrease in disorganized attachment among maltreated children [2]More positive self-representation and mother–child relationships expectations [3] Reduced behavior problems and trauma-related symptoms	[1]Cicchetti et al., 2006; Stronach et al., 2013 [2]Toth et al., 2002 [3]Lieberman et al., 2006 [1]Toth et al., 2006
Child First	Children 0–6 years and families with multiple risk factors	Integration of CPP and intensive case management to address emotional trauma, improve child development, and prevent child maltreatment	Improved language and reduced externalizing symptoms; lower parenting stress and psychopathology symptoms, less involvement with CPS	Lowell et al., 2011

Cognitively Enhanced Home Visitation	High-risk mothers of infants/toddlers	Twenty home visits to prevent risk of abuse of young children; cognitive behavioral therapy to teach parents to seek support and engage in problem-solving tactics	[1]Less physical punishment, fewer child injuries, higher safety standards [2]Less child aggression with mothers with higher social-emotional availability; less avoidant and withdrawn mothers	[1]Bugental & Schwartz, 2009 [2]Bugental et al., 2012
Integrated Treatment of Complex Trauma for Children (ITCT-C)	Children aged 8–12 years who have been exposed to complex trauma	Multimodal, component-based, assessment-driven treatment over 16–36 primarily child therapy sessions; focus on safety, affect regulation, trauma exposure, cognitive therapy, relationship processing, attachment, and posttraumatic stress and related symptoms	Reductions in anxiety, depression, posttraumatic stress, anger, dissociation, and sexual concerns	Lanktree et al., 2012
Intergenerational Trauma Treatment Model (ITTM)	Children aged 3–18 years and their families	Twenty-one sessions with 3 phases: trauma information, caregiver treatment regarding: trauma, child-caregiver conjoint session to address trauma-related behaviors and symptoms and promote stronger parent–child relations; cognitive-behavioral treatment methods, with focus on improving caregiver ability to respond to child and be change agent	Improvements in children's conduct and social relations; reduction in caregiver depression	Copping et al., 2001

(continued)

Table 7.4 *(continued)*

Program Name	Target Population	Program Description	Program Outcomes	Citation
Parent-Child Interaction Therapy (PCIT)	Children ages 2–12 years and their families	12–14 home visits focused on improving parent–child relationship and fostering new parenting skills, specifically positive behavior supports such as following child's lead, alternative discipline strategies, increased attention toward child	[1]Increased maternal sensitivity [2]Prevented new reports of physical abuse [3]Reduced child welfare recidivism [4]Reduced behavior problems [5]Reduced internalizing and externalizing behavior problems in foster children [6]Decreased disruptive behaviors, reduce parental depression, increased use of new parenting skills in PCIT-T (for toddlers)	[1]Thomas & Zinner-Gembeck, 2011 [2]Chaffin et al., 2004 [3]Chaffin et al., 2011 [4]Timmer et al., 2005 [5]Mersky et al., 2016 [6]Kohlhoff & Morgan, 2014
Real Life Heroes (RLH)	School-aged children (aged 8–12 years) with post-trauma and complex trauma symptoms	Relationship-based approach addressing traumatic stress, attachment, and complex trauma; 6 to 18 months of weekly sessions utilizing cognitive-behavioral therapy/psychoeducation; focus on three elements: emotional regulation, attachments, and life story	Reductions in trauma symptoms, child problem behaviors, and greater secure attachment to caregivers	Kagan et al., 2008

		integration; goals regarding: enhancing safety, repairing attachments and enhancing caregiver attunement, building capacity to process and integrate trauma memories		
Trauma-Focused Cognitive-Behavior Therapy (TF-CBT)	For people of all ages, but current focus on school aged children	Cognitive-behavioral treatment of child trauma, involving exposure to trauma reminders, skill-building, trauma narrative and processing, consolidation of traumatic experience	[1]Reductions in post-traumatic stress; [2]Child improvements regarding: PTSD, depression, behavior problems; and parent improvements regarding: depression, abuse-specific distress, support of the child, and effective parenting practices	[1]Konanaur et al., 2015; [2]Cohen et al., 2004

Tertiary prevention programs are designed to prevent the recurrence of a problem by addressing individual-level factors. Programs listed are evidence-based.

included interventions that have rigorous evaluations, including randomized controlled trials and quasi-experimental designs. However, given the paucity of strong evidence in specific areas, some interventions have only been evaluated with a single-group, pretest/posttest design.

As is evident, there are multiple programs that have been documented to be effective with children at risk for or who have experienced maltreatment and their families. The primary/universal prevention programs aim to reduce the incidence of maltreatment and related outcomes (e.g., infant mortality) through improving behaviors associated with child maltreatment. These programs are generally targeted to low-income families, particularly those with young children and new parents. Many of these programs employ comprehensive home visitation approaches, which focus on improving parenting.

The secondary/selective prevention models target families with specific risk factors that are associated with maltreatment and related adverse outcomes. Interventions have been created to prevent maltreatment through embedded treatment of mental health disorders, in particular, maternal depression, a major risk factor for child maltreatment (Conron, Beardslee, Koenen, Buka, & Gortmaker, 2009; Lovejoy, Graczyk, O'Hare, & Neuman, 2000). Many are designed to enhance parent–child interactions and relationships, including children's attachment to their caregivers.

The tertiary/indicated programs are designed to address maltreatment that has already occurred. Thus, treatment interventions can be viewed as components of tertiary preventive programs—for example, emerging evidence points to the benefit of interventions that employ cognitive-behavioral treatment strategies with children who have been exposed to complex trauma, particularly for school-aged children (Leenarts, Diehle, Doreleijers, Jansma, & Lindauer, 2013). Similarly, there is evidence that attachment-based interventions may also promote better outcomes for maltreating families, particularly those with young children (Fraser et al., 2013). Given their goal to prevent maltreatment recurrence, tertiary programs may entail involuntary services. There is a paucity of evidence regarding involuntary interventions, as well as those designed to facilitate reunification between birth parents and their children, especially around visitation or family time.

Programs at all prevention levels should employ a developmental perspective with regard to the strategies and activities embedded in the interventions. Many of the programs delineated in Tables 7.2–7.4 address maltreatment in the infant, toddler, and early childhood years (zero to six years of age). The elevated rates of maltreatment during early childhood highlight the need for prevention and intervention programs during this developmental phase. Consistent with the goal of prevention programs, these programs are designed to offer intervention early in development, so that they can positively alter children's developmental trajectories and adults' parenting trajectories before negative the consequences of maltreatment are crystallized. These early childhood prevention and intervention programs typically include both parent and child in the intervention sessions. They often have a foundation in attachment therapy, with a goal of supporting enhanced parent–child relationships.

Some of the early childhood interventions extend to the school-age years (e.g., Parent-Child Interaction Therapy [PCIT]) and thus focus on the child maltreatment processes that are characteristic of this developmental period. Thus, these interventions often capitalize on knowledge about the use of positive behavior supports and coach parents to use such methods. Other interventions geared for school-aged children fall within the tertiary level of prevention. These interventions are designed to capitalize on the capacity for advanced language and thinking characteristic of children in this developmental phase. Thus, there are more child-directed intervention modalities for families with children in this age group. These interventions often overlap with treatment approaches and are designed to assist children to cope with and overcome the developmental vestiges of trauma.

Overall, there is substantial evidence that preventive interventions can modulate the risk for and impact of maltreatment at the primary, secondary, and tertiary levels. However, these interventions are not broadly utilized by clinicians (Toth & Manly, 2011). Further, with few exceptions, child welfare agencies have not availed themselves of these programs and incorporated them into their service delivery system. It is critical that mechanisms be established by which these programs can be provided through or in collaboration with local child welfare entities.

Trauma-Informed Child Welfare Service Delivery

In addition to the integration of evidence-based preventive interventions within child welfare systems, the creation of trauma-sensitive child welfare agencies is essential. The National Child Traumatic Stress Network (NCTSN, 2013) has advocated for the development of trauma-informed service delivery across child-serving systems. Trauma-informed systems instill the knowledge about the impact of traumatic stress on children, caregivers, and service providers into their organizational cultures, policies, and practices (e.g., Gilkerson et al., 2013). Specifically, a trauma-informed service delivery system would aim to achieve the following objectives: (1) maximize physical and psychological safety for children and families; (2) identify trauma-related needs of children and families; (3) enhance the well-being and resilience of children, families, and providers; and (4) partner with children, families, agencies, and systems that interact with children and families (NCTSN, 2013). Specific to the child welfare system, the NCTSN has devised a Child Welfare Trauma Training Toolkit to assist child welfare agencies to become more trauma-informed through training and other resources.

Child welfare is arguably the major service delivery system contending with child and family trauma. Many of the trauma-informed objectives delineated here are already addressed within this system; however, there is a need to enhance specific strategies. For example, as is argued in the preceding section, child welfare systems should implement empirically grounded trauma interventions for children and parents at all levels (Institute of Medicine, 2012). It is also critical that child welfare systems attend to the secondary trauma of the child welfare workforce through staff well-being promotion strategies and strong, supportive supervision (Chen & Scannapieco, 2010; Denmark & Jones Harden, 2011; Sprang, Craig, & Clark, 2011). In addition, Osofsky and Lieberman (2011) have recommended that principles and intervention strategies from the field of early childhood mental health be integrated into child welfare practice. Specifically, child welfare systems should incorporate parent–child interaction into all interventions and should consider the trauma experienced by caregivers when they were children in the context of service delivery.

To meet the objectives of a trauma-informed service delivery system, child welfare must prioritize the following practices, which are aimed at reducing child trauma exposure and buffering them against the impact of trauma:

Screening and Assessment

Many child welfare agencies incorporate risk screenings and family assessments as part of the front-end and other services. With the recent child well-being mandate for child welfare entities (U.S. Department of Health and Human Services, 2012), it is important to gather information about children and parents' traumatic experiences and deliver services that address the consequences of these for children and parents' developmental outcomes. Further, given that trauma exposure can substantially derail children's development, it is essential that children be assessed for the potential consequences of trauma and be provided with supportive opportunities to promote normative development (e.g., high-quality child care and schools).

Universal screening for trauma exposure and/or symptoms can be conducted by child welfare staff at all levels (e.g., investigative workers, permanency workers, case aides). For those children who screen positive, a more comprehensive assessment should be completed by professional staff with knowledge and skill relative to child trauma. Thus, children and parents could be referred to mental health or trauma programs for more comprehensive evaluations of trauma exposure and its consequences, and for related service planning. Specifically, child sexual abuse evaluations, permanency evaluations (i.e., to inform decisions about whether a parent's rights should be terminated), and evaluations for posttraumatic stress disorder symptomatology or trauma-related developmental delays should be conducted by professionals who are trained and licensed to do so and who have experience with children of different ages and developmental levels.

Child Interventions

Child interventions are designed to address directly and individually the trauma-related concerns that pertain to the child. Although there is a growing evidence base on interventions for children who experience trauma, it is important for programs to ascertain whether specific interventions are developmentally appropriate for certain age groups and whether there is evidence of intervention effectiveness with this age group. As Wulczyn et al. (2007) state, all child welfare services should be development-centered so that the most effective interventions are used for different age groups of children (e.g., parent–child interaction approaches for young children, child cognitive-behavioral individual therapy for older children). It is notable that the child-specific interventions that are included in Tables 7.2–7.4 are often targeted toward school-age children, who are more likely to benefit from this modality than are younger children.

Parent Interventions

Partly due to the development of services for victims of war and other forms of violence, there are many intervention strategies for adults who have experienced trauma. However, these interventions are not typically designed to support maltreating parents. Given that parental mental health is strongly related to child maltreatment (Conron et al., 2009; Cort,

Toth, Cerulli, & Rogosch, 2011), it is critical to provide services that facilitate adults' coping with the trauma they have experienced. For example, some interventions for parents may address emotion regulation and impulse control, whereas other interventions support parents to reflect on their own experiences of early trauma. Both of these approaches may be beneficial to parents who are involved in the child welfare system. However, it is equally important to improve these adults' parenting behaviors, which serve to buffer their children against the impact of trauma and/or reduce their experience of trauma. As is evident in Tables 7.2–7.4, the majority of prevention and intervention programs focus on improving parenting behaviors within families at risk for or having prior experiences of maltreatment.

Child welfare programs would benefit from integrating the available evidence-based programs into their ongoing service delivery. These interventions should address parents' own experience of trauma, promote parental support of children who have experienced trauma, as well as enhance parent–child relationships and interactions. It is critical to consider how to implement these interventions in culturally appropriate ways for families who participate. Given the burden on child welfare systems to respond to so many families with such diverse and intensive needs, collaboration with mental health and parenting services in the community could potentially allow for the delivery of these services. These community-based collaborators should be selected based on their experience with the provision of trauma-informed treatment and intervention, their capacity to work with children of varying ages, as well as their awareness and provision of evidence-based models to address trauma.

Staff Support

Providers who serve children and families who experience trauma may experience secondary traumatic stress and are thus traumatized themselves from the stress of their work. Child welfare staff are particularly vulnerable to secondary traumatic stress (Pearlman & MacIan, 1995) due to their continual exposure to child trauma at varying levels of severity. Thus, child welfare staff should receive training, supervision, and consultation that improve their capacity to provide trauma-informed intervention (e.g., Gilkerson et al., 2013; Osofsky, Putnam, & Lederman, 2008; Sprang et al., 2011). Further, staff should be encouraged to reflect on their own traumatic experiences and feelings about their work with families who experience maltreatment and other forms of trauma. Staff self-care strategies, such as meditation and wellness activities, can also be helpful in reducing secondary traumatic stress (Denmark & Jones Harden, 2011). Foster and adoptive families, who care for young children who have experienced trauma, would also benefit from strategies used for staff, including training, consultation, and support around the effects of trauma exposure for children's development and behavior, as well as how caring for traumatized children can affect their mental health.

Collaboration

Due to the policy mandate to address children's well-being, child welfare agencies have to collaborate with other child-serving agencies to ensure that children's well-being is addressed. The child welfare system should work with pediatric, educational, and mental health settings to specifically meet the needs of children and families who have been exposed to trauma. Child welfare programs can contract with other service systems, which have trauma-informed approaches, to provide services to their populations of children, the overwhelming majority of whom are traumatized. One example of a collaboration between child welfare services and a trauma-specific intervention exists in San Francisco, California, where clinicians at the University of California San Francisco and San Francisco General Hospital support the local child welfare system through early childhood mental health consultation, assessment, and treatment regarding infants and toddlers who have been exposed to trauma (Lieberman & Van Horn, 2011). Another example is the Safe Babies Court Teams that have been implemented in several jurisdictions across the country, in which court systems collaborate with child welfare and mental health agencies to promote the safety, permanency, and well-being of infants and toddlers in the child welfare system (Katz, Lederman, & Osofsky, 2011; McCombs-Thornton & Foster, 2012). Overall, the complexity of the needs of these children and families requires cross-system collaboration across child-serving agencies and trauma-specific programs, which could foster case coordination such as sharing resources, exchanging family data, and joint decision making about service delivery (e.g., calendar of contacts, the role of each interventionist).

Thus, a trauma-informed child welfare service delivery system would institute the following practices: (1) screening and assessment for trauma; (2) trauma-based interventions for children and parents; (3) staff support around addressing families' and their own trauma; and (4) collaboration with other programs to alleviate the impact of trauma on children. The trauma-based interventions should encompass preventive interventions at multiple levels and should be derived from the base of evidence in this field. In this manner, child welfare systems could move closer to addressing the needs of the children and families they serve, such as the family presented in the following case vignette.

Case Vignette: The Rios/Sherman Family

The experiences of the Rios/Sherman family illustrate the vestiges of trauma on children and parents, as well as how the child welfare system can address trauma and its consequences. This is a two-parent family, with four children. The parents—Mr. Sherman and Ms. Rios—are not married but have had a stable relationship for the past four years. The father is a 30-year-old African American man, who dropped out of school when he was 15 years old and is currently unemployed. He is a former foster child and is very invested in caring for his children and "keeping them out of the system." He is the children's primary caregiver. The mother is a 22-year-old woman of Puerto Rican descent, who has a high school diploma. She works full-time as a medical assistant. Although she was never in the child welfare system, she reports being "abandoned" by her mother and father, both of whom had substance abuse problems, and left to live with her loving but troubled grandparents, whose marriage was marked by intimate partner violence. She has also stated that her grandfather had many infidelities and a long-standing alcohol abuse problem.

The children in this family are one 8-year-old daughter, one 6-year-old son, one 3-year-old son, and one 13-month-old daughter. The two older children are from the father's previous relationship with a woman who was documented to have physically abused her children. Their father was given full custody of the children after an incident in which teachers discovered bruises and burns on the children's bodies that were found inconsistent with the mother's explanations. The children were living with Mr. Sherman when he began his relationship with Ms. Rios. The older boy shows typical signs of trauma exposure, including self-regulatory and behavioral difficulties, hypervigilance and hyperarousal, as well as challenges in his relationships with his peers and siblings. The older daughter's teacher reports that she seems sad, anxious, and disengaged from school. Both children are performing poorly academically.

The father presents as a loud, boisterous man who has no history of maltreating his children. Although he is a strict disciplinarian, he has consistently been observed to provide his children with very good psychological and custodial care. However, he tends to be controlling of his spouse, and there have been reports from the mother and older children that he has physically abused her. He tends to become very angry when the mother has failed to do something for the children (e.g., missed a doctor's appointment, forgotten to purchase formula, allowed them to become too disruptive in the house). She has been observed to be disengaged from her children and to have flat affect. She has also reported several symptoms of depression and high levels of parenting stress. She works hard to keep her husband calm, so she is more responsive to the children when he is present. However, she describes spending her weekends and evenings asleep in her bed when she is at home alone with the children and her husband is out with his friends for long periods of time. It is important to note that there was no evidence that either parent abused alcohol or drugs.

This family was referred to child protective services (CPS) by the school where the older children attend because they had come to school inappropriately clothed in the winter and had severe dental caries in their mouths. When confronted by the school, both parents expressed concern about their children but stated that they did not have the money for winter clothing and that they could not find a dentist who accepted Medicaid. Subsequently, the CPS worker came to the school to question the children, and they spontaneously informed her of their experience of past abuse from their birth mother, which was confirmed by CPS case records. Upon visiting the family's home, the child welfare worker was met with a barrage of loud epithets from the father who demanded that the worker leave his home because he was "not going to let her take his kids away." The worker returned with a policeman who was able to subdue the father and convince him to cooperate with child welfare. The mother came home from work in the midst of the meeting. The social worker observed that the younger children did not acknowledge her return. The youngest son was running around the room, ignoring his mother's pleas to sit down and play. The infant daughter remained very still in a car seat sucking a pacifier and just staring blankly around the room.

First, the child welfare social worker acknowledged the parents' concerns about losing their children and stated her desire to help the parents take the best care of their children. She collaborated with the family to have the children seen by a dentist and to go to a clothing bank to obtain coats for each child. Because she did not see overt evidence of other aspects of abuse and neglect, and because of the father's clear investment in all four of the children, she decided to leave the children in the home with the support of community-based resources. She ensured that the family had access to other concrete resources (e.g., WIC, pediatric care) and worked with the school to monitor and support the family. She supported the parents to enroll the two younger children in an Early Head Start center-based program through which their developmental needs could be met. She also connected the mother to a program for women victims of intimate partner violence, where she could attend a victims group, but the mother did not attend the group, citing lack of time and energy. However, the father stated his willingness to work on his "anger issues" so that his children did not see him get out of control and did follow through with attendance to a men's group that focused on improving men's treatment of women.

Because of the observations and reports about trauma and depression, the social worker had encouraged the parents to complete trauma and depression screeners. Although both endorsed past and current traumatic experiences, and the mother reported clinical levels of depressive symptomatology, neither parent wanted any treatment for these issues. However, they stated they wanted to give their children the best home lives they could, so they agreed to obtain support around their parenting. Thus, the child welfare social worker linked the family to a local agency that had clinicians trained in early childhood prevention, intervention, and mental health approaches, including Child Parent Psychotherapy (CPP), Parent-Child Interaction Therapy (PCIT), and In-Home Cognitive Behavioral Therapy for Depression. She was fortunate enough to have the family assigned a clinician who had certifications in both CPP and PCIT. Although there was another clinician at the agency who could have provided the mother with support for her depression, the mother initially refused these services. The social worker ensured that the families were not overburdened with clinicians by discussing with them what the optimal times and places would be for their full participation in the interventions. The family opted for visits at their home, so the social worker brought the CPP/PCIT clinician to the home and provided a "warm handoff" to the family. It was agreed that the social worker and clinician would remain in close contact and would attempt to do monthly joint visits with the family. This allowed the social worker to have another set of eyes on the family while she was attending to the multiple other families on her caseload.

First, the CPP/PCIT clinician found as many ways as possible to validate the parents' love for their children and identified the many ways they had been good caregivers. For example, she applauded their efforts at keeping their children safe (e.g., the father's decision to remove them from their abusive mother's care). Employing the CPP approach, she engaged them in weekly interactions with their children, sometimes visiting the home a second time in the week if the family was not home when she arrived for the scheduled visit. She used the parent–child interaction to promote the parents' (particularly the mother's) attachment to their children and the children's use of the parents as a secure base from which to explore and play. In these interactions, she scaffolded the older children to explore their own perspectives on their traumatic experiences (e.g., abuse by birth mother, removal from home, moving to another city with another mother) and encouraged the parents to join the children in creating a shared narrative about these experiences. She also helped the parents to recognize when their own past experiences of being parented interfered with their capacity to be nurturing, responsive, patient, and supportive with their own children. Specifically, she helped the parents to reflect on the trauma they had experienced as children and how it affected their relationship with each other and their parenting of their children (e.g., intrusiveness, punitiveness, harshness, disengagement). She often took these opportunities to provide psychological nurturance to the parents, empathizing with the difficulties of parenting in their challenging lives and acknowledging how hard it must be for them to give to anybody when they felt they were not given to in the ways they needed when they were children. Although neither parent was able to modulate their interactions with each other, the clinician observed that they became more and more responsive to their children over time.

Given the children's behavior problems (particularly the boys), the clinician coached the parents to use positive behavior management strategies and to be more responsive to their children's needs in general. Using PCIT strategies, she built on the parent–child relationships that emerged through CPP to address the children's behavior problems. Specifically, she encouraged the parents to devote more attention to their children, to look for times when the children exhibited positive behavior, and to praise the children for these small moments. She also helped the parents to follow the children's lead in play, ignore small behavioral infractions, and use nonphysical discipline strategies, such as redirecting and consistent consequences for major behavioral issues. When the parents made small and big attempts to alter their parenting behavior, the clinician offered lots of enthusiastic praise and pointed specifically to the parents' behaviors and the corresponding behaviors of the children.

Over time (and with intensive intervention), both parents stated and illustrated their capacity to approach parenting in a different way. The mother also stated that she felt more in control of the boys and that she was not feeling as sad and hopeless about her family situation. Nevertheless, she decided that she wanted to work on her own well-being and reluctantly agreed to receive in-home cognitive-behavior therapy. This proved very difficult at first as the family was still engaged in parenting intervention and the father never allowed the mother to be alone with either clinician. The clinicians collaborated and agreed with the family that they would finish their parenting work before the mother began the individual in-home therapy. Because the clinicians included the father in each of these service decision-making points, he was ultimately able to give the mother the time and space to work on her depression. After the culmination of the parenting work, the mother was assigned to an in-home therapist who worked with her individually on her depression, recognizing the importance of respecting the context of her role as a mother of four young children. The clinician focused on helping the mother understand how depression can affect parenting, as well as her own sense of well-being. They worked on monitoring her moods, identifying the triggers to negative moods (e.g., when the children overwhelmed her), managing her stress (e.g., mindfulness), changing her thoughts about the events in her life, and creating activities in which she could engage that would bring her some gratification. Although the mother reported that the relationship with the father was a major stressor, the mother continued to resist addressing this relationship directing in the therapeutic work (e.g., joint meetings with the father).

After approximately 18 months of intervention, the Sherman/Rios family clearly exhibited enhanced parenting of their children, as well as a capacity to acknowledge when they were overwhelmed and to seek assistance from their social worker or another provider. Although they continued to have difficulties in their relationship with each other (e.g., frequent arguments), neither parent reported that the father's physical abuse continued. The child welfare social worker had remained involved with the family through monthly visits, often in concert with the interventionist who was working with the family, and had collaborated consistently with the interventionists. Given the parents' improvement in their care of their children, the case was closed in the child welfare system. However, the family continued to receive services from the community-based agency that provided preventive and therapeutic services to families at risk for child maltreatment.

Practice Recommendations and Concluding Remarks

To meet the needs of families, such as the Rios/Sherman family presented in the case vignette, current policy requires that child welfare systems address child safety, permanency, and well-being (U.S. Department of Health and Human Services, 2012). Although there is limited consensus about whether and how these three mandates should be addressed, child welfare systems would be much closer to realizing these goals if they were undergirded by a trauma-informed approach to service delivery. Such an approach would at a minimum include screening for trauma, trauma-sensitive interventions for children and parents, and support for the child welfare workforce. Further, evidence-based programs that have been found to benefit maltreated children and parents should be disseminated more widely, with a focus on how they can be utilized across the range of child welfare settings that exist in the United States. Importantly, the child welfare field would benefit from efforts to implement and evaluate programs to respond to the question of which programs and therapeutic interventions work for which children and families, with respect to geography (i.e., rural vs. urban), culture, risk level, maltreatment type, and child age/developmental level.

Consistent with the collaboration objective of a trauma-informed approach, Wald (2015) argues for moving beyond the child welfare sector to providing a system of support services for parents at risk for maltreating their children. His approach would include broad outreach to families, capitalize on current service delivery systems, and incorporate evidence-based parenting interventions. As Thompson (2015) asserts, attention to parenting practices is essential in interventions for maltreating families but should be accompanied by the provision of emotional support and concrete resources to families. Such parenting interventions should focus more on experiential, contextualized parenting interventions that employ coaching strategies to improve parenting skills (Barth et al., 2005). Further, early childhood mental health practitioners underscore the need for services that support the parent–child relationship given that maltreatment reflects an extreme perturbation of this relationship (Osofsky & Lieberman, 2011).

Such interventions should be incorporated into prevention efforts at the primary level (e.g., early care and education programs, home visiting programs), at the secondary level (interventions to reduce depression and to improve parenting), and at the tertiary level (e.g., interventions to reduce instances of physical abuse and neglect, to support reunification, and to address children's reactions to traumatic experiences). Building on the prevention/intervention evidence and the three-tiered model, we offer the following specific recommendations for improving practices relative to children and families involved in the child welfare system.

Primary prevention

- Implement broad community engagement and outreach efforts that encourage and incentivize parents to participate in parenting activities and remove the stigma of receiving parent support.
- Provide universal support (e.g., parenting information, home visits) for families through existing service sectors (e.g., health clinics, Supplemental

Programs for Women, Infants, and Children) and in settings that families with children frequent (e.g., community centers, grocery stores).

- Reach out to schools to foster their support of high-risk families through after-school programs, linkages with community-based health and mental health clinics, family engagement activities, and school-based family support services.
- Expand availability of dual-generation programs, which explicitly include services for both parents and children, and focus on promoting child development, positive parenting, and functioning of parents (e.g., self-sufficiency, mental health, executive functioning).

Secondary prevention

- Screen parents in primary prevention settings for risks associated with maltreatment (e.g., depression, parental stress, childhood trauma exposure) and engage these families in more targeted services.
- Integrate evidence-based home visiting and other parenting programs into primary prevention settings (e.g., Head Start, health clinics, family support programs, schools).
- Develop, implement, evaluate, and expand the availability and use of interventions that target specific risk factors for child maltreatment (e.g., substance abuse, depression, intimate partner violence).
- Increase the availability and use of services designed to improve parenting, which are developmentally and culturally sensitive, and are derived from an evidentiary base.

Tertiary prevention

- Expand availability of and increase engagement of high-risk families in evidence-based parenting programs that have documented effectiveness in reducing child maltreatment recurrence.
- Incorporate such evidence-based interventions broadly into child welfare service delivery, including within family preservation programs, visitation/family time programs, and reunification services.
- Conduct ongoing screening of children whose families are enrolled in tertiary prevention programs for developmental and mental health concerns.
- Provide access to a variety of individual treatment options for children who have been subjected to maltreatment, which have been found to benefit trauma-exposed children, such as cognitive-behavioral approaches.
- Increase workforce of interventionists trained to provide mental health treatment to children of different developmental phases, cognitive-behavioral therapies, and other intervention services for families of children who have experienced maltreatment.

Maltreatment is undoubtedly one of the most pernicious problems facing policymakers and practitioners who are invested in improving outcomes for children being reared in environmentally at-risk families. The past few decades have witnessed a reduction and stabilization of the numbers of maltreated children, yet a large portion of the U.S. child population is still victimized by maltreatment. Although child welfare is the system responsible for responding to the very vulnerable children and families who experience maltreatment, this service delivery system cannot address the needs of this population alone.

It is critical that a system of care be established for maltreating children and families that has a trauma-informed child welfare system at its core. A network of prevention and intervention programs, implemented by the child welfare agency and other community-based agencies, should exist in every jurisdiction to provide the additional intensive, ongoing supports that maltreated children and their families need. These programs should be developmentally sensitive, trauma-informed, evidence-based, and formally linked to and incorporated into child welfare service delivery. Additionally, in keeping with the recommendations of Nation et al. (2003) regarding prevention programs for high-risk children and families writ large, programs should be comprehensive, delivered with sufficient dosage, be theory driven, promote positive relationships between providers and families, be socioculturally relevant, and be delivered by a well-trained staff. Through the use of these prevention and intervention approaches, the child welfare system can move closer to achieving its goal of improving the well-being of maltreated children and their families.

References

Barth, R. P., Landsverk, J., Chamberlain, P., Reid, J. B., Rolls, J. A., Hurlburt, M. S., . . . Kohl, P. L. (2005). Parent-training programs in child welfare services: Planning for a more evidence-based approach to serving biological parents. *Research on Social Work Practice, 15*(5), 353–371.

Bosquet Enlow, M., Blood, E., & Egeland, B. (2013). Sociodemographic risk, developmental competence, and PTSD symptoms in young children exposed to interpersonal trauma in early life. *Journal Of Traumatic Stress, 26*(6), 686–694.

Briggs-Gowan, M., Carter, A., & Ford, J. (2012). Parsing the effects of violence exposure in early childhood: Modeling developmental pathways. *Journal of Pediatric Psychology, 37*, 11–22. doi:10.1093/jpepsy/jsr063

Burns, B. J., Phillips, S. D., Wagner, H. R., Barth, R. P., Kolko, D. J., Campbell, Y., & Landsverk, J. (2004). Mental health need and access to mental health services by youths involved with child welfare: A national survey. *Journal of the American Academy of Child & Adolescent Psychiatry, 43*(8), 960–970.

Casanueva, C., Ringeisen, H., Smith, K., & Dolan, M. (2013). *NSCAW child well-being spotlight: Parents reported for maltreatment experience high rates of domestic violence*. OPRE Report #2013–04, Washington, DC: Office of Planning, Research and Evaluation, Administration for Children and Families, U.S. Department of Health and Human Services.

Casanueva, C., Smith, K., Dolan, M., & Ringeisen, H. (2011). *NSCAW II baseline report: Maltreatment*. OPRE Report #2011–27c, Washington, DC: Office of Planning, Research and Evaluation, Administration for Children and Families, U.S. Department of Health and Human Services.

Chen, S. Y., & Scannapieco, M. (2010). The influence of job satisfaction on child welfare worker's desire to stay: An examination of the interaction effect of self-efficacy and supportive supervision. *Children and Youth Services Review, 32*, 482–486.

Conron, K.J., Beardslee, W., Koenen, K.C., Buka, S.L., & Gortmaker, S.L. (2009). A longitudinal study of maternal depression and child maltreatment in a national sample of families investigated by Child Protective Services. *Archives of Pediatric and Adolescent Medicine, 163*, 922–930. doi:10.1001/archpediatrics.2009.176

Cort, N.A., Toth, S.L., Cerulli, C., & Rogosch, F. (2011). Maternal intergenerational transmission of childhood multitype maltreatment. *Journal of Aggression, Maltreatment & Trauma, 20*(1), 20–39.

Denmark, N., & Jones Harden, B. (2011). Meeting the mental health needs of staff. In S. Summers & R. Chazan-Cohen (Eds.), *Understanding early childhood mental health: A practical guide for professionals* (pp. 217–226). Baltimore, MD: Brookes.

Dorsey, S., Burns, B.J., Southerland, D.G., Cox, J.R., Wagner, H.R., & Farmer, E.M. (2012). Prior trauma exposure for youth in treatment foster care. *Journal of Child and Family Studies, 21*(5), 816–824.

Farmer, E., Murray, M., Dorsey, S. &, Burns B.J. (2005). *Enhancing and adapting treatment foster care*. Presented at the 18th Annual Research Conference Proceedings, A system of care for children's mental health: Expanding the research base, University of South.

Finkelhor, D., Turner, H., Ormrod, R., & Hamby, S. L. (2009). Violence, abuse, and crime exposure in a national sample of children and youth. *Pediatrics, 124*(5), 1411–1423. https://doi.org/10.1542/peds.2009-0467. Florida, Louis de la Parte Florida Mental Health Institute, Research and Training Center for Children's Mental Health, Tampa, FL.

Fraser, J.G., Lloyd, S., Murphy, R., Crowson, M., Zolotor, A.J., Coker-Schwimmer, E., & Viswanathan, M. (2013). A comparative effectiveness review of parenting and trauma-focused interventions for children exposed to maltreatment. *Journal of Developmental & Behavioral Pediatrics, 34*(5), 353–368.

Geeraert, L., Van den Noortgate, W., Grietens, H., & Onghena, P. (2004). The effects of early prevention programs for families with young children at risk for physical child abuse and neglect: A meta-analysis. *Child Maltreatment, 9*(3), 277–291.

Ghosh Ippen, C., Harris, W., Van Horn, P., & Lieberman, A. (2011). Traumatic and stressful events in early childhood: Can treatment help those at highest risk? *Child Abuse & Neglect, 35*, 504–513. doi:10.1016/j.chiabu.2011.03.009

Gilkerson, L., Graham, M., Harris, D., Oser, C., Clarke, J., Hairston- Fuller, T., & Lertora, J. (2013). Trauma-informed Part C early intervention: A vision, a challenge, a new reality. *Zero to Three, 34*, 34–45.

Hussey, D.L., & Guo, S. (2005). Characteristics and trajectories of treatment foster care youth. *Child Welfare, 84*(4), 485–506.

Institute of Medicine and National Research Council. (2009). Preventing mental, emotional, and behavioral disorders among young people: Progress and possibilities. Committee on the Prevention of Mental Disorders and Substance Abuse Among Children, Youth, and Young Adults: Research Advances and Promising Interventions. Mary Ellen O'Connell, Thomas Boat, & Kenneth E. Warner, (Eds.). Board on Children, Youth, and Families, Division of Behavioral and Social Sciences and Education. Washington, DC: The National Academies Press.

Institute of Medicine and National Research Council. (2012). Child maltreatment research, policy, and practice for the next decade: Workshop summary. Washington, DC: The National Academies Press.

Institute of Medicine and National Research Council. (2014). Harvesting the scientific investment in prevention science to promote children's cognitive, affective, and behavioral health: Workshop in brief. Washington, DC: The National Academies Press.

Katz, L.F., Lederman, C.S., & Osofsky, J.D. (2011). *Child-centered practices for the courtroom and community: A guide to working effectively with young children and their families in the child welfare system*. Baltimore, MD: Paul H. Brookes.

Leenarts, L. E. W., Diehle, J., Doreleijers, T. A. H., Jansma, E. P., & Lindauer, R. J. L. (2013). Evidence-based treatments for children with trauma-related psychopathology as a result of childhood maltreatment: A systematic review. *European Child & Adolescent Psychiatry*, 22(5), 269–283. https://doi.org/10.1007/s00787-012-0367-5

Lieberman, A.F., Chu, A., Van Horn, P., & Harris, W.W. (2011). Trauma in early childhood: Empirical evidence and clinical implications. *Development and Psychopathology, 23*(2), 397–410. doi:10.1017/S0954579411000137

Lieberman, A.F., & Van Horn, P. (2011). *Psychotherapy with infants and young children: Repairing the effects of stress and trauma on early attachment*. New York, NY: Guilford Press.

Lipschitz, D.S., Winegar, R.L., Hartnick, E., Foote, B., & Southwick, S.M. (1999). Posttraumatic stress disorder in hospitalized adolescents: Psychiatric comorbidity and clinical correlates. *Journal of the American Academy of Child and Adolescent Psychiatry, 38*(4), 385–392. https://doi.org/10.1097/00004583-199904000-00010

Lovejoy, M. C., Graczyk, P. A., O'Hare, E., & Neuman, G. (2000). Maternal depression and parenting behavior: A meta-analytic review. *Clinical Psychology Review, 20*, 561–592.

McCombs-Thornton, K. L., & Foster, E. M. (2012). The effect of the ZERO TO THREE Court Teams initiative on types of exits from the foster care system—A competing risks analysis. *Children and Youth Services Review, 34*, 169–178.

Nation, M., Crusto, C., Wandersman, A., Kumpfer, K. L., Seybolt, D., Morrissey-Kane, E., & Davino, K. (2003). What works in prevention: Principles of effective prevention programs. *American Psychologist, 58*(6–7), 449–456. http://dx.doi.org/10.1037/0003-066X.58.6-7.449

The National Child Traumatic Stress Network. (2013). *Child welfare trauma training toolkit*. Retrieved from http://www.nctsn.org/ nccts/nav.dopidctr_cwtool

Osofsky, J., & Lieberman, A. (2011). A call for integrating a mental health perspective into systems of care for abused and neglected infants and young children. *American Psychologist, 66*(2), 120–128. doi:10.1037/a0021630

Osofsky, J. D., Putnam, F., & Lederman, C. (2008). Vicarious traumatization and compassion fatigue: How to maintain emotional health when working with trauma. *Juvenile and Family Court Journal, 59*, 91–101.

Osofsky, J. D., Wewers, S., Hann, D. M., & Fick, A. C. (1993). Chronic community violence: What is happening to our children? *Psychiatry, 56*(1), 36–45.

Pearlman, L. A., & Maclan, P. S. (1995). Vicarious traumatization: An empirical study of the effects of trauma work on trauma therapists. *Professional Psychology: Research and Practice, 26*(6), 558–565. doi:10.1037/0735–7028.26.6.558

Rivard, J. C., Bloom, S. L., Abramovitz, R., Pasquale, L. E., Duncan, M., McCorkle, D., & Gelman, A. (2003). Assessing the implementation and effects of a trauma-focused intervention for youths in residential treatment. *Psychiatric Quarterly, 74*(137), 137–154. doi:10/1023/A:1021355727114

Shonkoff, J. (2010). Building a new biodevelopmental framework to guide the future of early childhood policy. *Child Development, 81*(10), 357–367.

Shonkoff, J., Boyce, T. & McEwen, B. (2009). Neuroscience, molecular biology, and the childhood roots of health disparities. *Journal of the American Medical Association, 301*(21), 2252–2259.

Sprang, G., Craig, C., & Clark, J. (2011). Secondary traumatic stress and burnout in child welfare workers: A comparative analysis of occupational distress across professional groups. *Child Welfare, 90*, 149–168.

Stein, B. D., Zima, B. T., Elliott, M. N., Burnam, M. A., Shahinfar, A., Fox, N. A., & Leavitt, L. A. (2001). Violence exposure among school-age children in foster care: Relationship to distress symptoms. *Journal of the American Academy of Child & Adolescent Psychiatry, 40*(5), 588–594.

Thompson, R.A. (2015). Social support and child protection: Lessons learned and learning. *Child Abuse and Neglect, 41*, 19–29. doi:10.1016/j.chiabu.2014.08.001

Toth, S.L., & Cicchetti, D. (2013). A developmental psychopathology perspective on child maltreatment. *Child Maltreatment, 18*(3), 135–139.

Toth, S.L., & Manly, J.T. (2011). Bridging research and practice: Challenges and successes in implementing evidence-based preventive intervention strategies for child maltreatment. *Child Abuse and Neglect, 35*(8), 633–636.

U.S. Department of Health and Human Services, Administration for Children and Families, Administration on Children, Youth and Families. (2012). *Information memorandum: Promoting social and emotional well-being for children and youth receiving child welfare services (ACYF-CB-IM-12–04).* Retrieved from https://www.acf.hhs.gov/cb/resource/im1204

U.S. Department of Health & Human Services, Administration for Children and Families Administration on Children, Youth and Families Children's Bureau. (2016). *Child maltreatment 2014.* https://doi.org/10.1016/j.mppsy.2008.05.001

Wald, M.S. (2015). Beyond CPS: Developing an effective system for helping children in neglectful families. *Stanford Law School, Public Law and Legal Theory Research*, Paper Series #2554074.

Weisz, J.R., Sandler, I.N., Durlak, J.A., & Anton, B.S. (2005). Promoting and protecting youth mental health through evidence-based prevention and treatment. *American Psychologist, 60*(6), 628–648. http://dx.doi.org/10.1037/0003-066X.60.6.628

Wulczyn, F., Barth, R., Yuan, Y., Jones Harden, B., & Landsverk, J. (2007). *Beyond common sense: Child welfare, child well-being and the evidence for policy reform.* New Brunswick, NJ: Aldine Transaction.

CHAPTER 8

Exposure to Terrorism and Disasters

Howard J. Osofsky, Joy D. Osofsky, Anthony H. Speier, and Tonya Cross Hansel

A disaster is a sudden, calamitous event that seriously disrupts a community or society's ability to function and cope using its own resources. Further, human, material, economic, and environmental losses sustained as the result of the incident contribute significantly to the disruption (International Federation of Red Cross and Red Crescent Societies, n.d.). Natural disasters refer to incidents with natural causes such as hurricanes, earthquakes, tornadoes, wild fires, tsunamis, and flooding. Technological disasters, in contrast, are the result of human causalities (oil spills, toxic exposure, failure of safety mechanisms, and nuclear accidents). Both natural and technological disasters have multiplied in frequency, severity, and magnitude in the past decade, increasing exposure for the general population that includes children and families. Currently, over 200 million people are impacted by disasters each year (International Federation of Red Cross and Red Crescent Societies, n.d.). In the United States, over half of all families have been impacted by some type of disaster (Save the Children, 2015). Further, many individuals who are survivors of disasters have been exposed multiple times.

Regardless of the type of disaster, children are more vulnerable than adults when exposed to disasters; however, child and adolescent survivors often receive insufficient attention (Masten & Osofsky, 2010; J. D. Osofsky, Osofsky, & Harris, 2007; Steinberg, Brymer, Steinberg, & Pfefferbaum, 2006). Learning from the negative experiences of individuals experiencing major disasters, in recent years, increased attention has been paid to the special needs of children, adolescents, and families during and following disasters. Currently, children are recognized in the Pandemic and All-Hazards Preparedness Reauthorization Act, Public Law No. 113–5 as a special population with unique vulnerabilities to disaster and terrorist events. The National Commission on Children and Disasters (2010) further specifies characteristics of children and how their vulnerabilities can be identified and addressed related to medical and public health needs in disasters. Both research and anecdotal reports indicate that children are exposed to additional risks and can be differentially affected based on age, gender, and socioeconomic status. The dose-response effect, which can include degree, intensity, type of exposure, and, in the case of individual or mass violence, familiarity with the victims or perpetrators, plays an important role in the degree of traumatization (Masten, Narayan, Silverman, & Osofsky, 2015; Masten & Osofsky, 2010). Factors associated with increased vulnerability to developing symptoms of anxiety, depression, or posttraumatic stress disorder (PTSD) relate to degree of exposure, duration of the traumatic event, prior exposure to trauma, preexisting behavioral health problems, neurobiological factors, and coping resources. In a study of 7,258 children and adolescents living in heavily affected Louisiana parishes after Hurricane Katrina, H. J. Osofsky, Osofsky, Kronenberg, Brennan, and Hansel (2009) found that experiences associated with personal loss, separation from family, lack of community support, as well as previous loss or trauma were related to increases in posttraumatic symptoms. Relocation from schools and communities following major disasters can also lead to longer-term psychological symptoms. In a study of 795 children in 5th through 12th grades who were forced to relocate away from New Orleans and unable to return two years after Hurricane Katrina, Hansel, Osofsky, Osofsky, and Friedrich (2013) found heightened symptoms in relocated children from similar zip codes when compared with those who could return. The amount of stability and support that can be provided by the family also relates to the degree of traumatization of caregivers as well as community, school, and social supports (Appleyard & Osofsky, 2003; Kerns et al., 2014; H. J. Osofsky et al., 2011).

With incidents of emergency situations on the rise, disasters touch the lives of millions of children each year (UNICEF, 2011). The purpose of this chapter is to describe the effects and response for children and adolescents regarding exposure to natural and technological disasters as well as incidents of terrorism.

Natural and Technological Disasters

Natural disasters can lead to many negative outcomes for children and families, including displacement, loss of homes and personal property, economic hardship, loss of community and social supports, and, in some cases, injury and death of loved ones. Natural disasters often follow regional and seasonal patterns, which can provide some degree of familiarity and predictability for communities and families (U.S. Department of Justice, n.d.). It should be noted, however, that the increased frequency of the occurrence and magnitude of natural disasters is, in part, related to environmental and climate change effects. For example, the Great Flood of 2016 that occurred in central Louisiana, an area unprepared for such flooding, has been thought to be related to recent climate changes. As a result of the flooding, families were displaced, schools were closed for months, children in foster care had to be moved to new families, and parents and family members, counselors, childcare workers, teachers, and other providers had to deal with their own personal losses even as they tried to be available to the children.

Technological disasters, such as the Deep Water Horizon Oil Spill in 2010 and the 2011 nuclear disaster in Japan, are less predictable than natural disasters. As a result, not only did children and families have to deal with hardships, but also there was a resultant mistrust of information provided by officials that could lead to more uncertainty about the future. Following technological disasters, traditional employment and community functions are affected, with concerns about toxic exposure affecting current residents and impacting on the future health of children. For example, data collected five years after the Gulf Oil Spill indicated that children remained concerned about the long-term impact on the environment, safety of seafood and animal products, and possibilities for future careers especially in the fishing and oil industries (King et al. 2015). An emphasis on the interconnectedness of humans and their environment has also led to a hybrid understanding of some natural and technological disasters. For example, in addition to the direct damage from the winds and flooding of Hurricane Katrina, many of the effects resulted from the breech of poorly constructed levees, the flooding from these levees, and an inadequate capacity of existing water pumping systems. These human-related factors contributed to additional flooding and loss of lives, family homes, and property.

Terrorism

Incidents of terrorism and mass violence are also human caused but are differentiated from technological disasters due to their deliberate intent. Terrorist incidents caused by premeditated human acts result in sudden and unexpected threat, horror, and destruction, inevitably impacting innocent and unsuspecting people in the course of their daily routines. Fostering terror, or fear, is a major goal of terrorist attacks in public settings (U.S. Department of Justice, n.d.). Parents are not only concerned about their own safety but are also especially fearful for their children and allowing them the freedom that children need for their activities and normal growth and development. Children may become more fearful related to what they know directly, what they hear from one another and adults, and what they learn from television and social media. After terrorist attacks, the resulting deaths and property destruction become reminders to many of their own vulnerability and inability to keep their loved ones safe and out of harm's way. Since the September 2001 terrorist attack in New York City, more attention has been paid to terrorist incidents as well as to the effects of both direct and indirect exposure (Otto et al., 2007; Pfefferbaum et al., 2002, 2005). The frequency of reported incidents of terrorism is resulting in growing exposure to terrorism, with fears of increasing vulnerability for children and families. As Garbarino, Governale, Danielle, and Nesi (2015) noted, most children in the United States are "growing up in a world in which terrorism in its many aspects is a salient cultural phenomenon" (p. 1) that indirectly affects their worldview and perceptions of risk.

Behavioral Health Effects

Regardless of disaster type, experiencing a disaster can result in a variety of short- and long-term trauma-related mental and behavioral health problems, with children being particularly vulnerable to such negative effects. Following a disaster, impacted children may exhibit a range of reactions, including, but not limited to, regression of developmentally achieved milestones, posttraumatic stress, behavioral and emotional dysregulation, depression, grief, school and academic difficulties, aggression, substance abuse/use, and risk-taking behaviors. The most common post-disaster behavioral health symptoms, which require helpful services and intervention, are depression, anxiety, and posttraumatic stress (La Greca, Silverman, Vernberg, & Prinstein, 1996; Pynoos, Steinberg, & Piacentini, 1999). Young children, because of their limited coping capacity, are most impacted by parental responses. When parents can respond, and provide safety and security, symptoms are likely to be limited. However, when families are displaced, with parents having reduced incomes (one or both being unemployed) and possibly living apart temporarily or in overcrowded situations with arguing and fighting, young children will likely reflect this difficult environment in their behaviors and emotions. In the aftermath of Hurricane Katrina, over 30 percent of parents of young children reported symptoms sufficiently worrisome to warrant a request for further services and treatment. Forty-five percent of older children had symptoms that were sufficiently elevated to meet the cut-off for further evaluation and provision of services. Middle school children complained and reacted to loss of friends who were also displaced, loss of pets, and difficulty in finding new peer group support. Adolescents sensed the need to undertake more responsibility but were often more prone to risk-taking behaviors and increased alcohol and substance use when displaced to new communities. Some experienced support in new communities while others felt unwelcome and excluded by peers. While evidence shows that most children and families cope well and demonstrate adaptive skills following traumatic exposure, this does not mean that they do not experience some distress or symptoms (Goenjian et al., 1997; King et al., 2015; H.J. Osofsky et al., 2009; J.D. Osofsky, Osofsky, Weems, King, & Hansel, 2015; Weems, Russell, Neill, Berman, & Scott, 2016). Therefore, it is important to understand risk factors that may contribute to more significant posttraumatic symptoms and ways to support all children regardless of their level of distress following disasters.

Risk Factors

Most children experience some period of distress following natural and technological disaster. The level of distress depends on a number of different factors that impact the family as well as the child. The abundance of evidence indicates that increased vulnerability in children relates not only to age, gender, race, and ethnic group; developmental status; and deviation from developmental norms but also to intensity of exposure (dose) to traumatic consequences of the incident, economic problems, and disparities in care (Cloitre et al., 2009; Greeson et al., 2011; Masten et al., 2015; J.D. Osofsky et al., 2007). As would be expected, children with prior behavioral health difficulties show more persistent symptoms (J.D. Osofsky, Osofsky, Weems, Hansel, & King, 2014). In a study of 7,258 children and adolescents living in heavily affected Louisiana parishes after Hurricane Katrina, H.J. Osofsky et al. (2009) found that experiences associated with previous loss or trauma were related to increases in posttraumatic symptoms. Similarly, children and adolescents reported more symptoms when they experienced prior and subsequent traumatic exposure following the Gulf oil spill. Importantly following Hurricane Katrina, over 30 percent of children endorsed being exposed to one or more traumatic experiences occurring either before or since the devastating hurricane (Osofsky et al. 2009).

Family and Community Resources

Children, adolescents, and families with fewer resources and those living in poverty are affected more significantly by terrorism and disaster incidents due to increased vulnerability and fewer supports. In Louisiana following Hurricane Katrina, data gathered from highly impacted areas indicated that children and adolescents were affected by loss of housing, school, community, and the lives they were used to experiencing (Kronenberg, et al. 2010). Further in a study on young children and disaster-related attachment problems, families living in poverty prior to Hurricane Katrina were more likely to experience postdisaster attachment and behavior problems (J. D. Osofsky, Kronenberg, Bocneck, & Hansel, 2015). After Hurricane Katrina, reports indicated that 90 percent of the children were displaced and 17 percent reported separation from parents; further experiences associated with separation from family were related to increases in posttraumatic symptoms (H.J. Osofsky et al., 2009). The amount of stability and support that could be provided by the family was inversely related to the degree of traumatization of caregivers, and the level of community, school, and social supports (Appleyard & Osofsky, 2003; Kerns et al., 2014; H.J. Osofsky & J.D. Osofsky, 2013). The data from Louisiana provide a window into the potential impact on children and families following incidents of terrorism and disasters as well as the increased vulnerability for those living in poverty.

Media Coverage

The media, including social media, allow rapid access to information related to disaster and terrorist incidents. Terrorist events that are highly traumatic and cause mass casualties receive considerable media coverage, exposing millions of U.S. citizens and people around the world to the horror and trauma of the tragedy (U.S. Department of Justice, n.d.). On one hand, access to information is helpful in preparation and response efforts. Social media provides important information about the safety and whereabouts of family members who have been impacted. While social media can provide accurate data and information about safety, both social media and media in general can also add to fears for children, adolescents, and families. The media provide a much wider exposure to the incident including repeated replaying of frightening events, which can contribute to traumatic experiences for the child and family viewers (Vernberg, Hambrick, Cho, & Hendrickson, 2016).

Prolonged Recovery

Studies have shown that disasters with a slow recovery, such as Hurricane Katrina, can result in acute and chronic psychological effects (Kessler, Galea, Jones, & Parker, 2006; Kronenberg et al., 2010; Masten & Osofsky, 2010; Osofsky & Osofsky, 2013; H.J. Osofsky et al., 2011) that negatively impact the child's developmental trajectory (Pynoos et al., 1999). The psychological, social, economic, and ecological consequences of technological disasters can extend for years into the future. There are concerns about the long-term impact on developmental trajectories for children exposed to a disaster with slow recovery, especially given the persistent stress on caregivers and lack of social and community supports. The concerns are consistent with an understanding of the impact of disasters with prolonged recovery or complex disasters with cumulative effects with the cascading effects of disasters (Masten & Cicchetti, 2010). Either of these situations can lead to both acute and chronic psychological effects on children's development (Kessler et al., 2006). Such traumatic exposure can likely have significant impacts on children over decades with possible cross-generational effects (J.D. Osofsky et al., 2015).

Resilience

It is important to note that most children and adolescents are resilient, over time demonstrating recovery even if they continue to exhibit some behavioral health symptoms. Data on the trajectories of recovery following Hurricane Katrina and the Gulf oil spill generally demonstrate continuing improvement with periods of temporary increases in symptoms with further trauma exposure (Osofsky, Osofsky, et al., 2015). Overall, patterns of recovery are consistent with the typical patterns of resilience over time described by Masten and Narayan (2012; see Chapter 4 on "Resilience" in Volume II of this series). The concept of resilience, meaning the capacity to effectively recover from significant disturbances that threaten adaptive functioning and development, has received attention for several decades (Masten et al., 2015; Rutter, 2006). Recent efforts focus on characterizing children's resilience postdisaster and terrorism, identifying response factors that promote adaptive reactions, and building interventions that support resilience (Bonanno & Mancini, 2008; Kronenberg et al., 2010; Masten & Narayan, 2012; Meyerson, Grant, Carter, & Kilmer, 2011; Osofsky, Osofsky, et al., 2015). Fostering resilience at the individual and community level is crucial to this work (Bonanno, Westphal, & Mancini, 2011; Masten et al., 2015; Masten & Obradovic, 2008).

Responding to Needs of Children and Adolescents

Disaster recovery responses, including mental and behavioral health services, are effective in reducing symptoms of PTSD and depression (Berger, Gelkopf, & Heineberg, 2012; Giannopoulou, Dikaiakou, & Yule, 2006; Hoagwood et al., 2006; Jaycox et al., 2010). An important part of disaster preparedness and response for children is the involvement of parents and caregivers to effectively plan and carry out the roles of protection, communication, and safeguarding children under very difficult circumstances. Following disasters, it is especially helpful for family and school routines to be maintained and some children and families will need additional services and supports. The Institute of Medicine (2015) has promoted a three-tiered approach of interventions to help children and families impacted by disasters, including:

- *universal interventions*, which are appropriate for all members of a community;
- *targeted interventions*, which are implemented in the short-term period following disasters for children who are exhibiting moderate distress; and
- *intensive interventions*, which are implemented for children with severe or long-lasting reactions.

These interventions are frequently provided in schools due to the natural fostering of supportive relationships through students, teachers, and school staff interactions (Hansel et al., 2013; La Greca, Vernberg, Silverman, & Prinstein, 1996; Pina et al., 2008).

Schools that provide safe environments for children to play and learn offer protective factors for children exposed to disasters (Masten & Osofsky, 2010; J. D. Osofsky et al., 2007) and can be crucial in reestablishing routines (Masten & Narayan, 2012). Not only is school accessible for both children and parents, but it is also a familiar environment that encourages normalcy and minimizes the stigma related to accessing mental health services through community clinics (Cohen et al., 2009; Ehntholt, Smith, & Yule, 2005). Child and adolescent populations are often easier to locate postdisaster due to the concentration of this group in school settings (Pfefferbaum, Call, & Sconzo, 1999; Stuber et al., 2002). For all of these reasons, a variety of school-based postdisaster interventions have been designed for youth following exposure to disaster (CATS Consortium, 2010; Dorsey, Briggs, & Woods, 2011; Pfefferbaum, Newman, & Nelson, 2014). Findings suggest that clinical interventions in schools are successful in reducing psychological symptoms in children and adolescents (Catani et al., 2009; Weems et al., 2007).

Community Response to Child Needs

Large-scale complex disasters, such as Hurricane Katrina, the Gulf Oil Spill, earthquakes, and tsunamis, are of particular importance related to children's development. They not only directly affect the child and family but also trigger disturbances across multiple systems, including microsystems, exosystems, and macrosystems in which the lives and development of children and families are interconnected (Goldstein, Osofsky, & Lichtveld, 2011; Masten & Obradovic, 2008; Osofsky, Palinkas, & Galloway, 2010). A whole community perspective is needed for disaster response frameworks with families, individuals, and households as main components of the whole community. Bronfenbrenner's ecological systems model supports a whole community perspective relevant to disaster response in which individuals are nested within their families, schools, and communities, and changes that occur at the community level influence individual outcomes (Bronfenbrenner, 1999). Response and recovery expansion using a whole communities approach is needed to ensure that communities are addressing the unique needs of children and families as highlighted in the National Commission on Children and Disasters report (2010). In addition, collaboration with local community members in developing interventions that address racial, cultural, and community values and traditions, as well as socioeconomic issues and disparities in care, is very much needed. This approach is particularly important since the workforce delivering services in the acute phases after disasters or terrorism is sometimes not familiar with the traditions and characteristics of the affected communities (Masten et al., 2015; J. D. Osofsky, Osofsky, & Harris, 2007). Systems interactions (i.e., child, family, school) can also be applied to resilience following incidents of disaster and terrorism.

Community factors that facilitate recovery include both the perception of available community support and the actual availability of community resources. Connectivity to social groups, trust in the local government, and the integrity of local leaders further empower individual recovery, which in turn further enhances community cohesion and recovery.

It is important to underscore the building of community as well as individual resilience in order to improve well-being across multiple systems (Berkes & Ross, 2013; Boon, Cottrell, King, Stevenson, & Millar, 2012; Keim, 2008; Wyche et al., 2011). Norris, Stevens, Pfefferbaum, Wyche, and Pfefferbaum (2008) have proposed that community resilience is a set of "network adaptive capacities," including social capital, economic development, information and communication, and community competence. Similarly, Abramson et al. (2015) have proposed a "conceptual framework for resilience activation" emphasizing the importance of both community and individual attributes in activating resilience through engagement in social resources.

One example of a macro systems level response network is the National Child Traumatic Stress Network (NCTSN) authorized by Congress in 2000. NCTSN provides assessment, treatment and intervention development, training, data analysis, program evaluation, policy analysis and education, systems change, and the integration of trauma-informed and evidence-based practices in all child-serving systems. Since 2001, the NCTSN, under the direction of the Terrorism and Disaster Program, has responded to 75 natural and technological disasters, including Hurricanes Katrina and Sandy, the Joplin tornado, the Deepwater Horizon oil spill, and the mudslides in Oso, Washington. During the past decade, NCTSN has developed intervention protocols for all tiers of intervention, including Psychological First Aid (Tier 1), Skills for Psychological Recovery (Tier 2; adopted by the SAMHSA Crisis Counseling Program), and Trauma-Focused Cognitive Behavioral Therapy (Tier 3). These culturally relevant recovery intervention strategies recognize the diversity of individuals and communities and the many ways to address needs and recovery following disasters. Successful intervention strategies emphasize the importance of parallel and interactive individual and community recovery processes for the overall recovery experience. Individuals struggling with recovery need assistance learning how to build and blend their personal strengths while also addressing individual challenges and finding ways to enhance community resources. This bidirectional process of accepting assistance while sharing strengths is recognized as a crucial aspect for reestablishing personal competency and a sense of mastery.

Accomplishing these tasks provides the basis for achieving both individual and community resilience.

The Louisiana State University Health Sciences Center (LSUHSC) Terrorism & Disaster Coalition for Child and Family Resilience (TDC4CFR) is a five-year center funded through NCTSN. TDC4CFR is grounded in a three-tier public health model identified by the NCTSN for organizing response to events of extreme terrorism, mass violence, and major disasters (Pynoos, Goenjian, & Steinberg, 1998). Tier 1 focuses on general postdisaster support to a wide population of children and adolescents through schools, community agencies, and religious institutions; Tier 2 identifies children and families who have experienced extreme exposure and losses and high levels of current distress and adversity and are at developmental risk; and Tier 3 identifies children and adolescents with serious psychiatric disorders. Through these three tiers, TDC4CFR will adapt and disseminate important NCTSN products/interventions, including Psychological First Aid for Schools (PFA-Schools), the Help Kids Cope App, Skills for Psychological Recovery (SPR), and Post-Trauma Stress Management (PTSM).

To organize systemic response, TDC4CFR will develop four coalitions across the United States that will assist communities in developing preparation, response, and recovery efforts to support child and family resilience. The coalitions will be composed of state and community child behavioral health and disaster leaders, other NCTSN sites, and stakeholder groups that will include child and family input. Local and national consultants will provide expertise in each stage of the process that includes coalition development, implementation, and evaluation. Addressing the importance of establishing community and regional sustainable resources through collaborative networks is consistent with the aforementioned public health approach of understanding preparation, response, and recovery needs at the individual and community level and activating evidence-informed interventions across all three tiers of intervention when necessary. This will provide communities with access to empirically demonstrated resources on a renewable basis as long as the coalition remains engaged.

Local Collaborative Response

Well-developed mass trauma and disaster response knowledge residing within academia and the professional scientific literature do little good if it is not translated from the context of academic science to community utility and scientist to community responders. Complex severe events (acts of terrorism or natural or human-caused technological disasters) begin in a very direct and uncomplicated fashion. Typically, when an extreme event occurs, people have been busy conducting their routine daily life activities. Suddenly, they experience what becomes an overwhelming and terrifying experience forever impacting them. Life was going one way, and now it is very different.

It is within this context that building coalitions or local community collaborative service models, capable of blending the resources of (1) federal, state, and local government; (2) community-based social capital; and (3) the scientific intervention knowledge of disaster behavioral health, is essential for the sustainable recovery of families and communities (Speier and Sherman, 2017). The emerging resilience of communities within locally driven recovery initiatives is reinforced through processes that honor and respect all community members and is actively committed to adapting recovery resources that fit the needs of individuals and their communities.

Case Examples

Two case studies are presented demonstrating the lessons learned from work following Hurricane Katrina and illustrating the power of local leadership, action, and individual caring relationships in both cases.

As noted, on August 29, 2005, Hurricane Katrina devastated much of metropolitan New Orleans. Individuals and families who could not leave the city were stranded for many days in the Superdome and in the Convention Center. First responders, already struggling from concerns for their inability to fully protect the city, also lost their homes and had displaced families, at times not knowing where spouses and children were living. The Federal Emergency Management Agency (FEMA) leased two ships from the Carnival Cruise Line to allow first responders and city workers to temporarily live onboard with the provision for family members to join them. A team for the LSUHSC Department of Psychiatry lived with the police and their families for six months onboard one of the cruise ships. Of the many informal interactions, after a week on the ship, it was apparent that one little five-year-old boy, the son of a police officer, was distraught and withdrawn. His loving grandparents, who were caring for him, were very worried about him. Utilizing principles of PFA, the clinician sat down with him and proceeded to get to know him and try to understand his concerns. The little boy cried when he talked about being stranded at the Superdome but then described how his father, a police officer, had not joined them (he was stranded at the Convention Center). The boy then said that his father had not brought the cake he had promised for his birthday. When the clinician explained to him that his daddy was also upset that he missed his birthday but would be joining him soon and would bring him a cake, the little boy's face lit up and he clearly expressed how much better he felt. From that point on, he was more like his normal self; his grandparents were very appreciative, as was his father when he was able to join him and bring the celebratory birthday cake.

St. Bernard Parish, adjacent to New Orleans, was particularly devastated with virtually every home, church, and business heavily damaged by winds, rain, and a toxic oil spill, which made the parish virtually uninhabitable. Some of the displaced population either never returned or returned slowly after the floor waters receded. The courageous superintendent of schools was determined to open the school even before FEMA funds could be appropriated. As she pointed out, families could not return if there were no schools and the schools should become a home to the many families returning. In October 2005, she reopened a temporary school on the site of one of the heavily impacted high schools (there had been three high schools in the community before Hurricane Katrina) with trailers and a temporary structure for education. The LSUHSC Department of Psychiatry team worked closely with her, beginning on the first day that students came back to the parish. In the spring of 2006, St. Bernard Parish Public School system and LSUHSC developed a collaborative program, the St. Bernard Family Resiliency Project (SBFRP, 2010) to provide additional support and resilience to returning high school students. SBFRP was aided considerably by consultations from Robert Pynoos, MD, co-director, National Child Traumatic Stress Network; Ann Masten, PhD, renowned expert in resilience; and Albert Bandura, PhD, the father of social learning theory and self-efficacy. Guided by mental health professionals from our team, the students and teachers engaged in projects to help clear trash, build a school garden, assist returning younger children, provide support to the elderly, and express appreciation to volunteers from other parts of the country. Toward the end of the summer session, each of the students was interviewed by the team to gain further input from them as well as their understanding of how the program was personally helpful.

One 15-year-old explained how his family had been displaced to another parish. His father's job was no longer available, and it would not be available for another two to three years. As the family sat crowded around the television, he realized that his parents were as traumatized as him and that he needed to "grow up" and be of support to them. From that point on, with the help that he was receiving from SBFRP, he took on more family responsibility and functions and was able to be helpful to his sister and his parents during further recovery. Of note, his very meaningful growth and resilience have continued, and even while in college and then in law school, he volunteered time to help SBFRP and the schools.

Conclusion

While the majority of children show psychosocial resilience over time to the psychological impact of exposure to terrorist and disaster incidents, nearly all experience some period of distress. There is abundant evidence (Cloitre et al., 2009; Greeson et al., 2011; Masten et al., 2015; J. D. Osofsky et al., 2007) that increased vulnerability in children is related not only to gender, race, and ethnic group but also to economic problems, disparities in care, exposure to multiple traumas, and preexisting behavioral health problems. In their 2015 National Disaster Report Card on Protecting Children in Disasters, Save the Children highlights that 79 percent of the Commission's recommendations have remained unfulfilled since Hurricane Katrina.

It is crucial that the special needs of children and adolescents be addressed following both natural and technological disasters and following acts of terrorism. A whole community approach is needed involving parents and other caregivers (who themselves may be traumatized and in need of services), community providers, schools, spiritual leaders, and other supportive groups. While children and adolescents may expectably develop age and developmentally related regressive symptoms and behavioral dysregulation, most will be resilient and demonstrate normal patterns of resilience over time. Interventions should focus on efforts that will be universally helpful, those that should be targeted for children with specific reactions, and those that are useful for children with preexisting and long-term difficulties. It is important to include a community participatory approach in the establishment of supportive services. Respect needs to be given to the strengths and cultures of the impacted communities. Further attention should be given both to individual and community resilience. Important models are available and have been described in this chapter to help meet the needs of children and adolescents during preparation, response, and recovery.

References

Abramson, D. M., Grattan, L. M., Mayer, B., Colten, C. E., Arosemena, F. A., Bedimo-Rung, A., & Lichtveld, M. (2015). The Resilience Activation Framework: A conceptual model of how access to social resources promotes adaptation and rapid recovery in post-disaster settings. *The Journal of Behavioral Health Services and Research*, 42(1), 42–57.

Appleyard, K., & Osofsky, J. D. (2003). Parenting after trauma: Supporting parents and caregivers in the treatment of children impacted by violence. *Infant Mental Health Journal*, 24(2), 111–125.

Berger, R., Gelkopf, M., & Heineberg, Y. (2012). A teacher-delivered intervention for adolescents exposed to ongoing and intense traumatic war-related stress: A quasi-randomized controlled study. *Journal of Adolescent Health, 51*(5), 453–461.

Berkes, F., & Ross, H. (2013). Community resilience: Toward an integrated approach. *Society and Natural Resources, 26*(1), 5–20.

Bonanno, G. A., & Mancini, A. D. (2008). The human capacity to thrive in the face of potential trauma. *Pediatrics, 121*(2), 369–375.

Bonanno, G. A., Westphal, M., & Mancini, A. D. (2011). Resilience to loss and potential trauma. *Annual Review of Clinical Psychology, 7*, 511–535.

Boon, H. J., Cottrell, A., King, D., Stevenson, R. B., & Millar, J. (2012). Bronfenbrenner's bioecological theory for modeling community resilience to natural disasters. *Natural Hazards, 60*(2), 381–408.

Bronfenbrenner, U. (1999). Environments in developmental perspective: Theoretical and operational models. In S. L. Friedman & T. D. Wachs (Eds.), *Measuring environment across the life span: Emerging methods and concepts* (pp. 3–28). Washington, DC: American Psychological Association Press.

Catani, C, Kohiladevy, M., Ruf, M., Schauer, E., Elbert, T., & Neuner, F. (2009). Treating children traumatized by war and Tsunami: A comparison between exposure therapy and meditation-relaxation in North-East Sri Lanka. *BMC Psychiatry, 9*(22), 1–11. doi:10.1186/1471–244X-9–22

CATS Consortium. (2010). Implementation of CBT for youth affected by the World Trade Center disaster: Matching need to treatment intensity and reducing trauma symptoms. *Journal of Traumatic Stress, 23*(6), 699–707. doi:10.1002/jts.20594

Cloitre, M., Stolbach, B. C., Herman, J. L., Kolk, B. V. D., Pynoos, R., Wang, J., & Petkova, E. (2009). A developmental approach to complex PTSD: Childhood and adult cumulative trauma as predictors of symptom complexity. *Journal of Traumatic Stress, 22*(5), 399–408.

Cohen, J. A., Jaycox, L. H., Walker, D. W., Mannarino, A. P., Langley, A. K., & DuClos, J. L. (2009). Treating traumatized children after hurricane Katrina: Project Fleur-de Lis™. *Clinical Child and Family Psychology Review, 12*(1), 55–64.

Dorsey, S., Briggs, E. C., & Woods, B. A. (2011). Cognitive behavioral treatment for posttraumatic stress disorder in children and adolescents. *Child and Adolescent Psychiatric Clinics of North America, 20*, 255–269.

Ehntholt, K. A., Smith, P. A., & Yule, W. (2005). School-based cognitive-behavioral therapy group intervention for refugee children who have experienced war-related trauma. *Clinical Child Psychology and Psychiatry, 10*, 235–250.

Garbarino, J. Governale, A., Danielle, P., & Nesi, H. (2015). Sharing child and youth development knowledge: Children and terrorism. *Society for Research on Child Development Social Policy Report, 29*(2), 1–39.

Giannopoulou, I., Dikaiakou, A., & Yule, W. (2006). Cognitive-behavioral group intervention for PTSD symptoms in children following Athens 1999 earthquake: A pilot study. *Clinical Child Psychology and Psychiatry, 114,* 543–553.

Goenjian, A.K., Karayan, I., Pynoos, R.S., Minassian, D., Najarian, L.M., Steinberg, A. M., & Fairbanks, L. A. (1997). Outcome of psychotherapy among early adolescents after trauma. *The American Journal of Psychiatry, 1544,* 536–542. https://doi.org/10.1176/ajp.154.4.536

Goldstein, B.D., Osofsky, H.J., & Lichtveld, M.Y. (2011). The Gulf oil spill. *New England Journal of Medicine, 364,* 1334–1348.

Greeson, J.K., Briggs, E.C., Kisiel, C.L., Layne, C.M., Ake, G.S., III, Ko, S.J., & Fairbank, J.A. (2011). Complex trauma and mental health in children and adolescents placed in foster care: Findings from the National Child Traumatic Stress Network. *Child Welfare, 90*(6), 91–108.

Hansel, T.C., Osofsky, J.D., Osofsky, H.J., & Friedrich, P. (2013). The effect of long term relocation on child and adolescent survivors of Hurricane Katrina. *Journal of Traumatic Stress, 26*(5), 613–620. doi:10.1002/jts.21837

Hoagwood, K.E., Radigan, M., Rodriguez, J., Levitt, J.M., Fernandez, D., & Foster, J. (2006). *Final report on the Child and Adolescent Trauma Treatment and Services (CATS) Project for the Substance Abuse and Mental Health Services Administration* (SAMHSA). New York, NY: Office of Mental Health.

International Federation of Red Cross and Red Crescent Societies. (n.d.). *Disaster and crisis management.* Retrieved from http://www.ifrc.org/en/what-we-do/disaster-management/about-disasters/what-is-a-disaster/

Jaycox, L.H., Cohen, J.A., Mannarino, A.P., Walker, D.W., Langley, A.K., Gegenheimer, K.L., & Schonlau, M. (2010). Children's mental health care following Hurricane Katrina: A field trial of trauma-focused psychotherapies. *Journal of Traumatic Stress, 23,* 223–231.

Keim, M.E. (2008). Building human resilience: The role of public health preparedness and response as an adaptation to climate change. *American Journal of Preventive Medicine, 35,* 508–515.

Kerns, C.E., Elkins, R.M., Carpenter, A.L., Chou, T., Green, J.G., & Comer, J.S. (2014). Caregiver distress, shared traumatic exposure, and child adjustment among area youth following the 2013 Boston Marathon bombing. *Journal of Affective Disorders, 167,* 50–55.

Kessler, R.C., Galea, S., Jones, R.T., & Parker, H.A. (2006). Mental illness and suicidality after Hurricane Katrina. *Bulletin of the World Health Organization, 84,* 930–939.

King, L.S., Osofsky, J.D., Osofsky, H.J., Weems, C.F., Hansel, T.C., & Fassnacht, G.M. (2015). Perceptions of trauma and loss among children and adolescents exposed to disasters: A mixed-methods study. *Current Psychology, 34*(3), 524–536.

Kronenberg, M.E., Hansel, T.C., Brennan, A.M., Osofsky, H.J., Osofsky, J.D., & Lawrason, B. (2010). Children of Katrina: Lessons learned about postdisaster symptoms and recovery patterns. *Child Development, 81*(4), 1241–1259.

La Greca, A. M., Silverman, W. K., Vernberg, E. M., & Prinstein, M. J. (1996). Symptoms of posttraumatic stress in children after Hurricane Andrew: A prospective study. *Journal of Consulting and Clinical Psychology, 64*, 712–723. doi:10.1037/0022-006X.64.4.712

Masten, A. S., & Cicchetti, D. (2010). Developmental cascades. *Development and Psychopathology, 22*, 491–495.

Masten, A. S., & Narayan, A. J. (2012). Child development in the context of disaster, war, and terrorism: Pathways of risk and resilience. *Annual Review of Psychology, 63*, 227–257.

Masten, A. S., Narayan, A. J., Silverman, W. K., & Osofsky, J. D. (2015). Children in war and disaster. In R. M. Lerner (Ed.), M. H. Bornstein, & T. Leventhal (Vol. Eds.), *Handbook of child psychology and developmental science. Vol. 4. Ecological settings and processes in developmental systems* (7th ed., pp. 704–745). New York, NY: Wiley.

Masten, A. S., & Obradovic, J. (2008). Disaster preparation and recovery: Lessons from research on resilience in human development. *Ecology and Society, 13*(1), 9–24.

Masten, A. S., & Osofsky, J. D. (2010). Disasters and their impact on child development: Introduction to the special section. *Child Development, 81*(4), 1029–1039.

Meyerson, D. A., Grant, K. E., Carter, J. S., & Kilmer, R. P. (2011). Posttraumatic growth among children and adolescents: A systematic review. *Clinical Psychology Review, 31*(6), 949–964.

National Commission on Children and Disasters. (2010, October). *Report to the President and Congress* (AHRQ Publication No. 10-M037). Rockville, MD: Agency for Healthcare Research and Quality

Norris, F. H., Stevens, S. P., Pfefferbaum, B., Wyche, K. F., & Pfefferbaum, R. L. (2008). Community resilience as a metaphor, theory, set of capacities, and strategy for disaster readiness. *American Journal of Community Psychology, 41*, 127–150.

Osofsky, H. J., & Osofsky, J. D. (2013). Hurricane Katrina and the Gulf oil spill: Lessons learned. *Psychiatric Clinics of North America, 36*, 371–383.

Osofsky, H. J., Osofsky, J. D., Arey, J., Kronenberg, M. E., Hansel, T. C., & Many, M. (2011). Hurricane Katrina's first responders: The struggle to protect and serve in the aftermath of the disaster. *Disaster Medicine and Public Health Preparedness, Suppl* 2, S214–S219. doi:10.1001/dmp.2011.53

Osofsky, H. J., Osofsky, J. D., Kronenberg, M., Brennan, A., & Hansel, T. C. (2009). Posttraumatic stress symptoms in children after Hurricane Katrina: Predicting the need for mental health services. *American Journal of Orthopsychiatry, 79*, 212–220. doi:10.1037/a0016179

Osofsky, H. J., Palinkas, L. A., & Galloway, J. M. (2010). Mental health effects of the Gulf oil spill. *Disaster Medicine and Public Health Preparedness, 4*(4), 1–3.

Osofsky, J. D., Kronenberg, M. E., Bocneck, E., & Hansel, T. C. (2015). Longitudinal impact of attachment-related risk and exposure to trauma among young children after Hurricane Katrina. *Child & Youth Care Forum, 44*(4), 493–510. doi:10.1007./s10566-015-9300-7

Osofsky, J. D., Osofsky, H. J., & Harris, W. W. (2007). Katrina's children: Social policy considerations for children in disasters. *Social Policy Report, 21*(1), 3–18.

Osofsky, J. D., Osofsky, H. J., Weems, C. F., Hansel, T. C., & King, L. (2014). The effects of stress related to the Gulf oil spill on child and adolescent mental health. *Journal of Pediatric Psychology, 41*(1), 65–72. doi:10.1093/jpepsy/jsu085

Osofsky, J. D., Osofsky, H. J., Weems, C. F., King, L. S., & Hansel, T. C. (2015). Trajectories of post-traumatic stress disorder symptoms among youth exposed to both natural and technological disasters. *Journal of Child Psychology and Psychiatry, 56*(12), 1347–1355.

Otto, M. W., Henin, A., Hirshfeld-Becker, D. R., Pollack, M. H., Biederman, J., & Rosenbaum, J. F. (2007). Posttraumatic stress disorder symptoms following media exposure to tragic events: Impact of 9/11 on children at risk for anxiety disorders. *Journal of Anxiety Disorders, 21*(7), 888–902.

Pfefferbaum, B., Call, J. A., & Sconzo, G. M. (1999). Mental health services for children in the first two years after the 1995 Oklahoma City terrorist bombing. *Psychiatric Services, 50*, 956–958.

Pfefferbaum, B., Doughty, M. D. E., Reddy, C., Patel, N., Gurwitch, R. H., Nixon, S. J., & Tivis, M. R. D. (2002). Exposure and peritraumatic response as predictors of posttraumatic stress in children following the 1995 Oklahoma City bombing. *Journal of Urban Health, 79*(3), 354–363.

Pfefferbaum, B., Newman, E., & Nelson, S. D. (2014). Mental health interventions for children exposed to disasters and terrorism. *Journal of Child and Adolescent Psychopharmacology, 24*(1), 24–31.

Pfefferbaum, B. J., Devoe, E. R., Stuber, J., Schiff, M., Klein, T. P., & Fairbrother, G. (2005). Psychological impact of terrorism on children and families in the United States. *Journal of Aggression, Maltreatment and Trauma, 9*(3–4), 305–317.

Pina, A. A., Villalta, I. K., Ortiz, C. D., Gottschall, A. C., Costa, N. M., & Weems, C. F. (2008). Social support, discrimination, and coping as predictors of posttraumatic stress reactions in youth survivors of Hurricane Katrina. *Journal of Clinical Child and Adolescent Psychology, 37*(3), 564–574. doi:10.1080/15374410802148228

Pynoos, R. S., Goenjian, A. K., & Steinberg, A. M. (1998). A public mental health approach to the post-disaster treatment of children and adolescents. *Child and Adolescents Psychiatric Clinics of North America, 7*(1), 195–210.

Pynoos, R. S., Steinberg, A. M., & Piacentini, J. C. (1999). A developmental psychopathology model of childhood traumatic stress and intersection with anxiety disorders. *Biological Psychiatry, 46*, 1542–1554. doi:10.1016/S0006–3223(99)00262–0

Rutter, M. (2006). Implications of resilience concepts for scientific understanding. *Annals of the New York Academy of Sciences, 1094*(1), 1–12.

Save the Children. (2015). *National disaster report card on protecting children in disasters.* Retrieved from http://www.savethechildren.org/site/c.8rKLIXMGIpI4E/b.8777053/k.F31D/Get_Ready_Get_Safe_Disaster_Report_Card.htm

Speier, A., & Sherman, R. (2017). Why is integrating emergency management essential to disaster behavioral health challenges and opportunities. In B. Flynn & R. Sherman (Eds.), *Integrating emergency management & disaster behavioral health—one picture through two lenses* (pp. 73–98). Cambridge, MA: Elsevier.

St. Bernard Family Resiliency Project. (2010). APA Achievement Awards: Promoting recovery and providing trauma treatment for students and their families after Hurricane Katrina. *Psychiatric Services, 61*(10), 1039–1041.

Steinberg, A. M., Brymer, M. J., Steinberg, J. R., & Pfefferbaum, B. (2006). Conducting research on children and adolescents after disaster. In F. H. Norris, S. Galea, M. J. Friedman, & P. J. Watson (Eds.), *Methods for disaster mental health research* (pp. 243–253). New York, NY: Guilford Press.

Stuber, J., Fairbrother, G., Galea, S., Pfefferbaum, B., Wilson-Genderson, M., & Vlahov, D. (2002). Determinants of counseling for children in Manhattan after the September 11 attacks. *Psychiatric Services, 53*, 815–822. doi:10.1176/appi.ps.53.7.815

UNICEF. (2011). *UNICEF and disaster risk and reduction.* Retrieved from https://www.unicef.org/malaysia/UNICEF_and_Disaster_Risk_Reduction.pdf

U.S. Department of Justice. (n.d.). *Office of Justice Programs Responding to Victims of Terrorism and Mass Violent Crimes. Coordination and collaboration between American Red Cross workers and crime victim service provider.* NCJ209681: Retrieved from http://ojp.gov/ovc/publications/infores/redcross/ncj209681.pdf

Vernberg, E. M., Hambrick, E. P., Cho, B., & Hendrickson, M. L. (2016). Positive psychology and disaster mental health: Strategies for working with children and adolescents. *Journal of Clinical Psychology, 72*(12), 1333–1347. https://doi.org/10.1002/jclp.22289

Weems, C. F., Pina, A. A., Costa, N. M., Watts, S. E., Taylor, L. K., & Cannon, M. F. (2007). Predisaster trait anxiety and negative affect predict posttraumatic stress in youths following Hurricane Katrina. *Journal of Consulting and Clinical Psychology, 75*, 154–159. doi:10.1037/0022–006X.75.1.154

Weems, C. F., Russell, J. D., Neill, E. L., Berman, S. L., & Scott, B. G. (2016). Existential anxiety among adolescents exposed to disaster: Linkages among level of exposure, PTSD, and depression symptoms. *Journal of Traumatic Stress, 29*(5), 466–473.

Wyche, K. F., Pfefferbaum, R. L., Pfefferbaum, B., Norris, F. H., Wisnieski, D., & Younger, H. (2011). Exploring community resilience in workforce communities of first responders serving Katrina survivors. *American Journal of Orthopsychiatry, 81*(1), 18–30.

CHAPTER 9

Judicial Perspective on Violence and Trauma within the Family

Judge Constance Cohen (Ret.) and Joy D. Osofsky

The judicial and legal systems must consider the impact of domestic violence, as well as abuse and neglect from both adult and child perspectives in courtrooms every day. In Volume I, Betsy McAlister Groves (Chapter 5) provides an overview of domestic violence and the effects on children and families. The current chapter considers the issue of domestic violence in juvenile court and the importance of viewing domestic violence as well as frequently co-occurring abuse and neglect through a trauma-informed and collaborative lens in order to provide more support for children and families with an emphasis on the need for systems change.

Exposure to trauma and violence, including domestic violence, abuse, and neglect co-occurs in families, with reported exposure of between 30–70 percent of children depending on the way the data are collected (Margolin & Gordis, 2004; Summers, 2006). Violence exposure impacts children of all ages and for younger children especially can derail normal trajectories for physical, emotional, social, and cognitive development. Because the primary motivations in early childhood are attachment and exploration, exposure to trauma disrupts these processes, influencing the child's ability to learn to trust significant caregivers and feel free to explore their environment. Younger children are extremely dependent on their caregiving environment and exquisitely sensitive to changes in their caregiver. They also have not had the opportunity to develop individual coping capacities. For these reasons, they are especially impacted by the stress resulting from domestic violence. For children of all ages, the consistency and availability of parents or caregivers are crucial for development. Older children not only need guidance but also benefit from modeling of responsible and caring behavior by parents or caregivers. For these reasons, it is also important to understand the impact of trauma on caregivers and to support them in building their capacities to provide nurturance and to be available for their children. Unfortunately, exposure to trauma influences the caregiver's emotional availability as well as his or her ability to establish and maintain an empathic relationship with his or her child, which may disrupt the child's development. Adults may react to their own violence exposure by repeating the same behaviors with their children. They may also find maladaptive ways to cope with the stress through abusing alcohol and drugs. In addition, mental health problems can follow trauma exposure, creating a toxic environment for children. Depending on how the caregiver reacts, he or she may have a decreased capacity to recognize danger or stress. He or she may need to protect himself or herself from feelings of vulnerability and trauma, including traumatic reminders. Further, he or she may have more difficulty tolerating the child's sadness, anxiety, or aggression, which may also be a result of what the child has observed.

It is important for the court to be aware of the fact that children in families experiencing domestic violence may also be experiencing incest or child sexual abuse (Bancroft & Silverman, 2002) or may be injured during the violence or forced to watch the abuse (Weithorn, 2001). Children exposed to domestic violence may also suffer emotional, behavioral, and cognitive difficulties as a result of the exposure (Futures without Violence, 2013). Identifying domestic violence may be a critical context for understanding a parent's protective behaviors, inability to cooperate with service plans, or emotional reactions including fear, anger, or despondency.

The U.S. Department of Health and Human Services (HHS) recommends assessments throughout the life of the case for all child abuse and neglect reports received by the agency (Bragg, 2003). The agency should conduct a series of assessments as long as the case is open because they represent only the information available at that particular time for the child (National Council of Juvenile and Family Court Judges, 2011). In addition, a battered caregiver's willingness to provide more accurate and more detailed information may increase exponentially as he or she develops trusting relationships with providers and advocates.

Research has highlighted the low levels of service engagement among parents and an association between untreated maternal trauma and unstable affect and difficulty trusting service providers (Szilassy et al., 2016). Despite the difficulties engaging parents in treatment, many evidence-based interventions are available to children in the child welfare system. Of particular significance is the effect trauma may have on parents' ability to engage with service providers and child-serving systems. Compounding the difficulties of engaging parents is the fact that some evidence-based interventions available to children do not directly address issues of parental trauma (Checklist to Promote Perpetrator Accountability in Dependency Cases Involving Domestic Violence, 2011). The success of child welfare services depends in part on the willingness of parents to work with providers and create a safe home for their children. All trauma, including the family's ethnic, racial, or cultural experience of historical trauma, may impact parenting practices with young children (Lewis, Norona, McConnico, & Thomas, 2013).

From a judicial perspective, domestic violence, like exposure to other traumatic experiences, may impact the victim in different ways at the time the violence occurs and, over time, after the incident. It is important for judges to have more information about the science of early childhood development, brain development, and the impact of adverse childhood experiences and trauma exposure, including the developmental consequences for children of different ages who witness domestic violence. As mentioned, witnessing violence has been associated with emotional, behavioral and learning problems in children, with children's susceptibility affected by their developmental stage, the chronicity of exposure, the physical closeness to the incident, and the emotional closeness to the victim. Because domestic violence is perpetrated by the adults who are closest to the child and whose role should be to keep the child safe, exposure can be a particularly insidious event for the young child. Home is where the child is supposed to feel safe and protected. Therefore, this type of violence can be very confusing and frightening for the child. For these reasons, it is not unexpected that exposure to domestic violence is associated with a variety of problems in children.

In this chapter, we will consider the impact of domestic violence on children and parents or caregivers as well as abuse and neglect from a number of different perspectives that frequently emerge within the judicial system. We will also describe changes that have occurred in the past decade in knowledge and perspectives for juvenile judges regarding understanding, reacting to, and implementing case plans and procedures to benefit both the child who has experienced violence and her caregiver. We will present an illustrative example of an innovative program for young children, Safe Babies Court Teams (SBCT), to show how trauma-informed changes have been made in juvenile courts to support children exposed to abuse and neglect, domestic violence, and other traumatic experiences.

Historical Perspective on Courtroom Procedures Related to Domestic Violence

To provide an important historical perspective related to how changes have occurred in the treatment of children and families in some juvenile courts and other child-serving systems in the past several decades, case examples will be presented illustrating how domestic violence and other traumatic experiences can impact on children and their caregivers.

The year is 1972. The place is an elementary school in a midsized midwestern city. The neighborhood school strives to meet the needs of children and their families, many of whom struggle with poverty, unemployment, language barriers, and literacy. Laurena is an average student with a sweet disposition, always eager to help her fourth-grade teacher. One day the teacher notices that Laurena is struggling with multiplication facts. It confounds the teacher that she is having difficulty because these were skills Laurena had previously mastered. The teacher also observes that Laurena seems lethargic and withdrawn. Fortunately, her teacher did not have recess duty that afternoon, and she asked Laurena to stay back and help her with some tasks. As they worked beside each other, the teacher told Laurena she noticed that Laurena did not seem to be her usual self that day. Did she feel all right? Was anything bothering her that she wanted to talk about? Laurena then shared, in a very matter-of-fact way, that she hadn't slept much the night before because she was hiding behind the sofa while her stepfather chased her mother around the house trying to stab her.

The year is 1985. The prosecutor (P) is litigating a domestic abuse case in magistrate court. The defendant (D) takes the stand. On cross-examination:

P: In your earlier testimony, you said that you and your wife were arguing that night, correct?

D: Yeah . . . we were fighting about stuff.

P: When you say "fighting," what do you mean?

D: We fought, you know, like normal married couples do.

P: Well, I'm not sure I know what you mean . . . like normal couples do. Can you explain further?

D: I don't know . . . just like couples do.

P: Were voices raised?

D: Yes.

P: Was there any pushing or shoving?

D: Yes.

P: Did she fall down when you pushed or shoved her?

D: Yes.

P: Did she bang into any walls or furniture when you pushed or shoved her?

D: Yes.

P: Did you hit her?

D: Yes.

P: With what did you hit her?

D: Just my hand.

P: Was your hand in a fist or was your hand open?

D: I don't remember.

P: Do you remember where on her body your hand came in contact with your wife?

D: Yeah, on her stomach, shoulder, and maybe her head.

P: Did you kick her?

D: Yeah, maybe once or twice.

P: Were you wearing shoes?

D: Yeah.

P: What kind of shoes?

D: Cowboy boots.

P: Where on your wife's body did you kick her?

D: In her stomach. But not that hard.

P: Is your wife pregnant?

D: Yeah.

P: Is there anything you want to explain further?

D: No . . . we were just fighting, you know, like normal married couples fight.

The year is 1988. The prosecutor is training local law enforcement officers. Among their comments are the following:

> I don't know why I have to respond to a domestic call at that house. She uses us to calm things down and never wants to follow through as a prosecuting witness.

> She always takes him back, so she should know what's coming. After 3 times, there should be a policy that we don't have to respond to that caller.
>
> Domestics are the most dangerous calls for us. Both of them are usually drunk or high. By the time we get there, they've made up and we're the bad guy.
>
> I know that if one party has an injury the law requires arrest, but if she always wants us to drop the case, why bother? It's usually a very minor injury anyway.

The year is 1990. The prosecutor has a sworn deposition from the complaining witness in which she details serious violence and resulting injuries. Photographs depicting a shoe-shaped bruise on her back match the defendant's shoes. There is evidence of additional injuries that are consistent with her statements. At the pretrial conference two weeks before trial, she wants the case dismissed. The judge is displeased about her lack of cooperation and places her under oath. She testifies that she made a mistake during her sworn deposition and that the bruise on her back was caused when she fell down the steps. The judge is even more displeased but grants the prosecutor's motion to dismiss. He assesses court costs to the witness for "wasting the precious and limited resources of the criminal justice system." He told her she was lucky she was not being prosecuted for providing false information or being found in contempt of court for lying under oath during her deposition.

The year is 1992. The prosecutor has filed a case of domestic abuse with serious injury against a rural woman's husband. In addition to the violence, the victim's husband had disconnected the phone service, disabled her car, and otherwise isolated her. Their only neighbors for several miles were his parents and brothers who all farmed together with the victim's husband. The hog operation was on the victim's property. The routine abuse occurred at all times of day and night. The young children were not present to see the abuse but were typically within earshot. A no contact order was issued against the husband, giving the victim sole right to occupy the residence and maintain custody of the children. He was barred from being within 500 feet of the home. He was unable to complete livestock chores, and his family members blamed the victim for tearing the family apart. They would not help with the farming chores, and she was unable to manage it all on her own. She begged the prosecutor to drop the charges. The case was dismissed, and no interventions were implemented to help reduce the trauma to her or the children. No counseling was offered to the father. She never called for help again.

The year is 1994. The prosecutor has filed a charge against a woman's boyfriend. She sustained broken bones and other injuries when the paramour assaulted her over the course of two days. He begged her forgiveness and sent her flowers as she healed. But, this was not the first episode. She was resolved this time to see it through and be safe. She knew all too well his pattern of assault—honeymoon—assault, and this time the injuries that had escalated over the months were frightening. This time she was pregnant. He began treatment, proclaiming that this time it would be different, all the while violating the No Contact Order by contacting her directly and indirectly. She felt too vulnerable to report the violations. She called the prosecutor and told her she wanted to drop the charges. The prosecutor asked many questions, and they were answered unconvincingly. The prosecutor then asked whether the defendant was with her. She was able to answer simply, "Yes." Did he make you call me? "Yes." Did he pressure you to ask me to dismiss the case? "Yes." After a series of yes/no questions, the prosecutor told the victim that she should tell the defendant that the prosecutor was unwilling to ask the court to dismiss the case at that time. Because the parties to the case were the state and the defendant, as a witness she was not a party with the power to dismiss the case. The prosecutor then arranged for a victim advocate and deputy to go to the house immediately to assure her safety.

The year is 2000. It is dependency court, a juvenile court that hears cases about children who are abused and neglected in order to protect minors in juvenile court. A 10-month-old infant has been removed from the custody of his parents due to illegal drug use (methamphetamine and marijuana) and domestic violence. The case came to the attention of the court when neighbors heard violent fighting. The voices, screams, and sounds of items crashing were so loud that the next-door neighbors, 50 feet away, with doors and windows closed, clearly heard the disturbance. The judge is presiding over the initial removal hearing to determine whether the emergency removal should be confirmed. The father is also facing criminal charges for domestic abuse. The attorney representing the father zealously argues that there was no nexus between the parents' fighting and harm to the child because the child was sound asleep in another room when the alleged violence occurred. And, because the child was only a baby, there was no harm to him because he wouldn't remember any of this. The judge discounted this explanation, confirmed the removal, educated the parties and counsel as to the harm to the baby, and ordered appropriate protective and remedial services.

The Response of the Court Is Changing

What was different about these last two scenarios? How did the prosecutor know to listen for signs of coercion? Why had law enforcement responded to protect her through numerous violent episodes and reunions? How did the judge know that children need not be physically present or directly assaulted in order to suffer trauma from the violent events in his midst?

The answer to these questions is the result of collaborative training and courageous conversations. Law enforcement, judges, lawyers, social workers, psychologists, and others were brave enough to leave the comfort of their respective silos to try an approach based on science and education instead of saying "that's the way we've always done it." They learned together about power and control issues in domestic violence and about the numerous times a victim typically leaves a perpetrator before leaving for good. They made time to listen to and learn from the victims themselves. Victims helped them understand realities such as, "It was safer for my children and me to keep him near. I could gauge when he was cycling toward a violent episode, and send the children to grandma's before it happened." Similarly, another victim preferred knowing where he was in the cycle firsthand so she could anticipate and steel herself for the inevitable assault, as opposed to living in a constant state of hypervigilance and stress, never knowing exactly when she might be ambushed. They also learned from collaborative relationships with child development and clinical colleagues who shared with them relevant and important issues from the science of early childhood development.

There are several nationally recognized organizations that have helped support professionals in applying the best approaches to keeping families impacted by domestic violence safe and enabling them to heal. The National Council of Juvenile and Family Court Judges (NCJFCJ) was among the first to take on this difficult topic decades ago in *Effective Intervention in Domestic Violence & Child Maltreatment Cases: Guidelines for Policy and Practice* (Schechter & Edleson, 1999).

NCJFCJ recognized the tension between the domestic violence victim advocates and the child welfare advocates. Judges struggled to find the tipping point where the drastic measure of removal of a child from a battered parent was necessary to protect the child's safety. Domestic abuse victim advocates recoiled at the prospect of "further punishing the victim" by removing children to foster care, and child welfare advocates stressed the need to place the child's best interest ahead of the adult parent's needs, regardless of the circumstances. Instead of taking one side or the other, NCJFCJ provided a format for developing understanding and common ground. Policies, procedures, and protocols grounded in sound research emerged.

Before the publication of *Effective Intervention*, two decades of research had confirmed that adults and children were often victimized in the same family, yet most communities treated the abuse of a parent and the maltreatment of a child in the same family as separate phenomena, having little to do with each other. Two examples are illustrative of this issue. Consider the reactions of law enforcement officers who responded to the reported crime of domestic assault described earlier and saw no reason to intervene because she always took him back. Reports of child abuse stemming from these police calls were few and far between. Further, at least in the past, child abuse and domestic violence cases in the same family might be treated in different courtrooms without sufficient communication that the same family is involved.

The publication of *Effective Intervention* offered a framework for communities to improve their responses to families experiencing domestic violence and child maltreatment. They developed a more comprehensive set of responses to eliminate or decrease the enormous toll that individual domestic violence takes on children and their battered parents, as well as caseworkers, law enforcement, health-care systems, extended family members, judges, lawyers, community-based agencies, and even the batterer. It is important to remember the batterer described previously who testified he was only doing what he had likely observed as a child, that is, adults physically "fighting like normal married couples do."

Effective Intervention focuses on three primary systems: child protection, the network of community-based domestic violence programs, and courts exercising jurisdiction over child maltreatment cases. Three core values have emerged:

1. To ensure stability and permanency, children should remain in the care of their nonoffending parent(s) whenever possible. Making adult victims safer and stopping batterers' assaults are two important ways to do this.
2. To provide safety and stability for families, the community service system should create many points of entry.
3. Leaders should design interventions and responses that are appropriate to the diverse range of families experiencing domestic violence and child maltreatment. Because domestic violence encompasses a wide range of behaviors, families require a range of interventions, some voluntary and some mandated.

The principles and recommendations from *Early Interventions* ring true today even in the wake of many years of new research.

The key to the success of collaborative efforts, like so many innovative programs in courts, is the leadership role of the judge. Judges have a unique opportunity to identify and convene the community stakeholders necessary to improve outcomes for families who are involved in dependency court within juvenile court and impacted by domestic violence. Judges should collaborate with other disciplines in order to assess the availability of credible resources and services in the community, avoid duplication of efforts, and advocate for additional resources where gaps occur. Judges should also lead or colead efforts to make accessible cross-disciplinary training opportunities occurring on a regular basis to ensure that the community is sharing information and learning together.

While these changes were taking place, cross-disciplinary training and collaborations were also occurring for other types of juvenile cases presenting in court. For example, the passage of the Adoption and Safe Families Act of 1997 (PL105–80 ASFA) clarified that the juvenile court judge had a duty to provide independent oversight for children who were adjudicated dependent by the court due to abuse or neglect and follow mandated timelines for the child to be placed in a permanent home with the biological parent, a relative, or through adoption. These laws were the result of a bipartisan effort in Congress designed to reduce the length of time that abused and neglected children were left "in limbo" in foster care. Priority was established for children's safety, permanency, and well-being to guide judicial decision making. ASFA also required judges to determine whether families in their jurisdiction were receiving sufficient services to accomplish the goals of the case permanency plan at each hearing. Judges must make "reasonable efforts," which means that the judge is required to preserve or reunify families and achieve a permanent home for children at prescribed times (usually during a 12-month period unless modified by the court) during the life of a case and to evaluate whether the family received supportive services that were needed and required to reunify with their children safely. If the court finds that "reasonable efforts" have not been made since the last hearing, the family is given additional time to complete the case plan successfully, and the agency charged with providing the services is sanctioned financially (PL105–80 ASFA).

At the time the law was passed, dependency judges, presiding over these cases in juvenile court, were ill-equipped to make informed decisions based on sound science and research. The lawyers representing the child or parent in these cases also did not have the information they needed to advocate for their clients because requirements for continuing legal education did not provide education on topics such as infant mental health, brain development, or mental illness. Even if legal professionals did attend courses to provide additional information about young children, they could rarely claim accreditation for these subjects. Many states were slow to recognize the value of education for judges and lawyers beyond the general fare of law school, including, among other areas, civil procedure, torts, federal jurisdiction, and property, until the Child Abuse Prevention Treatment Act (CAPTA) was enacted in 1996 and reauthorized in 2010 (42 U.S.C Sec. 5106). CAPTA required attorneys representing children to undergo training in the relevant areas of education, child development, substance abuse, and mental health. Also, under CAPTA, states were required to develop or expand effective collaborations between child protective services and domestic violence service entities in order to improve investigation and intervention procedures. The expansion was to include not only provisions for the safety of the nonabusing parent and children and provision of services to children exposed to domestic violence but also those that support the caregiving role of the nonabusing parent.

One Successful Approach: Safe Babies Court Teams

ASFA and CAPTA created a fertile climate for the birth of an innovative multidisciplinary team approach to serving younger maltreated infants and toddlers in the child welfare system. In 2000, the second author of this chapter, Dr. Joy D. Osofsky, teamed up with Miami, Florida, Judge Cindy Lederman when she participated in the ZERO TO THREE (ZTT) Advanced Fellowship Program. Together, they developed the prototype for what is now the ZTT Safe Babies Court Teams (SBCT). In 2002, they and others coauthored the NCJFCJ *Technical Assistance Brief, Questions Every Judge and Lawyer Should Ask about Maltreated Infants and Toddlers in the Child Welfare System* (Osofsky, Maze, Lederman, Grace, & Dicker, 2002) with a second revised and expanded brief published in 2017 (Osofsky et al., 2017).

With the expansion of the SBCT program through ZTT, attention was now being focused on both the impact of abuse and neglect and domestic violence on very young children. Because children this young could not protect themselves and did not yet have the language to describe their experiences and express their feelings, the consensus among legal professionals, unschooled in child development, was that there was no impact of any consequence. Most believed that they were not impacted, would not remember, and, if they were affected, they would get over it. So long as the child was not physically battered during the episodes, it was irrelevant that they heard the violence from their cribs in another room. Even in recent years, some legal professionals have not incorporated these ideas such as the one in the courtroom scenario described previously. These scenes play out across the nation, underscoring the ongoing need for training and materials. The SBCT approach focuses on younger children, ages 0–5, who are adjudicated dependent and under the supervision of child protection related to abuse and neglect. An important feature of the SBCT approach that significantly reduces the risk of a child being in limbo waiting for a permanency decision is the frequency of court hearings and family team meetings. It is far less likely that cases receiving close and frequent judicial oversight would go longer than a month with a finding of failure to make reasonable efforts.

The SBCT approach, led by ZTT, began in 2005 with five demonstration sites: Eastern Band of Cherokee Indians, Cherokee, North Carolina; Polk County, Iowa; Hattiesburg, Mississippi; Ft. Bend, Texas; and New Orleans, Louisiana. The multidisciplinary team approach with a focus on applying science to justice was evaluated by James Bell Associates and demonstrated substantially better outcomes for children and their families in achieving permanency and decreasing future abuse and neglect. Based on the early work, the SBCT approach earned the status of a "promising practice."

In 2014, the Children's Bureau awarded a grant to ZTT to expand the SBCTs and implement additional evaluation of the program. Several states continue the SBCT work with independent financing, and with new funding from the Children's Bureau, an additional program, the Quality Improvement Center for Research-Based Infant-Toddler Court Teams (QIC-CT), incorporated SBCTs and added several additional sites. The QIC-CT program was implemented in Polk County, Iowa; Hattiesburg, Mississippi; New Haven, Connecticut; Northern Band of Cherokee, North Carolina; and Hawaii and several sites in Florida.

In addition to expanding the SBCTs in additional jurisdictions, two important resources have been developed by the QIC-CT that contribute to increased scientific knowledge for those working in juvenile court. The first is a glossary of cross-disciplinary terms that are frequently used by those working with courts to improve communication among all team members. The second is an update to the *Technical Assistance Brief* originally published in 2002 with additional information and expanded research included in many of the existing sections as well as the addition of new topics reflecting the growth of knowledge in this area in the past decade. New information is provided on Exposure to Domestic and Community Violence, Trauma and Parenting, and Family Time (*Visitation*). Increased knowledge about the effects of early traumatic experiences on development is included based on what judges and lawyers have learned since 2002 from the Adverse Childhood Experiences Study (ACES; Felitti; et al., 1998; https://www.cdc.gov/violenceprevention/acestudy/index.html; see Chapter 3 in Volume I). We also have much more information about to how to work with systems to integrate trauma-informed practice available online at the National Child Traumatic Stress Network (www.NTCSN.org) and the National Council of Juvenile and Family Court Judges (https://www.ncjfcj.org/trauma-informed-courts-and-role-judge). Increased information available about the biological and developmental impact of chronic stress has been extremely helpful for judges and others working in juvenile court (National Scientific Council on the Developing Child, 2014). Both the Glossary and the *Technical Assistance Brief* are available on the NCJFC (www.ncjfcj.org), Zero to Three (www.zerotothree.org), and QIC-CT (www.qicct.org) websites. Each section in the brief has a corresponding "Bench Card" guiding attorneys and providers in preparing to answer targeted questions. We provide an example of the Bench Card regarding Exposure to Domestic and Community Violence and questions designed to accompany the section:

- Has the child been exposed to domestic violence?
- What are the consequences of the domestic violence for the child?
- Has an assessment been initiated or mental health services provided to the child exposed to domestic violence?
- Can the child be kept safe and together with the nonoffending parent?
- Is there a safety plan in place to address domestic violence concerns related to the family, co-parenting, and visitation?

Bench Card questions relative to the "Trauma and Parenting" section are the following:

- Has the parent experienced unusual challenges related to high rates of poverty, childhood abuse, interpersonal violence, substance abuse, and mental health disorders?
- What additional services or assistance does the parent need in order to achieve reunification?
- Who does the parent depend on when he or she needs support or help?
- If the parent suffers from a mental health problem, has he or she had a psychological or psychiatric evaluation? Is the parent attending therapy sessions on a regular basis? If the parent is on medication, is he or she taking it as prescribed?
- Does the parent/caregiver use alcohol and/or illegal drugs? If so, when was the last time he or she used drugs? Is the parent attending a drug rehabilitation program?
- How has the parent made the home safe for the child?

Case Example

An example of the additional harm that can be done to young children in a less trauma-informed court is illustrated by the course of what happened to Janie. She was removed from her biological mother when she was six months old because of exposure to severe domestic violence and neglect and, due to delays in the family receiving services, Janie was "in limbo" during the period of focused attachment (the second half of the first year of life and almost all of the second year). The science of early childhood development shows clearly that experiences during the first two years of life are crucial for the development of a trusting attachment relationship as well as the support needed for optimal cognitive, social, and emotional development. Although 15 months may not seem that long, for a young child under the age of three, it is a large fraction of the child's life. With the SBCT model that includes family team meetings involving discussions with the family and caregivers and monthly in-court reviews. The child and families are provided both more comprehensive services and insurance against avoidable delays and unnecessary costs to the system.

Courts that are trauma-informed recognize that battered parents should be viewed as partners in the protection of their children. Routinely removing children from a battered parent can do more harm than good and fail to hold batterers accountable (Gatowski, Miller, Rubin, Escher, & Maze, 2016). Despite the potential harm for a child in experiencing domestic violence, not all children whose families experience domestic violence are traumatized or at risk of imminent harm. The most significant factors influencing a child's resiliency is his or her ability to remain connected to a protective parent. Likewise, one of the best ways to ensure a child's safety is to help the adult victim increase his or her own safety (Goodmark, 2008). Social services should work with the nonoffending parent to create a safety plan and provide the victim support to ensure that he or she can keep himself or herself and his or her children safe (Rennison, 2003). This safety plan may include supports that do not appear—on the surface—to be about safety, such as housing, child care, or access to health care. In addition, the availability of services to support the young child and parent (caregiver) and help them with the problems that led to the involvement with the court is extremely important to achieve reunification, safety, and permanency for the child.

Researchers estimate that as many as 75 percent of the parents who abuse or neglect their children were themselves maltreated in childhood (Widom, Czaja, & DuMont, 2015). Parents facing personal violence, or even the threat of it, often have low self-esteem and depression. Child Parent Psychotherapy (CPP; Lieberman, Ghosh-Ippen, & Van Horn, 2015), an evidence-based treatment designed to support and strengthen the parent–child relationship, can work effectively with both the young child and the parent to support the development of a healing and trusting relationship. Through that process, the therapist can also help the parent process his or her own childhood trauma in order for him or her to be able to parent his or her own child more effectively (Klain et al., 2009). Safety is also a concern during family time or visitation with the offending parent. Thus, the child's case plan should also address and account for the child's safety during visitation. In addition, courts can support the safety of children by providing appropriate services to the batterer to address the violence, such as batterer intervention programs, and can hold batterers accountable for not following through with required interventions (Schechter & Edleson, 1999). In cases with serious mental health or substance abuse issues, the intervention may include inpatient mental services that allow the adult victim and child to remain together (Goodmark, 2008). In addition, courts can order the offending parent to stay out of the home and into domestic violence–appropriate treatment to ensure that the adult victim and the child remain safe and together so long as the nonoffending parent is protected (Schechter & Edleson, 1999).

There are domestic violence shelters and transitional housing programs designed for battered parents and young children. In these cases, there can be close monitoring of parental compliance with services that focus on the parent's needs as well as the safety and well-being of the children (Klain et al., 2009). With proper services, social services may be able to keep the child in the care of the nonoffending parent and out of foster care and prevent the child from experiencing the trauma of removal. In addition, courts can order the offending parent to stay out of the home and into domestic violence–appropriate treatment to ensure that the adult victim and the child remain safe and together (Schechter & Edleson, 1999).

It is incumbent on the judge to convene stakeholders from all disciplines to learn from each other, maintain a current knowledge base of available services and resources, and grow those resources that are missing in the community. For example, there is typically a dearth of residential support services for fathers. Most inpatient domestic violence and substance abuse programs that can accommodate young children are for mothers only. Even though females comprise approximately 85 percent of the victims of family violence according to the Department of Justice, there is a need for this option in most communities (Osofsky et al., 2017).

In one Court Team site, a father who had previously been in the child welfare system, as well as the adult criminal system, pulled together a business plan for safe housing for fathers whose children had been removed. As of yet, there has not been the opportunity for children to live there with their nonoffending fathers; however, it is an appropriate setting for family time, and they continue to strive to accomplish the goal of housing fathers and children together.

Conclusion

When courts are both trauma-informed and work with collaborative teams, such as the SBCT, both procedure and outcomes for cases may be approached and conducted quite differently. In the concluding section, the five stories presented at the beginning of this chapter will be reconsidered with both a trauma-informed lens and better-informed systems that apply a collaborative approach such as SBCT to reconsider procedures and possible outcomes.

1972. Laurena's teacher, a mandatory reporter, notified the child welfare agency of the report of the violence that occurred in her home. Laurena's stepfather was criminally charged by trained officers who no longer considered domestic violence to be a "family matter." Protective orders barred him from contacting Laurena's mother and the children and from being within 500 feet of any place the mother or children were or were likely to be. The mother and children had exclusive rights to remain in the family home. Laurena continued to attend school in her neighborhood, with her friends and with the teacher she trusted. She lived with her two-year-old brother and her mother, who was pregnant. Her mother received appropriate medical treatment and had access to a trusted victim advocate to help guide her through the criminal proceedings. She also received and benefited from mental health and domestic violence counseling. Laurena received individual and joint counseling, and her younger brother and her mother engaged in CPP, a relationship-based treatment. Throughout the case, Laurena and her brother remained in a stable setting with their mother. The stepfather pled guilty to domestic abuse assault causing injury and was placed on probation. As terms of his probation, the protective order remained in place and he was to attend batterer's treatment as well as treatment for alcohol abuse. About three months after the incident, the stepfather violated the protective order, leaving flowers and cards, and repeatedly drove past the house. Laurena's mother reported these violations to authorities. He was arrested for violating probation. Bikers against Child Abuse (BACA), an organization with the goal of creating a safer environment for children who had been abused, worked with the family, empowering Laurena and her mother by their presence at both court hearings and times that the father violated the protective order by driving by the house. The child welfare case closed successfully without disrupting placement of the children with their mother. Services were able to continue as long as needed through Part C of the Individuals with Disabilities Education Act (IDEA) and Crime Victims Assistance funds.

1985. The criminal case formed the basis for the filing of a child welfare case in order to protect the defendant's infant son after the mother allowed the father to move back in with her. The well-trained judge recognized that the defendant and the mother both likely struggled with several traumatic events during their respective childhoods. As part of the evaluation and during therapy, it became apparent that the father had been exposed to many adverse childhood experiences, which placed him at high risk for having problems in relationships himself and having difficulty parenting a child effectively. The mother's Adverse Childhood Experiences (ACEs) scale experiences score was also high. During the first two months of the child welfare case, the baby was placed with a maternal aunt, who allowed the mother to visit every day and help with the child's care. She also welcomed the father into the home at times the mother was not there. Although the couple wanted to work things out, there was a legal order of protection that barred the father from contacting the mother or children. Over time, he was able to complete services successfully, and the parents began counseling together. The baby was returned to the mother after she began to benefit from services. She made impressive progress in protecting her child and keeping her safe, and in understanding the impact of violence on herself and her baby. The mother was fortunate to have a parent partner (a supportive person who had been successful previously in overcoming her own difficulties with child welfare and juvenile court) who was a great support to her and also remained in close contact after the family reunified.

1988. Judges, attorneys, law enforcement, social workers, medical professionals, providers, Court Appointed Special Advocates (CASAs), professionals providing early intervention, and others routinely plan and participate in cross-disciplinary training, which includes the dynamics of domestic violence, law updates, ACEs, trauma-informed approaches, brain development, mental health, substance abuse, and so forth. The trainings are free and qualify for accreditation. The judge also convenes stakeholders' meetings to keep current on the issues in the community that require a collaborative solution.

1990. The judge continues the hearing until a victim's advocate can counsel the victim and be present with her in court.

1992. The Court Team is aware of the unique issues that arise in rural settings where a family's financial well-being is connected so closely to the homestead. It can be very isolating, especially when the battered parent's support system consists of the batterer's family members and they all believe he is not abusive. The mother's desire to remain in the community with her children is strong; however, she can never feel safe again on the farm. She understands the cycle of abuse that she learned in counseling. Because the father is only going through the motions in treatment, and continuing to abuse alcohol and other drugs, and because the abuse has become increasingly violent, the mother has begun divorce proceedings. She is staying at a domestic violence shelter with her two preschool children. She is engaged in Child-Parent Psychotherapy and individual therapy. She is also receiving vocational rehabilitation services to improve her financial independence. The shelter offers child care so that she can also work part-time. The Volunteer Lawyers Project is handling her case without fee. She plans to relocate with her children to another part of the state where she will have support from her family and friends. The offending parent's contact with the children is supervised.

References

Bancroft, L., & Silverman, J. G. (2002). *The batterer as parent: Addressing the impact of domestic violence on family dynamics* (pp. 84–97). Thousand Oaks, CA: Sage Publications.

Bragg, H. L. (2003). *Child protection in families experiencing domestic violence*. Washington, DC: U.S. Department of Health and Humans Services.

Felitti, V. J., Anda, R. F., Nordenberg, D., Williamson, D. F., Spitz, A. M., Edwards, V., Koss, M. P., & Marks, J. S. (1998). Relationship of childhood abuse and household dysfunction to many of the leading causes of death in adults: The adverse childhood experiences (ACE) study. *American Journal of Preventive Medicine, 14*, 245–258.

Futures without Violence. (2013). *The facts on children's exposure to intimate partner violence*. Retrieved from https://www.futureswithoutviolence.org/the-facts-on-childrens-exposure-to-intimate-partner-violence/

Gatowski, S., Miller N., Rubin, S., Escher, P., & Maze, C. (2016). *Enhanced resource guidelines: Improving court practice in child abuse and neglect cases*. Reno, NV: National Council of Juvenile and Family Court Judges.

Goodmark, L. (2008). *Reasonable efforts checklist for dependency cases involving domestic violence*. Reno, NV: National Council of Juvenile and Family Court Judges.

Klain, E. J., Pilnik, L., Talati, E., Maze, C., Diamond-Berry, K., & Hudson, L. (2009). *Healthy beginnings, healthy futures: A judge's guide*. American Bar Association. National Council of Juvenile and Family Court Judges, and Zero to Three.

Lewis, M. L., Norona, C. R., McConnico, N., & Thomas, K. (2013). Colorism, a legacy of historical trauma in parent-child relationships: Clinical, research, & personal perspectives. *Zero to Three, 34*(2), 11–23.

Lieberman, A. F., Ippen, C. G., & Van Horn, P. (2015). *Don't hit my mommy!: A manual for child-parent psychotherapy with young children exposed to violence and other trauma* (2nd ed.). National Center for Clinical Infant Programs.

Margolin, G., & Gordis, E. (2004). Children's exposure to violence in the family and community. *Current Directions in Psychological Science, 13*, 152–155. doi:10.1111/j.0963–7214.2004.00296.

National Council of Juvenile and Family Court Judges (2011). *Checklist to promote perpetrator accountability in dependency cases involving domestic violence.* Retrieved from http://www.ncjfcj.org/sites/default/files/checklist-to-promote-accountability_0.pdf

National Scientific Council on the Developing Child. (2014). *Excessive stress disrupts the architecture of the developing brain. Working paper 3.* Updated Edition. Retrieved from http://www.developingchild.harvard.edu

Osofsky, J. D., Cohen, C. C, Huddleston, J., Hudson, L., Zavora, K., & Lewis, M. (2017). *Questions every judge and lawyer should ask about infants and toddlers in the child welfare system.* Reno, Nevada: National Council of Juvenile and Family Court Judges.

Osofsky, J. D., Maze, C. L., Lederman, J. C. S., Grace, M. P., & Dicker, S. (2002). Questions every judge and lawyer should ask about infants and toddlers in the child welfare system. *Juvenile and Family Court Journal, 55*(2), 45–51.

Rennison, C. M. (2003). *Intimate partner violence, 1993–2001.* U.S. Department of Justice, Office of Justice Programs Bureau of Justice Statistics Crime Data Brief, NCJ 197838.

Schechter, S., & Edleson, J. L. (1999). *Effective intervention in domestic violence & child maltreatment cases: Guidelines for policy and practice.* Reno, Nevada: National Council of Juvenile and Family Court Judges.

Summers, A. (2006). *Children's exposure to domestic violence: A guide to research and resources* (pp. 26–27). Reno, NV: National Council of Juvenile & Family Court Judges.

Szilassy, E., Drinkwater, J., Hester, M., Larkins, C., Stanley, N., Turner, W., & Feder, G. (2016). Making the links between domestic violence and child safeguarding: An evidence-based pilot training for general practice. *Health and Social Care in the Community, 25*(6), 1722–1732. doi:10.1111/hsc.12401

Weithorn, L. A. (2001). Protecting children from exposure to domestic violence: The use and abuse of child maltreatment statutes. *Hastings Law Journal, 53*(1), 82.

Widom, C. S., Czaja, S. J., & DuMont, K. A. (2015). Intergenerational transmission of child abuse and neglect: Real or detection bias? *Science, 347*(6229), 1480–1485. doi:10.1126/science.1259917

CHAPTER 10

The Ripple Effect of Trauma

Individuals, Organizations, and Society

Erika Tullberg and Nawal Muradwij

> Cases of horrible, sexual, predatory exploitation of children haunt me. I keep my balance and my job as a judge by profoundly guarding myself against being swept away by the gruesome evidence I have to confront. (Makin, 2002, p. 1)

As the impact of trauma on its victims has become increasingly recognized, there has also been a growing awareness of how trauma affects the people connected to trauma survivors or what Charles Figley called the "cost of caring" (Figley, 1995). Research in this area has considered the secondary impact of trauma on both family members and professionals who are in a helping capacity vis-à-vis trauma survivors. Researchers have also studied the impact of trauma on organizational functioning, noting parallels between how individuals and organizations respond to real and perceived threats in their environment. Overall, this work has shown that one does not have to experience trauma directly in order to be negatively impacted and that the failure to address secondary exposure to trauma can have serious implications for individuals, organizations, and the public more broadly.

This chapter will provide an overview of secondary trauma as well as the terminology used to describe how trauma affects those who are personally and professionally connected to trauma survivors. It will review the literature on secondary trauma, with attention given to addressing its impact on both individuals and organizations. It will also introduce the idea of looking at secondary trauma through a "trauma system" lens, integrating individual and organizational frameworks.

What Is Secondary Trauma?

There is a consensus in the field that exposure to trauma impacts not only those who are directly affected but also those who hear or learn about others' experiences through either professional or personal relationships (Baird & Kracen, 2006; Figley, 2002). There are different terms that are used both colloquially and in research to describe this phenomenon, which has led to some confusion in the field, and presents challenges in comparing responses and quantifying and comparing data across settings (Walsh, Mathieu, & Hendricks, 2017). The most common terms that are used are described in Table 10.1.

For the purposes of this chapter, we will use "secondary trauma" as an umbrella term to reference the many different ways people can be affected by working with and/or supporting trauma survivors. Because trauma also impacts organizations, we will also introduce the concept of a "traumatogenic environment," which we define as an environment, such as a workplace, that has been shaped by trauma and as a result functions in a way that can cause harm to others, including both clients and staff. We believe that individuals who work in traumatogenic environments can also experience the effects of secondary trauma, even if they don't have direct interaction with trauma survivors as part of their jobs. Secondary trauma symptoms can range from reactions to a discrete event to overall changes in people's relationships with others and their view of the world. Following is an example of someone who is experiencing different aspects of secondary trauma.

Case Example: Vanessa

Vanessa is a social worker who has been working in foster care since finishing her master's degree last year; she is married and the mother of a four-year-old boy, Andre. Up to this point Vanessa has worked with teenagers, but she recently moved to a new unit focused on younger children. She started working with the Smith boys, Jared (age seven) and Jayson (age five), two months ago. They were

Table 10.1 Secondary Trauma-Related Terminology

Burnout (Pines & Aronson, 1988)	Secondary Traumatic Stress (STS) (Figley, 2002)	Compassion Fatigue (CF) (Figley, 1995)	Vicarious Trauma (VT) (Rosenbloom, Pratt, & Pearlman, 1995)
• Caused by long-term involvement in emotionally demanding situations • Characterized by emotional exhaustion, depersonalization, and reduced sense of accomplishment • Not necessarily related to traumatic material, but common among trauma workers	• Reflected by symptoms of hyperarousal, avoidance, and reexperiencing • Can begin after a single encounter with a traumatized client • Directly related to hearing about a firsthand trauma experience	• Some definitions parallel that of STS; others include the combined effects of burnout and STS • Involves empathy for survivors of trauma • Has also been used to describe the general public's reaction to being oversaturated with news about war, poverty, and famine	• More global and pervasive effect of exposure to others' traumatic material • Impacts the ability to see the world as a safe, just, and predictable place • Change in perspective may be permanent, outlasting one's personal interaction with trauma survivors

reported to child protective services because of very infrequent school attendance, and, upon investigation, it was discovered that their mother's live-in boyfriend—who is unemployed and the boys' caretaker when their mother was at work—was molesting them. Jared told Vanessa about how he tried to protect Jayson by staying home from school with him when he was sick, and, as a result, was the more frequent target of the molestation.

Vanessa has met with the doctor and detective who saw Jared and Jayson after they were removed so she could include all of the details they had collected about the molestation in her court report and has talked repeatedly with the foster mother about her concern regarding the boys' sexualized behavior. The boys seem fairly shut down around strangers, but they love the same cartoon characters that Andre does, so Vanessa has used that as a way to engage them when she visits the foster home.

For the past several weeks, Vanessa has had the same nightmare about Andre being trapped in a room while she can't get to him, and she is exhausted and on edge from the lack of sleep. She has started calling his preschool program several times a day to make sure everything is going okay, sometimes abruptly leaving meetings at work in order to do so.

Last week, Vanessa was assigned another case involving two young boys; the next day, she came to work late and missed an appointment with their foster mother. Later in the week, she called in sick and also decided to stay home from her book club meeting, as the thought of engaging in the usual chit chat with everyone felt unbearable. When her husband got home from work that evening, he told Vanessa that the preschool had called to ask him if there is anything happening at home that they should know about. As he began asking her what was going on, she abruptly cut him off, accusing him of calling her a bad mother and saying he should just leave her alone. She went into their bedroom and slammed the door behind her. After feeding Andre and putting him to bed, he slept in the guest room.

Although Vanessa has worked with abused children before, working with boys who reminded her so much of her son impacted her differently. She began experiencing common STS symptoms, including reexperiencing (having nightmares), avoidance (coming into work late, calling in sick), and hyperarousal (checking up on her son, snapping at her husband). It is not uncommon for people to have a stronger response to clients' trauma when it reminds them of their own experiences or the vulnerability of their family members (Osofsky, 2009).

If such responses persist for over one month following exposure to traumatic material, some consider that to be "secondary traumatic stress disorder" (STSD; Figley, 1995). Although STSD is not a formal mental health diagnosis, the last update to the *Diagnostic and Statistical Manual of*

Mental Disorders (American Psychiatric Association, 2013) expanded the list of experiences that can lead to a posttraumatic stress disorder (PTSD) diagnosis to include "repeated or extreme exposure to aversive details of the traumatic event(s) (e.g., first responders collecting human remains; police officers repeatedly exposed to details of child abuse)," demonstrating a recognition of the profound impact that such secondary exposure can have. Despite this, it is uncommon for someone whose exposure to trauma is limited to workplace exposure to be formally diagnosed with PTSD. In fact, the kinds of symptoms that impact one's work, such as Vanessa's distraction, tardiness, and missing appointments, are often not recognized as responses to trauma but, instead, are seen—and inappropriately and ineffectively addressed—as poor work performance.

Vicarious trauma (VT) differs from STS in that it refers to broader changes, beyond the work context, that occur as a result of repeated secondary trauma exposure. Someone impacted by VT might see a father and daughter holding hands in a park and be worried that the girl is being sexually abused, have trouble pursuing interests outside of work because these activities feel trivial in comparison to the needs of their clients, or withdraw from religious practice because they don't understand how a God could allow for so much suffering in the world. In our case example, Vanessa's trauma exposure is more recent and limited, but she is already suffering physically and emotionally. Parts of her life that have been enjoyable and sources of support—her book club and her husband—feel stressful. As she continues working with young children who have been maltreated, she might experience broader changes in her daily activities, her commitment to her job (either becoming more avoidant or conversely finding it difficult to separate herself from work), her level of protectiveness toward her son, and her relationship with her husband, including her ability to be emotionally available to and physically intimate with him.

When people experience STS or VT symptoms, or a combination of both, it does not only affect how they feel; research has shown that trauma can also interfere with complex decision making, particularly when under stress (Bloom, 2013). One example of this comes from a study involving child protective staff that found that exposure to traumatic material made even experienced workers less able to identify signs of child abuse (Regehr, LeBlanc, Shlonsky, & Bogo, 2010). Why would such a result occur? One might assume that past trauma exposure would make a person more attuned to danger and threat in the environment, but this study showed that the avoidance accompanying trauma exposure can be a more powerful force. For those who work with trauma survivors, often in environments that are also dangerous for staff, an impaired ability to identify danger can have profound consequences for both them and their clients, making it a critical workplace concern.

Predictors of Secondary Trauma

If there are certain qualities that make people more or less susceptible to secondary trauma, individuals and organizations could hypothetically make more informed decisions about who is best suited for trauma work. Factors that have been shown to increase one's vulnerability to secondary trauma include a personal history of trauma (Killian, 2008; Pearlman & Mac Ian, 1995) and employing negative coping strategies such as denial and venting (Killian, 2008). Emotional self-awareness has also been shown to be negatively associated with secondary trauma symptoms (Killian, 2008), which means that people who are less able to identify their own emotional states typically have higher levels of such symptoms. This could be because people with less emotional self-awareness are more vulnerable to developing secondary trauma reactions and/or that secondary trauma itself reduces people's attunement to their own emotions—based on the cross-sectional nature of the research we cannot know the direction of this relationship.

Conversely, certain personal qualities, or even beliefs about certain qualities, can buffer the effects of secondary exposure to trauma. These protective factors include perceived coping ability (i.e., one's assessment of how well they manage stressful situations; Baird & Kracen, 2006; Killian, 2008), positive coping strategies such as reframing and seeking out social support (Killian, 2008), and participation in religious or spiritual activities (Sprang, Craig, & Clark, 2011). Additionally, the use of evidence-based clinical practices with clients has been shown to decrease levels of secondary trauma among mental health professionals (Craig & Sprang, 2010), perhaps due to their increased feelings of competence and ability to manage clients' reactions.

Empathy, the ability to understand and relate to others' feelings and thoughts, has been found to be both positively and negatively associated with secondary trauma. Some have found that empathy is essential to maintaining one's well-being in the midst of trauma exposure (Wagaman, Geiger, Shockley, & Segal, 2015), while others have found that having an empathic connection with trauma survivors puts one at higher risk for developing secondary traumatic reactions, perhaps because it is more likely that one will understand and therefore identify with others' traumatic experiences (Figley, 2002; Pearlman & Mac Ian, 1995).

People can also be vulnerable to secondary trauma based on their family or community connections. There is a body of research related to the secondary effect of trauma on children of survivors, including war veterans, Holocaust survivors, refugees, and torture victims (Palosaari, Punamäki,

Qouta, & Diab, 2013; van IJzendoorn, Bakermans-Kranenburg, & Sagi-Schwartz, 2003; Yager, Gerszberg, & Dohrenwend, 2016). Two modes of trauma transmission have been explored among these groups. The first is through hearing firsthand about a parent's traumatic experiences, which functions similarly to work-related transmission, except that children are perhaps even more likely to be overwhelmed by traumatic material because of their own age-related physical and emotional vulnerability, fear of losing their parent, and underdeveloped coping skills (Lombardo & Motta, 2008). Trauma can also have a negative impact on parenting practices, increasing the likelihood of harsh parenting and physical punishment and decreasing the parents' ability to soothe their child (Banyard, Williams, & Siegel, 2003). By themselves, these practices can elicit fear and helplessness in children; when they are paired with trauma reminders for the parent (e.g., events, smells, others' tone of voice), they can in effect transfer the parent's triggers to the child.

More recent research has examined the epigenetic transmission of trauma across generations. Epigenetics is the study of inherited changes in gene expression—whether a particular trait is turned "on" or "off"—that does not involve changes in the underlying DNA sequence but are instead prompted by environmental factors and stressors (Kellermann, 2013). These changes leave marks on chromosomes' chemical coating that can be passed down to trauma survivors' children and subsequent generations. Research in this area has shown that these changes can increase descendants' vulnerability to traumatic events or stories, potentially making them more likely to develop traumatic stress reactions compared with people who do not have this genetic sensitivity (Yehuda & Bierer, 2009).

There is also a body of research showing how trauma is transmitted within certain communities. This phenomenon, known as historical trauma, posits that the effects of long-term, mass trauma in populations can persist across generations (Sotero, 2006). While empirical literature on historical trauma is still relatively sparse, conceptual models have built on theories of trauma to explore the physiological, environmental, and social pathways through which trauma can be transmitted. Much of the existing research (Evans-Campbell, 2008; Sotero, 2006) has examined the experiences of American Indian/Alaskan Natives and the social and behavioral patterns that have developed in response to the traumas suffered by these populations. Additional work has focused on the ongoing impact of slavery, segregation, and racism in African American communities (National Child Traumatic Stress Network, n.d.).

The nature of one's work environment has also been linked with secondary trauma. The amount of time workers spend with trauma survivors, the percentage of their clients who are trauma survivors, and overall caseload size have all been associated with higher levels of traumatic stress (Craig & Sprang, 2010; Hensel, Ruiz, Finney, & Dewa, 2015). Other predictors of secondary trauma are related to one's field of work. While secondary trauma was first studied in mental health clinicians (Pearlman & Mac Ian, 1995; Schauben & Frazier, 1995), high levels of secondary trauma have been found among a range of professionals, including child welfare workers (Bride, 2007), domestic violence workers (Iliffe & Steed, 2000), emergency/disaster responders (Creamer & Liddle, 2005), law enforcement (Perez, Jones, Englert, & Sachau, 2010), judges and attorneys (Chamberlain & Miller, 2009; Jaffe, Crooks, Dunford-Jackson, & Town, 2003), medical staff (Beck, 2011), and school personnel (Borntrager et al., 2012). There is also evidence that organizations' culture and practices have an independent and perhaps stronger impact on posttraumatic stress among workers than individual-level characteristics (Killian, 2008; Regehr, Hemsworth, Leslie, Howe, & Chau, 2004).

Identifying and Addressing Secondary Trauma

The line distinguishing normal levels of work-related stress or anxiety and symptoms of secondary trauma is, naturally, a thin one. However, addressing the effects of secondary trauma is contingent on accurately identifying it. There are several validated measures that are used to assess whether someone has clinically significant secondary trauma symptoms; a sample of these tools are listed in Box 10.1. Many of them are in the public domain and are therefore available to individuals and organizations that are interested in assessing the impact of STS on themselves or their staff.

There is general agreement that secondary trauma is an inevitable part of working with trauma survivors and that the focus of such interventions should not just be on preventing its occurrence but also on mitigating its impact. In this chapter we describe approaches that are informed by research around secondary trauma.

Perhaps not surprisingly, PTSD treatment—focused on exposure methods, individual psychotherapy, and at times pharmacotherapy—has been used to treat secondary trauma, despite a lack of empirical support for their specific use with secondary trauma exposure (Motta, 2008). Other treatment models, such as the Accelerated Recovery Program (Gentry, Baranowsky, & Dunning, 2002), have taken trauma treatment

Box 10.1 Secondary Trauma Assessment Tools

- The Impact of Event Scale-Revised (Weiss & Marmar, 1996), the Secondary Trauma Scale (Motta, Hafeez, Sciancalepore, & Diaz, 2001), and the Secondary Traumatic Stress Scale (Bride, Robinson, Yegidis, & Figley, 2004) measure PTSD symptoms of intrusion, avoidance, and arousal.
- The Professional Quality Of Life Scale (Stamm, 2013) contains questions about burnout, STS, and compassion satisfaction.
- The Trauma and Attachment Belief Scale, previously the Traumatic Stress Institute Belief Scale (Pearlman, 2003), is directed at VT, measuring disruptions of safety, trust, esteem, intimacy, and control.
- The Secondary Traumatic Stress-Informed Organization Assessment Tool (Sprang et al., 2014) is used by organizations to assess how well they address secondary trauma experienced by their staff and to track changes in their practice over time.

approaches developed for trauma survivors and adapted them for use with those impacted by secondary trauma.

Psychological debriefing (Phipps & Byrne, 2003), an exposure-based group model that invites participants to share details of the events that are causing them distress with others and helps them manage their symptoms as they arise, has been controversial as a method of addressing secondary trauma exposure. Some studies have shown that a form of debriefing called Critical Incident Stress Debriefing can have adverse effects and increase trauma symptomology (Deahl, 2000), perhaps due to increased exposure to trauma material among debriefing participants. Others have found promising results for a debriefing adaptation known as Critical Incident Stress Management (Everly & Mitchell, 1999), which also teaches skills that can lower arousal when a person is exposed to traumatic material, such as muscle relaxation, breathing retraining, self-dialogue, and thought-stopping.

Self-care and self-reflection are widely recommended as strategies that can prevent or reduce secondary trauma reactions (Bober & Regehr, 2006). These approaches range from encouraging people to engage in self-care activities (e.g., eating well, getting enough sleep, exercising, engaging in social activities, creating separation between personal and work time) to taking a broader perspective on one's relationship with trauma work and making adjustments in one's work and daily practice that support wellness and balance. Despite the popularity of such recommendations, there is a lack of empirical evidence demonstrating that self-care practices are effective at ameliorating secondary trauma, and there have been at least two studies showing that engaging in such practices has *no impact* on one's level of secondary trauma symptoms (Bober & Regehr, 2006; Killian, 2008). Interestingly, one of these studies also found that even when individuals *believe* that self-care activities could improve their well-being and decrease the negative impact of secondary trauma, it is not reflected in their behavior, as they do not actively pursue such strategies (Bober & Regehr, 2006).

Self-care has other health- and work-related benefits and should be encouraged and supported at the organizational level. Agencies should also have policies that protect staff's nonwork hours and vacation/leave time, which can reduce burnout (Etzion, 2003). However, the lack of evidence supporting self-care's effectiveness at mitigating secondary trauma is relevant for both researchers and administrators, particularly those who may assume that the best way to support staff who have routine exposure to traumatic material at work is by promoting wellness and self-care. Just as ineffective treatment can turn people off to therapy and inadvertently prolong their suffering, insufficient secondary trauma interventions can create or exacerbate resistance within organizations and prolong its negative impact among staff. So what alternatives are available? To answer that question, one first needs to understand the parallels between trauma's impact on individuals and organizations.

Secondary Trauma and Organizations

Like families, organizations are living systems that respond to external forces, including trauma and stress (Bloom, 2012). Organizations that serve clients who have experienced trauma or that have gone through collective traumatic experiences—such as client deaths or threats or assaults on property or staff—can exhibit the same characteristics that traumatized individuals do, becoming hyperaroused, threat-focused, and ultimately psychologically unsafe for those who work for and are served by the organization.

Earlier we introduced the concept of a traumatogenic environment, defined as an environment that has been shaped by trauma and, as a result, functions in a way that can be harmful to others. One way to understand a traumatogenic environment is to think back to Vanessa, and imagine working in an office full of Vanessas. Your colleagues may avoid doing their work; they may be tense and irritable, easily triggered at the smallest misunderstanding. Others may be distracted and preoccupied, not following through with anything. If Vanessa were a supervisor, she might cancel meetings with her team as a way to avoid emotionally difficult details about cases, respond harshly to staff who express uncertainty about what to do in a certain situation, or just appear to be checked out. Over time, what was a cohesive work group could come to feel fractured, unsupportive, and even threatening, even to those staff who do not interact with trauma survivors as part of their day-to-day jobs. Another way that organizations can be traumatogenic environments is related to how they manage crises. An example of such an organization follows next.

Case Example: The Center for Women and Children

The Center for Women and Children (CWC) provides food, shelter, job training, and housing assistance to families impacted by homelessness and domestic violence. When its founder retired, it was absorbed into the operations of Johnson Charities, a larger social services agency. After a recent court hearing, a CWC client, Ms. Desai, was followed back to the shelter by her estranged husband, who fatally shot her and her two young children and then himself. The shooting led the evening news that night, and following an interview with the director where she defended her staff's actions, the local newspaper ran an editorial criticizing the CWC for trying to whitewash over problems at the shelter.

In response to the negative press coverage, the county administrator announced that the county was ending its contract with the CWC and reviewing all services run by Johnson Charities. The following day, Johnson's CEO sent out a press release saying that the organization was conducting an internal investigation to find out how this breach of security happened and that in the meantime the CWC director and those staff who worked directly with the family had been suspended without pay. An internal memo was distributed that informed all Johnson employees that the suspended staff were instructed not to contact each other or other employees during their suspension because of potential legal action.

Over the course of the following months, staff and supervisors who had worked in the field for years began questioning their own competence, expressing anger at their clients' lack of progress, and wondering if their efforts were making any positive difference. By the end of the year, about half of the CWC staff had resigned their positions, reporting high levels of stress and interpersonal conflict among staff and between staff and shelter residents, a lack of supervisory and organizational support, and the negative impact of work on their health and families. Johnson's human resource department reported that it was getting fewer inquiries about their job listings than usual, which had left vacancies throughout the agency.

One of the long-term Johnson managers met with the CEO to express safety concerns related to the low staffing and a lack of client engagement among those staff who remained and suggested measures aimed at increasing staff support. At the following senior leadership meeting, the CEO announced that Johnson Charities would be implementing a new review process designed to hold staff accountable for specific performance and productivity measures, meant to "right the ship."

This example demonstrates how when organizations feel threatened, they often respond reactively, in the same way an individual person does when threatened (Bloom, 2013). In the immediate aftermath of the Desai murders, the Johnson Charities' leadership was in survival mode, taking steps to restore the confidence of the county administrator and general public in its competence and operations. While these actions may have been effective in easing concerns of these external stakeholders, they ignored the needs of the staff and families who were most affected by the events and at highest risk for developing posttraumatic responses to them. By automatically responding in a punitive way, the leadership communicated a lack of caring for, and trust in, its staff. This led many staff to leave the agency; those who remained were left alone to grieve the loss of the Desai family, their colleagues, and their own sense of physical and psychological safety.

Although quick and immediate action is protective in the face of acute danger, it is generally less effective in addressing more complex and nuanced problems. When leadership is reactive and punitive following these kinds of incidents, staff can feel under attack, and as a result be both physically and psychologically unable to attend to the needs of their clients or even reflexively punitive toward them. This parallel process—between organizations and staff and staff and clients—is typical of traumatogenic environments and can have a pervasive and negative impact.

How can organizations stop this cycle? To understand how to intervene on both the individual and organizational level, we draw on the concept of a "trauma system." As described in the Trauma Systems Therapy (TST) treatment model (Saxe, Ellis, & Brown, 2015), a trauma system is comprised of (1) an individual who has a trauma response in specific, definable moments and (2) a broader environment that is not able to protect the individual from trauma reminders and/or regulate his or her trauma responses. According to this framework, individuals who are given strategies for understanding their trauma and managing their trauma responses, but remain in families, schools, workplaces, communities, and/or service systems that are unsafe or feel unsafe, will remain focused on survival and not have the mental or emotional ability to learn and/or use such strategies. From the TST perspective, in order for a traumatized individual to heal, both sides of the trauma system need to be addressed.

This idea of a trauma system is applicable to secondary trauma as well. As there are individuals who can thrive even in the face of abuse or violence, there are also staff who remain resilient despite the quality or nature of their place of work. But for many people working in traumatogenic environments—particularly those who are already vulnerable because of trauma experienced personally or in their communities—individual-level self-care strategies will be no match for the crisis-driven, reactive, and fear-inducing workplace they encounter every day. In addition to being inadequate, approaches that exclusively focus on individual-level changes put the onus on staff for solving the problem of secondary trauma and therefore implicitly "blame the victim" if and when they prove to be ineffective. Individual-level change is a necessary part of any secondary trauma-related intervention (just as it would be for someone who had a primary experience of trauma), but because of the nature of trauma systems, in most cases it will not be sufficient without attending to the broader work environment.

Building Trauma-Informed Organizations

While there are few empirically tested models available to address the impact of secondary trauma on staff and workplace culture, research has identified organizational qualities that help to mitigate its impact: fostering strong mutual support among staff, encouraging team-based work, having mechanisms for staff input and shared power in the workplace, providing staff with flexibility around work hours and client assignments, demonstrating a commitment to the protection of their workforce, and being transparent around decision making (Killian, 2008; Slattery & Goodman, 2009). Importantly, most of these strategies do not depend on additional financial resources. They do, however, require leadership buy-in and a commitment to a more democratic, inclusive, and flexible workplace culture, which is unlikely to exist if agency leadership is itself suffering the effects of secondary trauma.

Another key aspect of a trauma-informed workplace culture is the open and active recognition of secondary trauma's impact on the work. What do we mean by this? As noted by Leslie Anne Ross, many trauma professionals face the "unspoken message that to be successful, providers should be able to handle whatever stress or distress is related to this work" (2014). Even in organizations that provide trauma-informed interventions for clients, staff are too often left on their own to manage trauma's impact on them. It is rare, for example, for supervisors to receive training that would help them to distinguish between secondary trauma symptoms and poor performance and to intervene effectively with their staff, not to mention getting support for *their own* reactions to the work.

Additional approaches organizations can use to address the impact of secondary trauma include the following (see Box 10.2):

Box 10.2 Organizational Approaches to Addressing Secondary Trauma

- *Understanding how staff are impacted by secondary trauma through regular surveys, which may include trauma assessment tools referenced earlier and can be easily distributed through web-based platforms.* Ensuring that such surveys are confidential may increase staff's willingness to honestly share their experiences. Such tools can also serve as psychoeducation on the impact of secondary trauma and encourage staff to be more attuned to their own and their colleagues' responses.
- *Talking openly about secondary trauma during the hiring and onboarding processes, including inquiring about prospective staff's experience working with trauma survivors and how they manage personal and professional stress.* In some fields, such as child welfare and medicine, staff are sometimes simultaneously helping children and families that have been traumatized and causing trauma to those children and families through their interventions, which can lead to internal conflict and/or distress. Open communication about such issues not only sets an important tone, but if it includes information on individual-level risk factors, it can help prospective staff understand their personal vulnerabilities and make informed decisions around their fit with the job.
- *Providing ongoing education about secondary trauma-related risk factors and symptoms to all staff, including support staff and agency leadership, and creating spaces where people can openly discuss the personal impact of the work without concern about retaliation.* Such activities normalize people's response to trauma work and send the message that they are organizational priorities that impact all staff, rather than personal problems for direct service staff. One well-known model that approaches trauma's impact on all members of an organization holistically is Sandra Bloom's Sanctuary Model (2013), which is based on the concepts of physical, psychological, social, and moral safety for both staff and clients.
- *Providing skill-based training to increase staff resilience and positive coping.* The first author of this chapter was a collaborator on an intervention, called the Resilience Alliance (Chemtob, Avinadav, & Tullberg, 2011), that focused on enhancing staff optimism, mastery, and collaboration, on the individual, work unit, and office levels. In developing this intervention we heard from staff that they were often more stressed by their interactions with colleagues than their work with clients; given this, a large focus of the intervention involved consciously shifting the dynamic to one that recognizes the impact of the work on individual,

unit, and organizational functioning and sees mitigating that impact as the responsibility of everyone within the organization.

- *Thinking of self-care as both an individual and organizational responsibility.* Are staff told about the importance of work–life balance but still expected to respond to e-mails at night and on the weekend? Does the office culture implicitly reward those who work late every night and deride those who take vacations? Although trauma work is rarely "9 to 5," treating everything as an emergency will quickly deplete staff and affect the quality of their work. Identifying organizational-level strategies helps to ensure that everyone is "walking the walk" and that the responsibility of wellness and work–life balance is a shared one.
- *Ensuring that secondary trauma awareness and mitigation are integrated into support and supervision at all levels of the organization.* It can't be said enough: direct service staff are not the only ones impacted by secondary trauma and traumatogenic environments. Supervisors, managers, and leaders will not be able to be attuned to its impact among staff if they are suffering from its impact as well. Giving agency leadership, who often have less access to peer support, the mental and physical space to consider how secondary trauma affects decision making at all levels of the organization will translate into improved staff well-being and client care.
- *Looking at staff "performance issues" though a trauma lens.* When leadership is under stress, either following a critical incident or in the face of ongoing concerns about staff effectiveness, their decision making is more likely to be rigid and narrowly focused. It is important to have a process that allows leadership to take a step back and check in with their own reactivity before responding and provides an opportunity to see how secondary trauma might be impacting staff functioning.
- *Ensuring that crisis response protocols include support for staff impacted by client deaths and other serious incidents.* While some people will decline such services, it is important that they are consistently offered rather than left to the discretion of individual managers. Even if some people do not afford themselves this support, their routine provision sends an important message about how the organization values its staff.
- *Fostering a workplace culture that promotes both physical and psychological safety.* In settings such as health care and child welfare, providers have looked to promote the idea of "safety culture," which is the extent to which an organization and its staff's values, attitudes, and behaviors together focus on promoting safety, recognizing the impact of stress on staff performance, and pursuing consistent, harm-free operations (Vogus, Cull, Hengelbrok, Modell, & Epstein, 2016). An important aspect of safety culture is allowing individuals to report errors without fear of retribution and having mechanisms that use errors as opportunities for learning and improvement in individual and group decision making.

Additionally, tools such as the Secondary Traumatic Stress-Informed Organization Assessment Tool (Sprang et al., 2014) described earlier can help organizations identify areas of weakness and track their progress in changing their policies and practices. While more research is needed on organizational-level secondary trauma interventions, these kinds of approaches can have an important impact.

The Role of the Public in the Trauma System

As demonstrated in the earlier Johnson Charities example, organizational responses to crises often include responding to pressure and criticism received from the media, political leaders, and the general public. These players are usually external to trauma-serving organizations, but they nevertheless are important parts of the larger trauma system. In fact, in summarizing the literature on secondary trauma among child welfare staff, Osofsky, Putnam, and Lederman (2008) named "concerns about being publicly scapegoated for a tragic outcome when they did not have the means or authority to intervene effectively" as a common source of secondary trauma. It is likely that this is a source of traumatic stress for *many* people working for public/social services agencies, as it has the challenging combination of being out of one's control while carrying very high stakes for both individuals and organizations.

In the face of tragic events such as a client death, organizations and political leaders are responsible for identifying and addressing any gaps in practice that contributed to the event's occurrence. As described by a child welfare commissioner, however, this process is often driven by fear and a need to assign blame rather than reason:

> Atrocities to children are the most disturbing events that occur to us as humans. The culture is so horrified—and we should be so horrified, but we become irrationally obsessed with finding someone to blame . . . This is so primal, it's so deep, that the reporters themselves lose their minds. It's a shared phenomenon, culturally, and the crowd becomes mad in the wake of atrocities. (van Dernoot Lipsky, 2010, p. 235)

In the Johnson Charities scenario, the CWC director's message of support for her staff was interpreted and reported as her deflecting responsibility for the Desai family deaths, and she and the staff were punished accordingly. The agency's failure, rather than the estranged husband's violence, was the focus of negative press reports. Instead of fully understanding the factors that led to the shooting before taking any action, the leadership simply reacted. While this satisfied the public in the short term, it did not address the underlying problem, and in fact over time it undermined its staff and clients' well-being and safety.

It is important for members of the public to understand their own reactions to traumatic events in the public sphere, whether they are happening in their community or playing out on television or social media channels. Repeated exposure to such events can have a real impact, resulting in numbness or apathy on one extreme or anger or hypervigilance on the other. However, when there is a high-profile tragedy in the news, there is usually not an accompanying outcry over budget cuts, systemic inequalities, or other measures that may have contributed to the events in question. We call on the public to resist their own black-and-white thinking, encourage the media and others to realistically report on the nuances involved, and hold social service organizations, public systems, and political leaders accountable for ensuring that social service professionals have the resources and support needed to do their jobs safely and effectively.

Conclusion

Throughout this chapter, we have highlighted how secondary trauma impacts individuals and organizations, and what can be done both on the micro and macro level to reduce its adverse impact. By introducing the concept of a traumatogenic environment, we seek to highlight the fact that trauma's secondary effects can be broad, even touching people who do not have direct contact with trauma survivors as part of their jobs.

Despite the field's frequent emphasis on self-care, the research demonstrates that most people working in traumatogenic environments will likely receive limited benefit from individual-level interventions, whether they are informal wellness strategies or professional counseling, provided in isolation. We call on agency leaders to recognize their organizations' role in the trauma system and to approach the idea of secondary trauma intervention in a way that includes changes in workplace culture and practice.

An additional part of this shift toward a systems perspective is understanding the roles of the media, political leaders, and the broader public in either mitigating or exacerbating trauma experienced by social service professionals. People in helping professions are taking on the responsibility *we all share* for the most vulnerable members of our society; they are doing the necessary work that most others in our society are not willing to do. Their sacrifice should be honored by providing them with the tools they need to do their jobs effectively, without sacrificing their own personal well-being and professional effectiveness in the process.

References

American Psychiatric Association. (2013). *Diagnostic and statistical manual of mental disorders* (5th ed.). Arlington, VA: American Psychiatric Association.

Baird, D. K., & Kracen, A. C. (2006). Vicarious traumatization and secondary traumatic stress: A research synthesis. *Counselling Psychology Quarterly, 19*(2), 181–188. https://doi.org/10.1080/09515070600811899

Banyard, V. L., Williams, L. M., & Siegel, J. A. (2003). The impact of complex trauma and depression on parenting: An exploration of mediating risk and protective factors. *Child Maltreatment, 8*(4), 334–349.

Beck, C. T. (2011). Secondary traumatic stress in nurses: A systematic review. *Archives of Psychiatric Nursing, 25*(1), 1–10. https://doi.org/10.1016/j.apnu.2010.05.005

Bloom, S. L. (2012). Trauma-organized systems. In C. R. Figley (Ed.), *Encyclopedia of trauma* (pp. 741–743). Thousand Oaks, CA: Sage.

Bloom, S. L. (2013). *Creating sanctuary: Toward the evolution of sane societies* (revised ed.). New York, NY: Routledge.

Bober, T., & Regehr, C. (2006). Strategies for reducing secondary or vicarious trauma: Do they work? *Brief Treatment and Crisis Intervention, 6*(1), 1. https://doi.org/10.1093/brief-treatment/mhj001

Borntrager, C., Caringi, J. C., Pol, R. van den, Crosby, L., O'Connell, K., Trautman, A., & McDonald, M. (2012). Secondary traumatic stress in school personnel. *Advances in School Mental Health Promotion, 5*(1), 38–50. https://doi.org/10.1080/1754730X.2012.664862

Bride, B. E. (2007). Prevalence of secondary traumatic stress among social workers. *Social Work, 52*(1), 63–70. https://doi.org/10.1093/sw/52.1.63

Bride, B. E., Robinson, M. M., Yegidis, B., & Figley, C. R. (2004). Development and validation of the secondary traumatic stress scale. *Research on Social Work Practice, 14*(1), 27–35. https://doi.org/10.1177/1049731503254106

Chamberlain, J., & Miller, M. K. (2009). Evidence of secondary traumatic stress, safety concerns, and burnout among a homogeneous group of judges in a single jurisdiction. *Journal of the American Academy of Psychiatry and the Law Online, 37*(2), 214–224.

Chemtob, C., Avinadav, R., & Tullberg, E. (2011). *The Resilience Alliance: Promoting resilience and reducing secondary trauma among child welfare staff.* Retrieved from http://nctsn.org/sites/default/files/assets/pdfs/resilience_alliance_training_manual.pdf

Craig, C. D., & Sprang, G. (2010). Compassion satisfaction, compassion fatigue, and burnout in a national sample of trauma treatment therapists. *Anxiety, Stress, & Coping, 23*(3), 319–339. https://doi.org/10.1080/10615800903085818

Creamer, T. L., & Liddle, B. J. (2005). Secondary traumatic stress among disaster mental health workers responding to the September 11 attacks. *Journal of Traumatic Stress*, *18*(1), 89–96. https://doi.org/10.1002/jts.20008

Deahl, M. (2000). Psychological debriefing: Controversy and challenge. *Australian and New Zealand Journal of Psychiatry*, *34*(6), 929–939. https://doi.org/10.1046/j.1440-1614.2000.00828.x

Etzion, D. (2003). Annual vacation: Duration of relief from job stressors and burnout. *Anxiety, Stress, & Coping*, *16*(2), 213–226. https://doi.org/10.1080/10615806.2003.10382974

Evans-Campbell, T. (2008). Historical trauma in American Indian/Native Alaska communities: A multilevel framework for exploring impacts on individuals, families, and communities. *Journal of Interpersonal Violence*, *23*(3), 316–338. https://doi.org/10.1177/0886260507312290

Everly, G. S., Jr., & Mitchell, J. T. (1999). Critical Incident Stress Management (CISM): A proposed international standard of care in workplace crisis intervention. *APA PsycNET*, 11–12. https://doi.org/10.1037/e35973 2004-009

Figley, C. R. (1995). Compassion fatigue: Toward a new understanding of the costs of caring. In *Secondary traumatic stress: Self-care issues for clinicians, researchers, and educators* (pp. 3–28). Baltimore, MD: The Sidran Press.

Figley, C. R. (2002). *Treating compassion fatigue*. New York, NY: Routledge.

Gentry, J. E., Baranowsky, A. B., & Dunning, K. (2002). The Accelerated Recovery Program (ARP) for compassion fatigue. In C. R. Figley (Ed.), *Treating compassion fatigue* (pp. 123–137). New York, NY: Routledge.

Hensel, J. M., Ruiz, C., Finney, C., & Dewa, C. S. (2015). Meta-analysis of risk factors for secondary traumatic stress in therapeutic work with trauma victims. *Journal of Traumatic Stress*, *28*(2), 83–91. https://doi.org/10.1002/jts.21998

Iliffe, G., & Steed, L. (2000). Exploring the counselor's experience of working with perpetrators and survivors of domestic violence. *Journal of Interpersonal Violence*, *15*(4), 393–412. https://doi.org/10.1177/088626000015004004

Jaffe, P. G., Crooks, C. V., Dunford-Jackson, B. L., & Town, J. M. (2003). Vicarious trauma in judges: The personal challenge of dispensing justice. *Juvenile and Family Court Journal*, *54*(4), 1–9. https://doi.org/10.1111/j.1755-6988.2003.tb00083.x

Kellermann, N. P. F. (2013). Epigenetic transmission of holocaust trauma: Can nightmares be inherited? *The Israel Journal of Psychiatry and Related Sciences*, *50*(1), 33–7.

Killian, K. D. (2008). Helping till it hurts? A multimethod study of compassion fatigue, burnout, and self-care in clinicians working with trauma survivors. *Traumatology*, *14*(2), 32–44. https://doi.org/10.1177/1534765608319083

Lombardo, K. L., & Motta, R. W. (2008). Secondary trauma in children of parents with mental illness. *Traumatology*, *14*(3), 57–67. https://doi.org/10.1177/1534765608320331

Makin, K. (2002, August 14). *Judges live in torment, study finds*. Retrieved from https://www.fact.on.ca/news/news0208/gm020814.htm
Motta, R. (2008). Secondary trauma. *International Journal of Emergency Mental Health*, *10*(4), 291–298.
Motta, R.W., Hafeez, S., Sciancalepore, R., & Diaz, A.B. (2001). Discriminant validation of the Modified Secondary Trauma Questionnaire. *Journal of Psychotherapy in Independent Practice*, 2(4), 17–25. https://doi.org/10.1300/J288v02n04_02
National Child Traumatic Stress Network. (n.d.). *Racial injustice and trauma: African Americans in the U.S.* Retrieved from http://nctsn.org/sites/default/files/assets/pdfs/racialinjusticeandtrauma_101816_final.pdf
Osofsky, J.D. (2009). Perspectives on helping traumatized infants, young children, and their families. *Infant Mental Health Journal*, *30*(6), 673–677. https://doi.org/10.1002/imhj.20236
Osofsky, J.D., Putnam, F.W., & Lederman, J.C.S. (2008). How to maintain emotional health when working with trauma. *Juvenile and Family Court Journal*, 59(4), 91–102. https://doi.org/10.1111/j.1755-6988.2008.00023.x
Palosaari, E., Punamäki, R.-L., Qouta, S., & Diab, M. (2013). Intergenerational effects of war trauma among Palestinian families mediated via psychological maltreatment. *Child Abuse & Neglect*, *37*(11), 955–968. https://doi.org/10.1016/j.chiabu.2013.04.006
Pearlman, L.A. (2003). *Trauma and Attachment Belief Scale (TABS) manual*. Los Angeles, CA: Western Psychological Services.
Pearlman, L.A., & Mac Ian, P.S. (1995). Vicarious traumatization: An empirical study of the effects of trauma work on trauma therapists. *Professional Psychology: Research and Practice*, *26*(6), 558–565. https://doi.org/10.1037/0735-7028.26.6.558
Perez, L.M., Jones, J., Englert, D.R., & Sachau, D. (2010). Secondary traumatic stress and burnout among law enforcement investigators exposed to disturbing media images. *Journal of Police and Criminal Psychology*, *25*(2), 113–124. https://doi.org/10.1007/s11896-010-9066-7
Phipps, A.B., & Byrne, M.K. (2003). Brief interventions for secondary trauma: Review and recommendations. *Stress and Health*, *19*(3), 139–147. https://doi.org/10.1002/smi.970
Pines, A., & Aronson, E. (1988). *Career burnout: Causes and cures* (Vol. xiv). New York, NY: Free Press.
Regehr, C., Hemsworth, D., Leslie, B., Howe, P., & Chau, S. (2004). Predictors of post-traumatic distress in child welfare workers: A linear structural equation model. *Children and Youth Services Review*, *26*(4), 331–346. https://doi.org/10.1016/j.childyouth.2004.02.003
Regehr, C., LeBlanc, V., Shlonsky, A., & Bogo, M. (2010). The influence of clinicians' previous trauma exposure on their assessment of child abuse risk. *The Journal of Nervous and Mental Disease*, *198*(9), 614–618. https://doi.org/10.1097

Rosenbloom, D. J., Pratt, A. C., & Pearlman, L. A. (1995). Helpers' responses to trauma work: Understanding and intervening in an organization. In B. H. Stamm (Ed.), *Secondary traumatic stress: Self-care issues for clinicians, researchers, and educators* (pp. 65–79). Baltimore, MD: The Sidran Press.

Ross, L. A. (2014). Creating a culture of wellness for providers in harm's way. In R. M. Reece, R. F. Hanson, & J. Sargent (Eds.), *Treatment of child abuse: Common ground for mental health, medical, and legal practitioners* (2nd ed., pp. 255–261). Baltimore, MD: Johns Hopkins University Press.

Saxe, G. N., Ellis, B. H., & Brown, A. D. (2015). *Trauma Systems Therapy for children and teens* (2nd ed.). New York, NY: Guilford Publications.

Schauben, L. J., & Frazier, P. A. (1995). Vicarious trauma: The effects on female counselors of working with sexual violence survivors. *Psychology of Women Quarterly, 19*(1), 49–64. https://doi.org/10.1111/j.1471-6402.1995.tb00278.x

Slattery, S. M., & Goodman, L. A. (2009). Secondary traumatic stress among domestic violence advocates: Workplace risk and protective factors. *Violence against Women, 15*(11), 1358–1379. https://doi.org/10.1177/1077801209347469

Sotero, M. (2006). A conceptual model of historical trauma: Implications for public health practice and research. *SSRN Scholarly Paper, No. ID 1350062.* Retrieved from https://papers.ssrn.com/abstract=1350062

Sprang, G., Craig, C., & Clark, J. (2011). Secondary traumatic stress and burnout in child welfare workers: A comparative analysis of occupational distress across professional groups. *Child Welfare: Arlington, 90*(6), 149–168.

Sprang, G., Ross, L., Blackshear, K., Miller, B., Vrabel, C., Ham, J., . . . Caringi, J. (2014). *The Secondary Traumatic Stress-Informed Organization Assessment.* Retrieved from http://www.uky.edu/CTAC/

Stamm, B. H. (2013). *Professional Quality of Life Scale.* https://doi.org/10.1037/t05192-000

van Dernoot Lipsky, L. (2010). *Trauma stewardship: An everyday guide to caring for self while caring for others.* Retrieved from ReadHowYouWant.com

van IJzendoorn, M. H., Bakermans-Kranenburg, M. J., & Sagi-Schwartz, A. (2003). Are children of Holocaust survivors less well-adapted? A meta-analytic investigation of secondary traumatization. *Journal of Traumatic Stress, 16*(5), 459–469. https://doi.org/10.1023/A:1025706427300

Vogus, T. J., Cull, M. J., Hengelbrok, N. E., Modell, S. J., & Epstein, R. A. (2016). Assessing safety culture in child welfare: Evidence from Tennessee. *Children and Youth Services Review, 65*, 94–103. https://doi.org/10.1016/j.childyouth.2016.03.020

Wagaman, M. A., Geiger, J. M., Shockley, C., & Segal, E. A. (2015). The role of empathy in burnout, compassion satisfaction, and secondary traumatic stress among social workers. *Social Work, 60*(3), 201–209. https://doi.org/10.1093/sw/swv014

Walsh, C. R., Mathieu, F., & Hendricks, A. (2017). Report from the secondary traumatic stress San Diego think tank. *Traumatology*, *23*(2), 124–128. https://doi.org/10.1037/trm0000124

Weiss, D. S., & Marmar, C. R. (1996). The Impact of Event Scale-Revised. In J. Wilson & T. M. Keane (Eds.), *Assessing psychological trauma and PTSD* (pp. 399–411). New York, NY: Guildford.

Yager, T. J., Gerszberg, N., & Dohrenwend, B. P. (2016). Secondary traumatization in Vietnam veterans' families. *Journal of Traumatic Stress*, *29*(4), 349–355. https://doi.org/10.1002/jts.22115

Yehuda, R., & Bierer, L. M. (2009). The relevance of epigenetics to PTSD: Implications for the DSM-V. *Journal of Traumatic Stress*, *22*(5), 427–434. https://doi.org/10.1002/jts.20448

CHAPTER 11

From Adverse Childhood Experiences to Adverse Community Experiences

Addressing and Preventing Community Trauma[1]

Howard Pinderhughes and Rachel Davis

Over the past decade, there has been a growing awareness of the impacts of the exposure to violence on children, youth, and adults in communities with high rates of violence. While nationally there has been a reduction in the rates of violence and violence crime, communities with historically high rates of violence continue to be plagued with persistently high rates of violence and trauma. Many of these communities are working to prevent violence and promote community safety. Through comprehensive, multisector actions, a number of cities, including Minneapolis, Seattle, Los Angeles, and Boston, have seen violence decrease in recent years (Davis & Tsao, 2014). However, trauma continues to be a serious issue in communities with high levels of violence, and it functions as a barrier to successfully implementing violence prevention strategies and other health-promoting strategies. For those communities with ongoing violence, traumatic stress is a significant risk factor. This chapter will examine the links between individual trauma and community health.

The U.S. Service Administration of Mental Health and Substance Abuse (SAMHSA) defines "trauma" in this way: "Individual *trauma* [emphasis added] results from an event, series of events, or set of circumstances experienced by an individual as physically or emotionally harmful or life-threatening with lasting adverse effects on the individual's functioning and mental, physical, social, emotional, or spiritual well-being." Children and adults may be affected by trauma in many different ways, and some are more acutely affected than others.

Trauma and its associated symptoms of mental and psychological illness are more prevalent in the United States than in most other countries in the world (Kessler & Üstün, 2008), with posttraumatic stress disorder (PTSD) ranging from 9 to 12 percent in the general population (Breslau, Davis, Andreski, & Peterson, 1991; Resnick, Kilpatrick, Dansky, Saunders, & Best, 1993). There is evidence that boys and men of color are at higher risk of traumatic stress than other groups due to multiple factors, including higher rates of incarceration and more exposure to violence. Indeed, there is an epidemic of trauma in many communities.

The increased awareness of the scope and depth of trauma and its impacts have resulted in important advances in the diagnosis and treatment of trauma and PTSD among children, youth, and adults. This awareness has been amplified by the widespread dissemination and adoption of the Adverse Childhood Experiences Study (ACES) to understand trauma and PTSD. The Adverse Childhood Experiences framework has made a vital contribution to understanding the link between traumatic events in childhood and adverse health outcomes in adulthood. It has also shifted the focus and questions raised about children, youth, and adults who have been exposed to adversity from the question of "What is wrong with them?" to "What happened to them?"

The predominant approach to dealing with trauma in the United States today is through the expansion of mental health services and the adoption of "trauma-informed" care, which has become a standard of care both in health-care and mental health-care realms. This approach focuses on screening and treatment of individuals, which is a vital first step in dealing with the effects of exposures to violence. It also includes protocols in a growing number of schools, hospitals, and juvenile detention centers, which recognize that individuals being served by these institutions may be traumatized, and they are designed so as not to exacerbate the trauma.

In communities with high rates of violence, trauma is not just a problem for the individuals who directly witness or experience violence.

Service providers, first responders, and residents also experience trauma, including vicarious or secondary trauma, resulting from the indirect exposure to a traumatic event through firsthand accounts or narratives of that event. Additionally, any person who has a significant relationship with a survivor of trauma may also experience vicarious trauma (McCann & Pearlman, 1990). Community violence contributes to high levels of trauma across the population *and* a breakdown of the community's social networks, social relationships, and positive social norms—all of which could otherwise help *protect* both individuals and the community from violence and trauma.

Treating individuals who have experienced trauma is vitally important, but it is only part of a comprehensive solution. As mental health expert Dr. George Albee said, "No epidemic has ever been resolved by paying attention to the treatment of the affected individual" (Albee, 1983). As an epidemic, trauma must be addressed at the *population* level—and that means expanding from, and adding to, trauma-informed care of individuals. It means going beyond addressing Adverse Childhood Experiences to addressing community traumas, which we have termed "Adverse *Community* Experiences." It means addressing the broader external factors that contribute to trauma, such as community violence, and structural violence, which includes structural racism, the lack of educational and economic opportunity, and deteriorating physical environments.

For years, public health and violence prevention leaders who work in high-violence neighborhoods have helped inform emerging models to counter the effects of trauma, promote community healing, and foster community resilience. Yet there was not a full framework for understanding, addressing, and preventing trauma at a community or population level until Prevention Institute published its Adverse Community Experiences and Resilience (ACE|R) framework in late 2015 (Pinderhughes, Davis, & Williams, 2015) with support from Kaiser Permanente Northern California Community Benefit Program. The ACE|R framework shifts the question about communities from "What is wrong with this community and these people?" to "What happened to this community?" and "How do we help it to heal?"

Fundamental Terms: Violence and Trauma

Violence and trauma are closely entwined. *Trauma* is caused by experiences or situations that are threatening, dangerous, and/or overwhelming. *Violence* is the intentional use of physical force or power, threatened or actual, against oneself, another person, or a group or community that either results in or has a high likelihood of resulting in injury, death, psychological or emotional harm, maldevelopment, or deprivation (WHO, 2017). From the community perspective, *interpersonal violence* is an act by an individual or group that inflicts harm on another individual or group. *Structural violence* refers to harm that individuals, families, and communities experience from the economic and social structure; social institutions; and relations of power, privilege, inequality, and inequity that may harm people and communities by preventing them from meeting their basic needs (Burtle, 2013; Pinderhughes, Davis, & Williams, 2015). It includes structural social processes like racism and multiple forms of discrimination and oppressions. Interpersonal and structural violence often go hand in hand and result in trauma to both individuals and communities. Both contribute to, exacerbate, and are exacerbated by individual and community trauma—as will be explained in more detail later in this chapter.

Individual Trauma

As previously mentioned, research indicates that PTSD ranges from 9 to 12 percent in the general population (Breslau et al., 1991; Resnick et al., 1993), and these figures probably underestimate the disorder's prevalence in urban areas that have been economically disadvantaged. Children and youth who are exposed to violence often suffer PTSD and trauma, and research indicates trauma greatly impacts development, health, and well-being (Felitti et al., 1998; Funk, Bechtoldt Baldacci, Pasold, & Baumgardner, 2004; Gorman-Smith & Tolan, 1998; Hart, 2007).

Although researchers identified trauma as a major problem in inner-city neighborhoods and communities with high rates of violence in the early 1990s, it took two decades for trauma-informed practices to be developed and adopted by health-care providers, practitioners, and educators. Trauma-informed care and mental health services now exist in many communities across the country. Trauma-informed care is defined by SAMHSA as "a program, organization, or system that realizes the widespread impact of trauma and understands potential paths for recovery; recognizes the signs and symptoms of trauma in clients, families, staff and others involved with the system; and responds by fully integrating knowledge about trauma into policies, procedures, and practices, and seeks to actively resist re-traumatization" (SAMHSA, 2017).

Individual approaches and strategies for healing from trauma are vital and important—and they are most effective when we also address the sociocultural, physical, and economic factors that influence individual health at the same time. These factors encompass everything from levels of violence in the community to access to quality education, housing, employment, and healthy food.

Community Trauma: An Overview

Residents who live in communities with high levels of violence know that an entire *community* can be traumatized en masse by violence. Indeed, this is the reality in many inner-city neighborhoods. Members from nearly two dozen U.S. cities in the UNITY Network (Urban Networks to Increase Thriving Youth—a Centers for Disease Control and Prevention (CDC)-funded national network that *supports U.S. cities in advancing more effective, sustainable efforts to prevent violence before it occurs so that urban youth can thrive in safe environments with supportive relationships and opportunities for success*), as well as public health/violence prevention practitioners in Northern California, were interviewed about trauma for Prevention Institute's ACE|R report (Pinderhughes, Davis, & Williams, 2015). All reported that many children, youth, and adults in neighborhoods with high levels of violence were traumatized and that many exhibited the symptoms of PTSD. In recent years, researchers have defined this situation as an example of *collective trauma*—an aggregate of trauma experienced by individual members. War, genocide, slavery, terrorism, and natural disasters can cause collective trauma.

Community trauma is not just the aggregate of individuals in a geographic area who have experienced emotional trauma from violence and other sources, nor is it tied to a single event. Community trauma is *the common experience of chronic adversity* from systemic factors such as discrimination, racism, sexism, poverty, and oppression—all of which intersect with interpersonal and community violence. Community trauma can thus be characterized as a set of community-level symptoms such as disconnected and damaged social relations and networks; deteriorated physical environments and unhealthy public spaces; disinvestment, including the relocation of businesses; failing public education systems; long-term unemployment and limited employment; and intergenerational poverty.

Communities with high levels of community trauma may also have lower levels of collective efficacy—that is, the ability for people to come together to develop and implement health-promoting strategies for the community, including solutions to prevent violence. As one violence prevention practitioner noted, "Trauma gets in the way of us doing what we need to do . . . When it is chronic and not episodic, it is really damaging. I see it impacting how people . . . problem solve, how they interact with their friends" (Pinderhughes, Davis, & Williams, 2015). In summary, social connections between people (the social environment), the physical environment, and economic opportunities interact in ways that either bolster a community or keep it from thriving.

Manifestations of Trauma in the Three Domains of the Community Environments

Healthy communities contribute to the fabric and foundation of resiliency for individual children, youth, and families. A healthy community is made up of factors in three interrelated domains—the sociocultural environment (the people), the physical/built environment (the place), and the economic and educational environment (equitable opportunity). Initially identified by Prevention Institute for the U.S. Office of Minority Health (Davis, Cook, & Cohen, 2005) as part of THRIVE (Tool for Health and Resilience in Vulnerable Environments), these three domains contain factors that research has shown as relating to health and safety outcomes—factors such as quality *education* in the equitable opportunity domain, *housing* in the place domain, and *social networks and trust* in the people domain (see Figure 11.1). The factors themselves are shaped by structural drivers—that is, how the distribution of power, money, and resources plays out at the community level, influencing daily living conditions (CSDH, 2008). A community that lacks its fair share of power, money, and resources is more likely to experience lower-quality education and housing; similarly, social networks and trust may be damaged or compromised.

In a healthy community, these three domains promote community health, safety, and resiliency for individuals and families. When a community is traumatized, however, each of the domains is damaged and undermined, threatening the sense of safety, decreasing opportunity, and

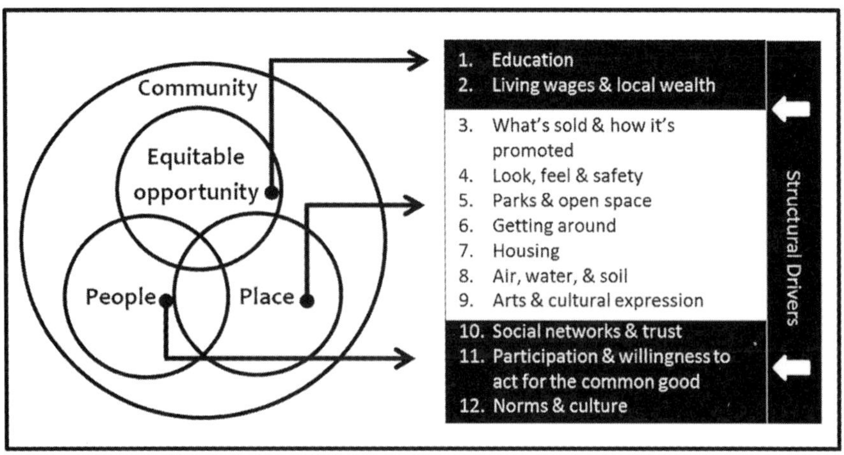

Figure 11.1 THRIVE Diagram Featuring Three Domains and Associated Factors

negatively affecting resilience. The following sections describe how trauma manifests in each of the three domains of the community environment (see Figure 11.2).

People: The Sociocultural Environment

The symptoms of community trauma are especially apparent in the sociocultural environment. They can be seen in damaged social relations and networks, destructive social norms that may encourage violence and unhealthy behavior, and a decreased sense of collective political and social efficacy.

In highly impacted communities, high rates of violence are accompanied by high rates of incarceration and family disruption, with family members and neighbors often separated from one another, and intergenerational relationships undermined. Familial and communal love and bonds are negatively impacted by fear, distrust, and social distance. The infrastructure of community organizations and community social support networks are underdeveloped or damaged. Sadly, it is strong social relationships, networks, and supports that are most needed by children, youth, and adults who are exposed to violence and trauma, in order to boost their resiliency.

Community trauma also manifests in the sociocultural domain as social norms that encourage violence and unhealthy behaviors instead of community-oriented, positive social norms. Cultural and social norms are highly influential in shaping individual behavior—norms can either protect against violence or support and encourage the use of violence. When violence is culturally and socially accepted, either as a normal method of resolving conflict or as a usual part of child-rearing, it is a risk factor for all types of interpersonal violence, including violence within families, peer groups, communities, and societies (WHO, 2009).

Violence is also correlated with lower rates of social cohesion and less sense of collective efficacy (informal social control) in a community (Sampson, Raudenbush, & Earls, 1997). Collective efficacy might be measured, for example, by residents' willingness to intervene when trouble arises, including on behalf of the community's youth or a willingness to participate in collective action for the common good, such as preventing violence. Social cohesion is a critical component of collective efficacy, and the presence of both correlates with lower rates of violent crime and better health outcomes (Cohen, Farley, & Mason, 2003; Lochner, Kawachi, Brennan, & Buka, 2003). In communities that have higher rates of community trauma, there is less capacity to take collective action, thus reducing levels of political and social efficacy.

Place: The Physical/Built Environment

Community trauma manifests within the physical environment as dangerous public spaces and a high availability of unhealthy products such as alcohol and cigarettes. Economic and social changes over the past 50 years have created communities where high rates of poverty are concentrated in certain neighborhoods with crumbling infrastructure: dilapidated buildings and deteriorating roads, poor transportation services, and crippled local economies. There is a mutually reinforcing relationship between these deteriorated and unhealthy physical environments, violence, and community trauma.

In the past two decades, many inner-city neighborhoods have seen increased government and private investment, which has led to an improvement in the infrastructure and physical/built environment, higher property values, and large-scale displacement of poor and working-class communities. As a result of this process of gentrification, many communities that are poor in affluent cities have been displaced to suburbs and smaller cities with fewer resources, where the poor quality of the physical environment is replicated with fewer social services available. The result of this process is the increased isolation of communities and the intensification of community trauma.

Equitable Opportunity: The Economic Educational Environment

Within the community environment, trauma is interwoven with intergenerational poverty, relocated businesses and jobs, long-term unemployment and limited employment, and government- and private-sector disinvestment. Over the past 40 years, multiple studies have shown the role of concentrated poverty in creating "neighborhood effects," including violence, crime and delinquency, poor education, psychological distress, and various health problems. The stressors of living with inadequate access to economic and educational opportunities, and/or inequitable opportunities, play a big role in trauma at the community level. What's more, the economic and social processes that result in the concentration of poverty and the urban decay of inner-city neighborhoods can damage the sociocultural environment of many inner-city communities, exacerbating the potential for community trauma. Figure 11.2 describes how the three domains intersect and interact.

The symptoms of community trauma in the three domains are the product of decades of economic, political, and social isolation; lack of investment in the maintenance and improvement of the built environment; loss

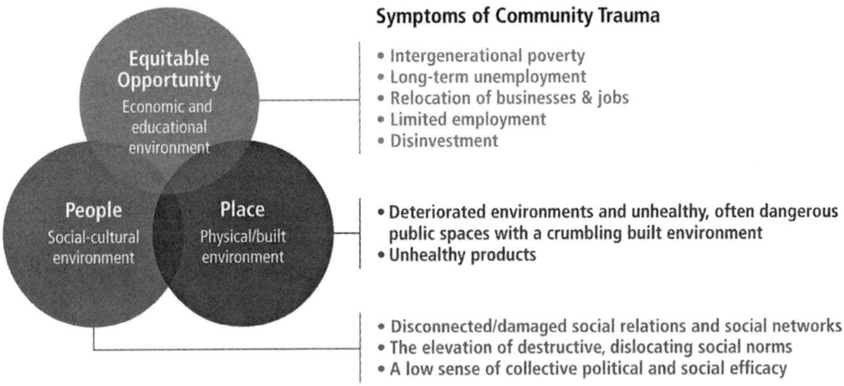

Figure 11.2 Symptoms of Community Trauma across Three Domains

Source: Adverse Community Experiences and Resilience: A Framework for Addressing and Preventing Community Trauma (Pinderhughes, Davis, & Williams, 2015).

of social capital with the flight of middle-class families; concentrated poverty; and exposure to high levels of violence. In traumatized communities, these three domains comprise an environment that does not promote resiliency. Instead, the community environment contributes to poor health, illness, and injury by exacerbating trauma and contributing to the production of violence.

Violence and Trauma at the Community Level

Violence, including experiencing violence, the threat of violence and loss as a result of violence, as well as structural violence, all contribute to individual and community trauma. At the community level, trauma means both that multiple people are traumatized and that community processes, environments, and relationships are negatively impacted.

The community-level symptoms in the three THRIVE domains, as well as individual symptoms of trauma (e.g., emotional numbing, avoidance, and increased arousal), increase the risk of future violence. The relationship is cyclical: violence contributes to the production of trauma, and trauma, in turn, contributes to the production of violence. A community that experiences community trauma without healing does not necessarily have the full capacity and efficacy to organize effectively around solutions to address threats against being a healthy community, including violence and structural violence. What's more, the symptoms of community trauma may provide a basis for legitimizing structural violence—such as justifying enhanced suppression and containment tactics—and this can further contribute to community trauma. Figure 11.3 illustrates how violence produces individual and community trauma and how trauma symptoms then feed back into, and exacerbate, violence.

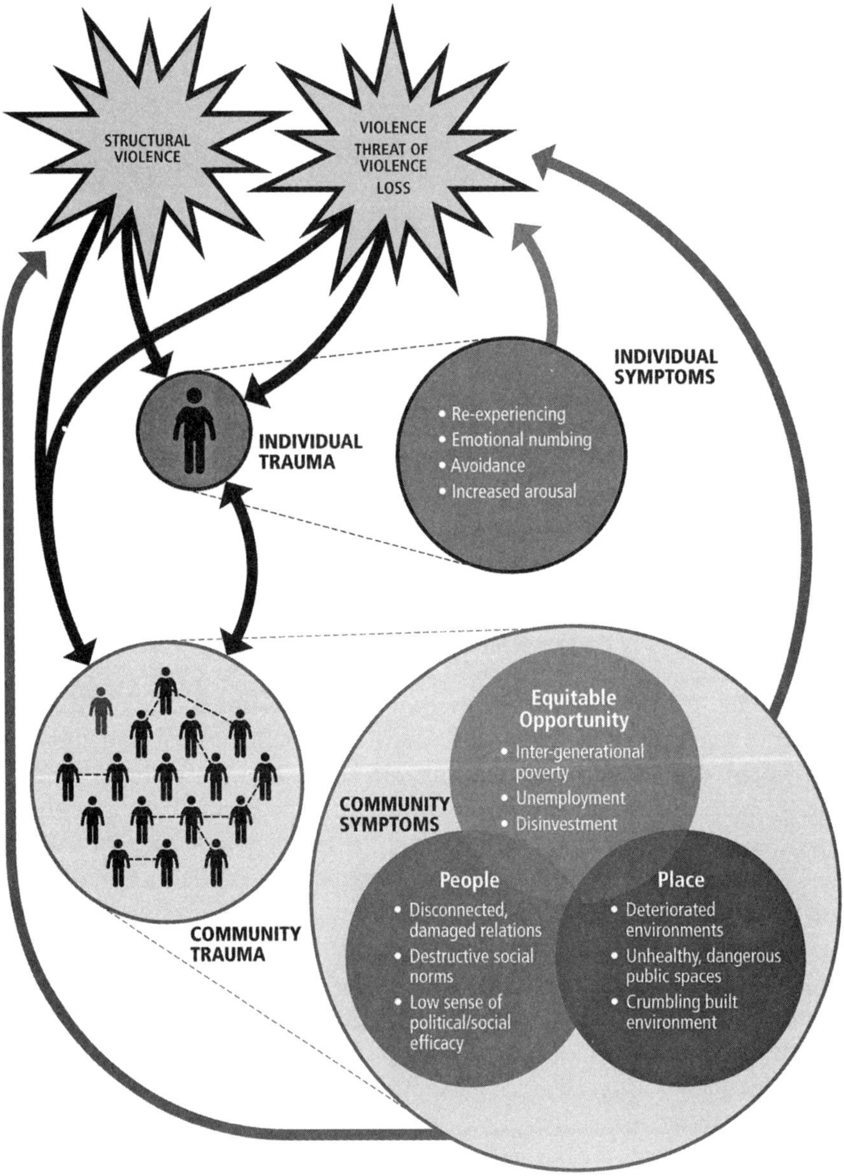

Figure 11.3 The Production of Trauma from Violence

Source: Adverse Community Experiences and Resilience: A Framework for Addressing and Preventing Community Trauma (Pinderhughes, Davis, & Williams, 2015).

Healing as a Starting Point to Sustainably Address Trauma

In neighborhoods with high rates of interpersonal and structural violence, both individual and community trauma need to be addressed. Healing from this violence is a starting point toward community agency, which is necessary for effective collective action to find solutions to improve community health. Individual approaches to healing include trauma-informed care and mental health services. At the community level, healing may take different forms, including healing circles and vigils or instituting restorative justice practices and community dialogs that acknowledge transgressions and identify solutions for moving forward. Healing circles are a collective community approach to psychological and emotional healing that is deeply rooted in the traditional practices of indigenous people. Many Native American communities have used the healing circle as a way of bringing people of all ages together for the purposes of collective teaching, listening, learning, and healing.

Mental health practitioners, youth workers, teachers, and community organizers have noted the importance of recognizing the pain that has been endured by young people for generations and the value of lifting up usually silenced or missing voices and bringing them to the table (Nunez, personal communication, April 6, 2015). Many communities around the country have developed healing approaches that draw on culturally based knowledge and practices. The case study in this chapter, from Tacoma, Washington, provides one example. Some of the most effective strategies are based in indigenous, black, and Latino cultural practices, values, and rituals. By engaging intergenerational community members, they utilize reconnection to and reaffirmation of cultural identity to support the healing process.

Just as individual and community trauma exacerbate each other, individual healing contributes to community healing, and vice-versa. Both individual and community healing contribute to reductions in trauma. This, in turn, contributes to reductions in the risk associated with the likelihood of violence and increased well-being and resilience for individuals, families, and communities. Healing also paves the way for implementing specific strategies within the three domains of people, place, and equitable opportunity. In the following case study, we describe how a coalition in Tacoma began to heal community trauma by including community members in the planning process of an initiative to improve the mental health and well-being of men and boys—a powerful example of collective efficacy.

Addressing and Preventing Community Trauma: Strategies in Three Domains

Some of the most effective community-level strategies to address community trauma build on indigenous knowledge, expertise, and leadership to build culturally relevant and appropriate strategies. Strategies that address community trauma strengthen community resilience, which prevents future community trauma and lessens the impact of future adversity. Just as individuals develop resiliency in the face of adversity, strategies that address community trauma build a community's capacity to handle continued adversity and to take action to reduce violence and structural violence. Ideally, community strategies focus simultaneously on the sociocultural environment, physical/built environment, and economic environment, since the symptoms of community trauma manifest within and across them (see Figure 11.4). Case study no. 2 describes improvements to the built environment through replacing substandard public housing while improving the sociocultural environment in the southeast section of San Francisco.

Figure 11.4 Community Strategies to Address and Prevent Community Trauma

Source: Adverse Community Experiences and Resilience: A Framework for Addressing and Preventing Community Trauma (Pinderhughes, Davis, & Williams, 2015).

Sociocultural strategies to address and prevent community trauma include rebuilding social relationships, particularly intergenerational relations; revitalizing damaged or broken social networks and social support infrastructure; holding healing circles that provide spaces for expression of and healing from individual trauma while reinforcing and strengthening intergenerational relationships; changing the narrative about the community and its people; and strengthening and elevating social norms that promote or encourage healthy behaviors, community connection, and community-oriented positive social norms. Others include organizing and promoting regular positive community activity, providing a voice and element of power for community members to shift and change environmental and structural factors, and promoting and restoring a connection to cultural identity.

Case Example 1: Making Connections—Building Community Power to Heal and Thrive

In Tacoma, Washington, a coalition was formed to develop a community-based approach to improve men and boys' mental health. Addressing community trauma immediately became a priority. The coalition was funded as a part of Making Connections for Mental Health and Wellbeing among Men and Boys (Prevention Institute, 2014), a national initiative, funded by the Movember Foundation, of 16 communities that are transforming community conditions that influence mental well-being. In the Tacoma coalition, the initial concerns that emerged about men and boy's health included needs around mental health; individual and community trauma stemming from high rates of violence, poverty, displacement, and unjust policing; and unsafe physical environments. The Tacoma-Pierce County Health Department (TPCHD) led the development of the coalition, which includes many community organizations and service providers working with boys and young men of color. The coalition operates on a collaborative leadership model, where all members have equal say in efforts.

"Our communities have known for a very long time . . . that structures like racism and inequality and unequal distribution of power create the foundation for how we experience trauma and how we respond to trauma, and therefore should drive how we undo that," said Victor Rodriguez, of TPCHD, a partner in the Making Connections initiative.

Using Prevention Institute's THRIVE tool, the Tacoma coalition developed community-level strategies to understand and improve social, physical, and economic conditions in the community environment that influence mental health and well-being for men, boys, and LGBTQ people of color. Their overarching strategy was to build community power to heal and thrive, in part by intentionally engaging community members each step of the way, starting with the early planning process. TPCHD and its partners, Hilltop Urban Gardens, the Tacoma Urban League, and Centro Latino, started by working with 16 partner organizations to conduct surveys, lead focus groups, and gather life stories from community members to inform their priorities.

The coalition then convened a People's Movement Assembly (PMA), a community organizing tool to collectively analyze and develop solutions to community problems. As part of the data collection process, the PMA incorporated culturally grounded activities, including a community altar, music, and art. Young men used theater, spoken word, and other approaches to teach and share their experiences with everything from police brutality to job interviews. Young children also participated, painting messages on rocks to contribute to the community Black Lives Matter memorial garden hosted by the Hilltop Urban Gardens.

The community emerged with three key findings: (1) community trauma is pervasive in the forms of police brutality, violence, discrimination (racial as well as gender), and inequitable access to resources to meet basic needs; (2) authentic social connections support healthy interpersonal relationships and neighborhood cohesion; and (3) there is a need to build and support community-level action and civic engagement in local fiscal and policy decision making. These findings informed their goals for their upcoming work: (1) strengthen social connections, (2) strengthen community resilience, and (3) improve access and utilization of quality resources.

Rodriguez said that using a truly community-based data collection process has been essential in fostering trust, resilience, and healing. "We wanted to move away from traditional data collection approaches that are very extractive, where you only come to communities when you need something or when a group needs to produce a report," he said. "What ends up happening is that communities lose respect and trust. We were trying to counter some of these structural norms that produce structural violence. We don't have all the answers, but at a minimum we hope to bring these norms to light."

Case Example 2: Trauma-Informed Community Building

Founded in 1983, BRIDGE Housing was hired to redevelop two large public housing developments, Jordan Downs in the Watts neighborhood of Los Angeles and Potrero Terrace and Annex (PTA) in San Francisco. Both developments suffered from years of physical neglect. It was also evident that public housing's historical practices in the United States, along with those of other government and private sectors, had resulted in a lack of trust between residents and the housing developer.

BRIDGE Housing's Trauma-Informed Community Building (TICB) model emerged out of the need to acknowledge and address the trauma that had been experienced by public housing residents. TICB addressed the challenges to traditional community building by taking into account residents' emotional needs and recognizing the impact of pervasive trauma on a community (Weinstein, Wolin, & Rose, 2014). In working with residents of the PTA public housing complex, BRIDGE engaged them in a way that felt comfortable to them by hosting a series of listening sessions to understand what the community wanted, what they saw as their strengths, and how they envisioned their future. Then residents were offered accessible and predictable opportunities that most everyone could engage in, such as a walking club, Zumba, monthly cooking workshops, and a community garden. As a result of participating in TICB activities, BRIDGE residents have experienced improved health and safety outcomes, including reduced depression, improved self-esteem, greater feelings of happiness and relaxation, increased physical activity, a healthier diet, and maintenance of a healthy weight (Hope SF Learning Center, 2015). Residents also reported that they felt a sense of safety while participating in the activities, even if the immediate surroundings were unsafe (Hope SF Learning Center, 2015). The location of activities in neutral territories and the presence of consistent staff help to create these localized "Zones of Safety," which can, in turn, promote cohesion and connectedness among residents.

By engaging over 520 residents in TICB activities in 2015 alone, BRIDGE has helped ensure that more residents become active community members and feel increasingly connected within their community (BRIDGE Housing Corporation, 2016). Community-building activities have fostered new and meaningful connections between residents and have served as the foundation for the development of cross-cultural and multigenerational relationships (Hope SF Learning Center, 2015). Another major outcome of BRIDGE's work in PTA has included breaking down the barriers between residents of PTA public housing and the neighboring North Potrero neighborhood (BRIDGE Housing Corporation, 2016). As one resident put it, "You meet a lot of different people from different races that live up here in the community with me that I would never have known if I wouldn't come to these activities. I probably would have seen them but I wouldn't have known them, but now I know them" (Hope SF Learning Center, 2015).

Through BRIDGE's work in the PTA community, they have built an innovative, successful, and replicable approach to community building that accounts for community trauma. BRIDGE has also led a major shift in how affordable housing developers imagine their role, develop partnerships, and engage with residents. BRIDGE's work highlights the role that the community development sector can play in addressing trauma and promoting community healing and serves as a model for multiple sectors coming together to promote community resilience and healing.

Toward Community Resilience in the Context of Adversity

The elements of a resilient community are spelled out in THRIVE (see Figure 11.5). As a whole, THRIVE is a *framework* for fostering community resilience; a *process* for engaging community members and practitioners in changing community conditions to achieve better health and safety outcomes; and *a tool* for assessing the status of community conditions and setting priorities to improve health, safety, and health equity (Davis, Cook, & Cohen, 2005). Using THRIVE starts with identifying the factors in the sociocultural, physical/built, and economic environments that affect health, safety, and health equity and then determining community-led strategies for improving those factors. These strategies have a twofold mission regarding community trauma: to spur community healing and to build community resilience—that is, the ability to thrive in spite of adverse events or experiences. A resilient community reinforces community-level

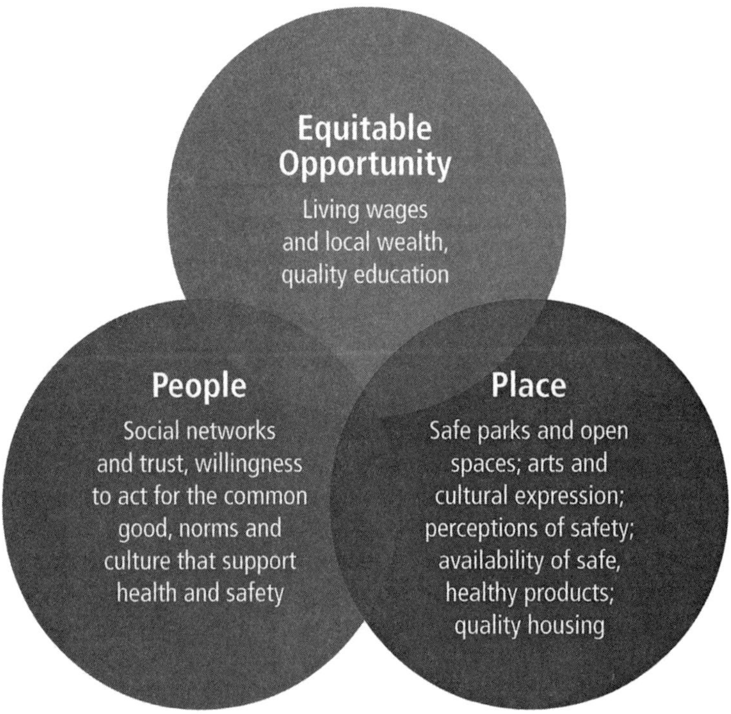

Figure 11.5 Elements of a Resilient Community

Source: Adverse Community Experiences and Resilience: A Framework for Addressing and Preventing Community Trauma (Pinderhughes, Davis, & Williams, 2015).

strategies to address trauma, which helps to protect against the onset of trauma in the first place, as well as contributes to healing.

Figure 11.6 depicts a model for moving from trauma to community resilience and increased well-being for individuals, families, and communities.

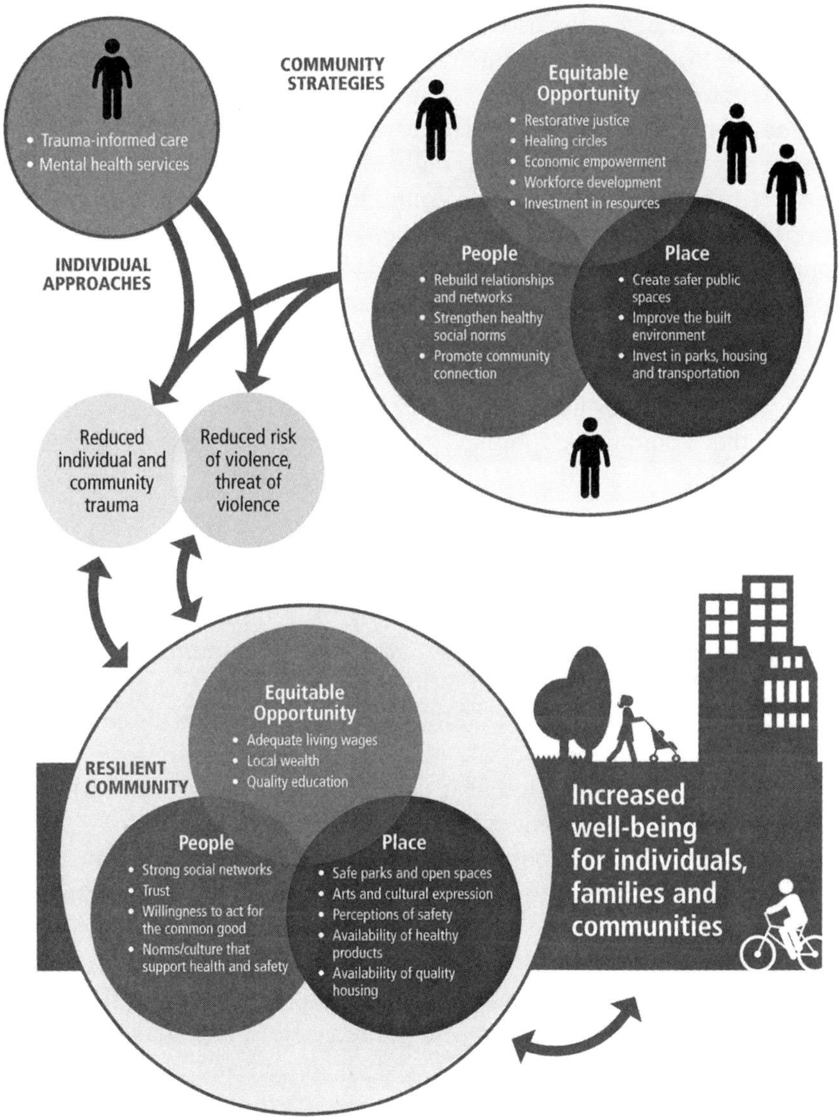

Figure 11.6 Promoting Community Resilience: From Trauma to Well-Being

Source: Adverse Community Experiences and Resilience: A Framework for Addressing and Preventing Community Trauma (Pinderhughes, Davis, & Williams, 2015).

In neighborhoods with high rates of interpersonal violence combined with exposure to structural violence, both individual and community trauma need to be addressed.

As depicted in Figure 11.6, individual approaches to trauma include trauma-informed care and mental health services. Effective approaches contribute to individual healing and, in part, to community healing. Community strategies focus on the sociocultural environment (people), the physical/built environment (the place), and the economic environment (equitable opportunity) because the symptoms of community trauma manifest within each. The community strategies contribute to community healing and also help build community resilience.

A resilient community is a community that can thrive in spite of adverse events or experiences. A resilient community in turn reinforces community strategies to address trauma, helping to protect against the onset of trauma and contributing to community healing.

Individual and community healing result in reductions in trauma. These, in turn, contribute to reductions in violence and increased well-being. Similarly, a resilient community contributes to reductions in individual and community trauma and violence, as well as increased well-being for individuals, families, and communities.

Conclusion: It Is Time to Take on Adverse Community Experiences

It is time to expand our understanding of trauma as something that does impact not only individuals but also whole communities. While the rise in trauma-informed care for individuals is incredibly important, it is essential that attention go beyond individuals, and beyond a sole focus on treatment after exposure to traumatic conditions. Addressing trauma effectively demands attention at a *population* level and consideration of what can be done to prevent trauma in the first place.

This is difficult but important and cutting-edge work. Since most systems and funding are set up neither to address trauma at the community level nor to prevent it in the first place, this work demands that communities, and those working on behalf of communities, think outside the box. Those working within communities must meet the communities where they are—drawing on solutions that emerge from and make sense for each community's needs, strengths, and challenges and keeping a broad variety of community members intricately involved in the work.

Many of those who live and work in impacted areas share the sense that whole communities can be traumatized, but until now there has been no framework for understanding the systematic effects of trauma at a community level—and how community trauma undermines both individual and collective resiliency in the face of violence and other kinds of adversity. The emerging set of strategies outlined in this chapter holds great promise for promoting community healing and developing safer, healthier, and more resilient communities. The time to take on Adverse *Community* Experiences is now.

Note

1. Some of the text and figures in this chapter have been reprinted with permission from Pinderhughes, H., Davis, R., & Williams, M.(2015). *Adverse community experiences and resilience: A framework for addressing and preventing community trauma.* Oakland, CA: Prevention Institute.

References

Albee, G.W. (1983). Psychopathology, prevention, and the just society. *Journal of Primary Prevention*, 4(1), 5–40.

Breslau, N., Davis, G.C., Andreski, P., & Peterson, E. (1991). Traumatic events and posttraumatic stress disorder in an urban population of young adults. *Archives of General Psychiatry*, 48(3), 216–222.

BRIDGE Housing Corporation. (2016). *Partners in progress case study.* Retrieved from http://www.bridgehousing.com/news-media/publications

Burtle, A. (2013). *What is structural violence?.* Retrieved from http://www.structuralviolence.org/structural-violence/

Cohen, D.A., Farley, T.A., & Mason, K. (2003) Why is poverty unhealthy? Social and physical mediators. *Social Science & Medicine*, 57(9), 1631–1641.

CSDH. (2008). *Closing the gap in a generation: Health equity through action on the social determinants of health.* Geneva, Switzerland: World Health Organization.

Davis, R., Cook, D., & Cohen, L. (2005). A community resilience approach to reducing ethnic and racial disparities in health. *American Journal of Public Health*, 95(12), 2168–2173.

Davis, R.A., & Tsao, B. (2014). *A multi-sector approach to preventing violence: A companion to multi-sector partnerships for preventing violence, a collaboration multiplier guide.* Oakland, CA: Prevention Institute.

Felitti, V.J., Anda, R.F., Nordenberg, D., Williamson, D.F., Spitz, A.M., Edwards, V., Koss, M.P., & Marks, J.S. (1998). Relationship of childhood abuse and household dysfunction to many of the leading causes of death in adults: The Adverse Childhood Experiences (ACE) Study. *American Journal of Preventive Medicine*, 14(4), 245–258.

Funk J.B., Bechtoldt Baldacci, H., Pasold T., & Baumgardner J. (2004). Violence exposure in real-life, video games, television, movies, and the internet: Is there desensitization? *Journal of Adolescence*, 27(1), 23–39.

Gorman-Smith D., & Tolan P. (1998). The role of exposure to community violence and developmental problems among inner-city youth. *Development and Psychopathology*, *10*, 101–116.

Hart, S. N. (2007). Reflections on the implications of re-victimization patterns of children and youth as clarified by the research of Finkelhor, Ormrod and Turner. *Child Abuse & Neglect, 31*(5), 473–477. doi:10.1016/j.chiabu.2007.03.014

Hope SF Learning Center. (2015). *Trauma informed community building evaluation: A formative evaluation of the ticb model and its implementation in potrero hill.* San Francisco, CA: Hope SF Learning Center.

Kessler, R. C., & Üstün, B. (Eds.). (2008). *The WHO World Mental Health Surveys: Global perspectives on the epidemiology of mental disorders.* New York, NY: Cambridge University Press.

Lochner, K. A., Kawachi, I., Brennan, R. T., & Buka, S. L. (2003). Social capital and neighborhood mortality rates in Chicago. *Social Science & Medicine, 56*(8), 1797–805. doi:10.1016/S0277–9536(02)00177–6

McCann, I. L., & Pearlman, L. A. (1990). Vicarious traumatization: A contextual model for understanding the effects of trauma on helpers. *Journal of Traumatic Stress, 3*(1), 131–149.

Pinderhughes, H., Davis, R., & Williams, M. (2015). *Adverse community experiences and resilience: A framework for addressing and preventing community trauma.* Oakland, CA: Prevention Institute.

Prevention Institute. (2014). *Making connections for mental health and wellbeing among men and boy in the U.S.* Oakland, CA: Prevention Institute.

Resnick, H. S., Kilpatrick, D. G., Dansky, B. S., Saunders, B. E., & Best, C. L. (1993). Prevalence of civilian trauma and posttraumatic stress disorder in a representative national sample of women. *Journal of Consulting and Clinical Psychology*, *61*(6), 984.

Sampson, R. J., Raudenbush, S. W., & Earls, F. (1997). Neighborhoods and violent crime: A multilevel study of collective efficacy. *Science, 227*(5328), 918–924.

Samhsa-HRSA Center for Integrated Health Solutions. (2017). *Trauma*. Retrieved from http://www.integration.samhsa.gov/clinical-practice/trauma

Weinstein, E., Wolin, J., & Rose, S. (2014) *Trauma informed community building: A model for strengthening community in trauma affected neighborhoods.* Retrieved from http://bridgehousing.com/PDFs/TICB.Paper5.14.pdf

World Health Organization. (2009). *Violence prevention, the evidence: Changing cultural and social norms that support violence.* Geneva, Switzerland: World Health Organization.

World Health Organization, Violence Prevention Alliance. (2017). *Definition and typology of violence.* Retrieved from http://www.who.int/violenceprevention/approach/definition/en/

CHAPTER 12

U.S. Federal Policy Efforts to Address Violence and Trauma in the Lives of Children

Ellen Gerrity, Diane Elmore Borbon, and Holly M. Strain

In recent decades, the impact of violence and trauma has become an important national issue and a larger part of federal policy, scientific research, and service delivery (Friedman, 2016; National Center for PTSD, 2017). In the 1990s and since, federal research and policy initiatives have had a greater focus on the short- and long-term health and mental health impact of trauma and violence on children (Centers for Disease Control and Prevention [CDC], n.d.; Felitti et al., 1998; Putnam, Harris, & Putnam, 2013; Substance Abuse and Mental Health Services Administration [SAMHSA], 2014), leading to increased federal funding and new research and policies in some areas.

Policy change is often driven by research findings that provide details about the scope and cost of trauma and violence and highlight the prevalence of exposure to traumatic events. The 2007 Great Smoky Mountains Study (Copeland, Keeler, Angold, & Costello, 2007), a representative longitudinal study of children, found that by age 16, more than 67 percent of the children had been exposed to one or more traumatic events, such as child maltreatment, domestic violence, or sexual assault. According to a 2011

Office of Juvenile Justice and Delinquency Prevention study of children ages 0 through 17, about 58 percent of the children surveyed were exposed to violence within the past year (Finkelhor, Turner, Shattuck, & Hamby, 2013).

Some areas of trauma, such as child abuse, have been specifically tracked by state or federal government agencies. The rate of substantiated reports of child maltreatment in fiscal year 2015 was 9.2 per 1,000 children ages 0 through 17, with children under age 1 having the highest rate of 24.2 reports per 1,000 children, according to the Administration for Children and Families (ACF; U.S. Department of Health and Human Services [HHS], 2017). Such early exposure to abuse can result in many health and other problems later in life. Early findings from the Adverse Childhood Experiences Study (ACES), and additional studies now coordinated by CDC, have shown that adverse experiences predispose children toward negative trajectories from infancy through adulthood (Felitti et al., 1998; Gilbert et al., 2015), with studies showing higher rates of mental health, substance use, and other health problems, increasing with greater exposure. A recent study (Mirhashem et al., 2017) found that maltreatment experienced as a child was associated with posttraumatic stress disorder, opioid use, and other substance-related problems as an adult and recommended that trauma history and symptoms be addressed as part of opioid addiction treatment.

Evidence is clear that early childhood exposure to trauma and violence can be costly. Findings from a 2012 CDC study estimated that the total lifetime economic burden associated with U.S. child maltreatment cases was approximately $124 billion (Fang, Brown, Florence, & Mercy, 2012). The Perryman Group (2014) calculated that the lifetime costs of child maltreatment go far beyond the physical and psychological consequences. When the effects related to social services, criminal justice, and education are included, costs can increase by hundreds of thousands of dollars per victim. Similar findings are illustrated in resources on the Childhood Adversity Narratives website (www.canarratives.org).

Research advances also contributed to policy changes that sought to integrate trauma-informed approaches in specific child-serving systems, such as education, child welfare, and juvenile justice. Larger mental health policy reform efforts that have been underway for many years, including the "parity" movement that pushed for fairness in insurance coverage of mental health and addiction treatment, and the integration of such parity principles into the Affordable Care Act health-care reform law (P.L. 111–148), have also expanded access to child trauma care.

In 2017, many programs and policies exist in the context of sweeping proposals to change federal policies and severely reduce funding for health-care and other domestic spending for children and families. The immediate and future impact of these changes is uncertain, but understanding the history and purpose of major child trauma-related initiatives can provide a context for what has been of value. To that end, we will highlight federal laws and agency programs that have historically focused on violence and child trauma services, indicate how these efforts have been part of other major health reform efforts, identify key policy gaps that remain, and describe the role that health and mental health providers can have in advancing policy change. This chapter will focus primarily on the legislative branch of government; federal policies for infants and very young children will be addressed separately in Chapter 13 in this volume.

Selected Landmark Federal Laws Related to Child Trauma and Violence

In this section, we review selected landmark laws related to child trauma and violence, listed in Box 12.1.

Child Abuse Prevention and Treatment Act

In 1974, Congress enacted a fundamental federal law to guide child protection, the Child Abuse Prevention and Treatment Act (CAPTA; P.L. 93–247). CAPTA provided federal funding to states in support of prevention, assessment, investigation, prosecution, and treatment activities (Child Welfare Information Gateway, 2011). Specifically, the law-authorized formula (state-administered) grants to improve their child protective services; competitive funds to institutions for research, technical assistance, and demonstration projects related to prevention, assessment, and treatment of child abuse and neglect; and funding to all states for community-based activities to prevent child abuse and neglect (Stoltzfus, 2017). The law also established the National Clearinghouse on Child Abuse and Neglect Information that supported the collection and dissemination of data related to prevalence, scope, and change over time.

Box 12.1 Landmark Laws Related to Child Trauma and Violence

- Child Abuse Prevention and Treatment Act (CAPTA)
- National Child Traumatic Stress Network (NCTSN)
- National Children's Alliance (NCA)/Children's Advocacy Centers (CACs)
- The Family Violence Prevention and Service Act and the Violence against Women Act (VAWA)

The original CAPTA also established a federal office to coordinate CAPTA activities, now known as the Office on Child Abuse and Neglect (OCAN) within the Children's Bureau in the U.S. Department of Health and Human Services (2012). OCAN administers state and discretionary grants, provides technical assistance to states, identifies issues of focus for research and demonstration programs, and creates training materials for the field. Since its enactment, CAPTA has been reauthorized seven times and refined by many amendments (Child Welfare Information Gateway, 2011; U.S. Department of Health and Human Services, 2011). Over time, CAPTA has focused on responding to the incidence and impact of child abuse, as well as prevention and multisector approaches and partnerships (National Low Income Housing Coalition, 2014), but funding levels have remained low.

Advocates continue to urge Congress to reauthorize, appropriately fund, and fully implement CAPTA. Current advocacy priorities have focused on increasing funding to states for community-based child abuse prevention, early intervention as part of disability programs such as those in the Individuals with Disabilities Education Act (U.S. Department of Education, n.d.), and support for children whose parents with substance use disorder (SUD) have led to child abuse or neglect (Prevent Child Abuse America, 2016).

National Child Traumatic Stress Network

In response to a growing understanding of the breadth and depth of childhood exposure to trauma, the U.S. Congress created the National Child Traumatic Stress Network (NCTSN; www.nctsn.org) as part of the 2000 Children's Health Act administered by SAMHSA. The NCTSN mission is to raise the standard of care and increase access to services for children and families who experience traumatic events. As of 2017, the NCTSN included 82 funded centers and over 160 affiliate (formerly funded) members working in hospitals, universities, and community-based programs in 44 states. Many centers also have funding for services or research from other federal, state, and local sources, and many of the children served rely on Medicaid for health, mental health, and addiction care. NCTSN members integrate trauma-informed and evidence-based practices in many types of child-serving systems by providing treatment, services, intervention development, training, data collection and analysis, program evaluation, product development, policy analysis, and rapid crisis response.

In 2016, the NCTSN was reauthorized to continue its work serving children and families involved in all child-serving systems, across all trauma types (including acute natural disasters and shootings) and all ages (including supporting first responders, frontline providers, caregivers, and adults with child trauma histories, in addition to children), and providing training, resources, and partnerships with many professional organizations, policymakers, and the public. The NCTSN has been built on a model of collaboration among researchers, clinicians, community providers, families, youth, and partners, integrating many perspectives to improve culturally appropriate and evidence-based care and move scientific advances quickly into practice across the United States (see later in this chapter for more information about the NCTSN's genesis and history).

National Children's Alliance/Children's Advocacy Centers

Formally established as the National Children's Alliance (NCA) in 1988, the Children's Advocacy Centers (CACs) program has a long history of advocating for children who experience child abuse and neglect. The NCA is the national association and accrediting body for the CACs, providing leadership, support, accreditation opportunities, financial assistance, training, technical assistance, and research. It also provides education to communities, child abuse professionals, and the 795 children's advocacy centers throughout the United States (NCA, n.d.).

In 2015, CACs were located in all 50 states and the District of Columbia where they served 311,688 children and provided prevention training and information to over 1.8 million individuals. Nearly all CACs are funded through multiple sources, including the Victims of Child Abuse Act.

CACs are designed to be child-focused facilities that offer safety, security, and a wide range of victim services for children and families who have been exposed to violence and abuse. These community-based centers and their staff serve as part of the team that responds to allegations of child physical and sexual abuse and neglect, bringing together law enforcement, criminal justice, child protection, forensic, prosecution, mental health, medical, and victim advocacy professionals in a safe setting to investigate abuse, hold offenders accountable, and help children heal from the trauma of abuse (NCA, 2016).

Current challenges for CACs are similar to those facing other programs serving children affected by trauma: increasing national need, insufficient funding, and an uncertain future related to federal policies. Based on an internal review of CAC member activities, the NCA is working to shape its future priorities to meet these challenges (NCA, 2016).

The Family Violence Prevention and Service Act and the Violence against Women Act

Two key federal laws aimed at addressing intimate partner violence are the Family Violence Prevention and Service Act (FVPSA) and the Violence against Women Act (VAWA).

FVPSA was signed into law in 1984 as part of the Child Abuse Amendments of 1984 (P.L. 98–457) and was the first federal law to address domestic violence (Fernandes-Alcantara, 2015). It served as the primary federal initiative to support emergency shelter and related assistance for domestic violence victims (U.S. DHHS, Family and Youth Services Bureau, 2016) and is administered by ACF and CDC. The law provided support for direct services to victims and families; a national domestic violence hotline, which maintains a national database of services and provides referrals for victims and families; and domestic violence prevention activities through the Domestic Violence Prevention Enhancement and Leadership through Alliances (Fernandes-Alcantara, 2015). Several programs within CAPTA provided support for children exposed to family violence, including services for children in the state grant program and in the services, research, and mental health and trauma programs of the National Resource Center on Domestic Violence (Fernandes-Alcantara, 2015).

VAWA was signed into law in 1994 as part of the Violent Crime Control and Law Enforcement Act of 1994 (P.L. 103–322). While FVPSA focused on prevention and domestic violence services, VAWA targeted the crimes of intimate partner violence, dating violence, sexual assault, and stalking by improving the law enforcement and legal response to domestic violence. The majority of VAWA programs are administered by the Office of Violence against Women within the Department of Justice (DOJ), first established in 1995 and officially codified by Congress in 2002. Additional VAWA grants are administered by other federal agencies, including CDC and the DOJ Office of Justice Programs (Sacco, 2015).

Since its 1994 enactment, VAWA has been reauthorized three times, most recently in 2013, with key amendments added: (1) the reauthorization of the Trafficking Victims Protection Act (TVPA) of 2000 that integrated measures to combat human trafficking; (2) the expansion of Indian tribe authority to enforce domestic violence laws and related crimes against non-Indian individuals; and (3) the inclusion of a nondiscrimination provision in VAWA grant programs. The reauthorization also included measures to address the rape kit backlog in states (Sacco, 2015).

Additional child-relevant provisions in VAWA included requirements for victim restitution for specific federal sex offenses, for example, sexual abuse, sexual exploitation, and other abuse of children; grant programs for special populations, such as children and youth; special protections for battered nonimmigrant women and children; and prevention programs to enhance the safety of youth and children who are victims of or exposed to domestic violence, dating violence, sexual assault, stalking, or sex trafficking. Experts and advocates continued to urge policymakers to protect, enhance, and expand VAWA programs and funding, including those that support the needs of children and adolescents.

High-Risk Populations and Violence and Trauma

Federal efforts to improve services for children affected by violence and trauma have also been extended to specific populations with unique needs not addressed in current laws. As specific national crises such as trafficking, growing refugee and immigration challenges, discrimination against LGBTQ populations, and the opioid epidemic have moved to the forefront of political and policy debates, federal legislation and initiatives were developed to provide direction and resources to meet these needs.

Trafficking

According to the TVPA (P.L. 106–386), the sex trafficking of minors is defined as the recruitment, harboring, transportation, provision, or obtaining of a person under the age of 18 for the purposes of a commercial sex act, that is, any sex act for which anything of value is given to or received by any person. In cases of sex trafficking, when the trafficked person is under age 18, no proof of force, fraud, or coercion is required because children cannot consent to participation in commercial sex. According to a 2015 Congressional Research Service report (Finklea, Fernandes-Alcantara, & Siskin, 2015), the exact number of child victims of sex trafficking in the United States is unknown because of the differences in definitions and methodologies involved in various systems. However, estimates are available through the Polaris Project, which coordinates the National Human Trafficking Hotline: over 8,000 U.S. cases were reported in 2016 (Polaris Project, 2016). Research has shown that the majority of trafficked girls had prior child welfare involvement due in part to prior sexual abuse (Gragg, Petta, Bernstein, Eisen, & Quinn, 2007; Raphael & Shapiro, 2002; Stoltz et al., 2007). Sexual abuse history has consistently been identified as a risk factor for involvement in commercial sex (Institute of Medicine and National Research Council, 2013).

In early 2017, U.S. trafficking policy continued to be a bipartisan issue, with several bills introduced in the Senate and the House. The bills included new provisions related to training, monitoring situations internationally, expungement of criminal records for victims, and extension of the statute of limitations for victims to file civil actions.

Refugees and Immigrants

The UN High Commissioner for Refugees (UNHCR, 2016b) reported that in 2015 the number of refugees worldwide reached an all-time high: 65.6 million, with one of every 113 persons designated as a refugee, internally displaced, or seeking asylum. About half of these individuals were children, with the number of unaccompanied minors from El Salvador, Mexico, Guatemala, and Honduras substantially higher after 2011. As part of a MacArthur Foundation-funded UNHCR study (UNHCR, 2016a), children were interviewed regarding their reasons for leaving their country of origin and their experiences. Of the representative sample of 404 children interviewed, 58 percent reported they were forcibly displaced because they suffered or faced harm that indicated a potential or current need for international protection. The harm experienced by the children fell into two major categories: violence by organized armed criminals (48%) and violence in the home (21%).

In 2017, as the U.S administration proposed changes in immigration and deportation policies, concerns increased about the trauma impact on children and families who are abruptly separated, living under constant threat, or deported to dangerous situations (Harvard Law School, 2017; Murphey, 2016; Stein, 2017a, 2017b). Uncertainty continued regarding which policies may be established, continued, or expanded.

LGBTQ

LGBTQ youth face multiple risk factors related to trauma and violence. According to the Gay, Lesbian, & Straight Education Network (GLSEN) survey (Kosciw, Greytak, Giga, Villenas, & Danischewski, 2016), many LGBTQ youth reported being physically and verbally bullied (including electronic harassment), feeling unsafe at school, missing school because of the lack of safety, being told to leave their homes, and attempting suicide. Many chose not to report their experiences to the authorities, and of those who did, many reported that nothing was done to protect them or prevent the bullying.

According to the Human Rights Campaign, several laws were introduced with broad support in the 114th Congress, including the Every

Child Deserves a Family Act (which prohibited discrimination against same sex couples in foster care decisions) and the Student Nondiscrimination Act (which prohibited schools from discriminating against students based on sexual orientation and gender identity). A third bill, the Safe Schools Improvement Act, introduced in early 2017, required school districts in states that receive Elementary and Secondary Education Act funds to adopt codes of conduct specifically prohibiting bullying and harassment that is based on race, color, national origin, sex, disability, sexual orientation, gender identity, and religion. In 2017, the future of these efforts was uncertain, due to changing federal policies.

Substance Use Disorder

Recent major advances in supporting the needs of individuals and families faced with the problems related to substance use disorders (SUD) include the enactment of the 2016 Comprehensive Addiction and Recovery Act (CARA) and the 21st Century Cures (CURES) Act that authorized $500 billion over two years to increase access to treatment and services. The CURES law is further described in this chapter; the comprehensive CARA law covered many issues related to substance use, with some sections focusing on children.

The CARA law included provisions to fund new recovery programs in local communities, increase access to medication for opioid overdose, provide training for health-care providers and pharmacists, collaborate with criminal justice stakeholders related to incarcerated individuals suffering from addiction, and fund prescription drug monitoring programs. Specific language addressed the needs of children of parents with SUD, providing funding for (1) treatment of pregnant and postpartum women and their children; (2) the development of plans for safe care for infants with addiction; (3) children who may enter the child welfare system if parents with SUD are incarcerated; (4) building connections with child welfare agencies; and (5) outreach to families, including providing support services to children (Community Anti-Drug Coalitions of America, n.d.).

Relevant Health-Care Policies

In recent years, several comprehensive federal health initiatives have been launched, following decades of advocacy and many legislative and public debates. These initiatives have far-reaching implications for health-care delivery in general but also specifically for mental health, addiction, and other child trauma-related problems.

Mental Health Parity and Addiction Equity Act: Insurance Parity

The Paul Wellstone and Pete Domenici Mental Health Parity and Addiction Equity Act (MHPAEA; P.L. 110–343) was enacted in 2008 to end discriminatory health-care insurance practices against those with mental illness and/or SUD. The statute provides that plans cannot apply financial requirements or treatment limitations to mental health or substance use disorder (MH/SUD) benefits that are more restrictive than those applied to medical/surgical benefits. Most notably, the law aims to remedy both the financial and nonfinancial ways that plans limit access to MH/SUD care, often more so than plans do for other health conditions (www.parityispersonal.org; https://www.paritytrack.org/). Full compliance with the law would allow children who have experienced trauma and need mental health or addiction treatment to have greater access to care.

Final parity implementation regulations went into effect on January 1, 2014, for all private plans covered by MHPAEA, with final regulations implementing parity protections for Medicaid-managed care plans released in March 2016. The SAMHSA (http://www.samhsa.gov/health-financing/implementation-mental-health-parity-addiction-equity-act), Department of Labor (https://www.dol.gov/ebsa/mentalhealthparity/), and Center for Medicare & Medicaid Services (https://www.medicaid.gov/medicaid/benefits/bhs/index.html) agencies provide coordination and oversight. These regulations provided greater clarity on how plans must apply the nonfinancial treatment limit requirements and what specific information and which documents must be given to patients, providers, and their advocates. In 2017, advocates are focused on full implementation and enforcement of regulations.

Patient Protection and Affordable Care Act

In 2010, the Affordable Care Act (ACA; P.L. 111–148) expanded health-care delivery systems in the United States, with a goal to increasing access to health care for millions of Americans. The law included new protections for individuals with mental illness and SUD, thus allowing those seeking treatment for trauma-related health and mental health problems to have greater access to insurance and services. This was done primarily through the expansion of protections provided by MHPAEA (as described earlier). As a result, qualified health plans (individual and small group health plans offered inside and outside of the health insurance exchanges) and the benefits offered to specific Medicaid populations were required to include MH/SUD benefits as an essential health benefit as part of complying with the ACA.

In addition, the ACA included several provisions that affected survivors of domestic, sexual, and dating violence. Most notably, the ACA prohibited insurance companies, health-care providers, and health programs that receive federal financial assistance from denying coverage to women based on being a survivor of domestic or sexual violence. The ACA also included victims of violence and abuse in several new protections and programs (Futures Without Violence, 2012), and a provision that allowed for domestic violence screening without cost sharing.

In 2017, with efforts to repeal the ACA law, the future of these MH/SUD and domestic violence protections (Pear, 2017; Pear & Kaplan, 2017) remained uncertain.

21st Century Cures (CURES)

On December 13, 2016, President Obama signed the 21st Century Cures Act (P.L. 114–255; https://energycommerce.house.gov/cures), a sweeping biomedical innovation bill, into law. Some of the law's key MH/SUD provisions relevant to children and youth, which are based on specific Senate and House legislation (the Mental Health Reform Act [S. 2680 and HR 2646]), are summarized in Box 12.2.

Box 12.2 Key Provisions in 21st Century Cures

- Reauthorization of the NCTSN
- Programs for Early Intervention and Improved Access to Care for Children and Adolescents
- MHPAEA implementation and enforcement
- Funding to address the opioids misuse and overdose epidemic

Children's Recovery from Trauma

This section reauthorized the NCTSN, strengthening its broad mission that includes the collection and analysis of child outcome data and training based on evidence-based and trauma-informed treatments, interventions, and practices for NCTSN grantees, providers, and partners.

Programs for Early Intervention and Improved Access to Care for Children and Adolescents

As part of this section, the Public Health Service Act was modified to include early identification of children and adolescents who are at risk of SUD, SUD treatment services for those with co-occurring mental health and SUD problems, and assistance in obtaining treatment and recovery support services for pregnant and parenting women. In addition to these provisions, pediatricians were included as eligible providers for consultations regarding the treatment of pregnant and parenting women, and a program was established for intensive early intervention for young children who are at risk of developing mental illness. As of January 2019, children receiving Medicaid-covered inpatient psychiatric hospital services would be eligible for the full range of early and periodic screening, diagnostic, and treatment services.

Federal Oversight

This section strengthened federal leadership and accountability over MH/SUD programs. Included is a new position of Assistant Secretary for Mental Health and Substance Use within the U.S. Department of Health and Human Services who will be responsible for overseeing SAMHSA and promoting best practices. Similarly, a SAMHSA chief medical officer was established to advise on evidence-based and promising best practices emphasizing a clinical focus.

Insurance Parity Enforcement and Implementation

This section included provisions to enhance enforcement and implementation of MHPAEA. Specifically, federal agencies were required to issue a compliance program guide, report on enforcement actions related to MHPAEA, and audit a health plan if it is found to have repeatedly violated the parity law.

Funds to Address the Opioids Misuse and Overdose Epidemic

As part of this provision, $1 billion was authorized over two years for grants to states to amplify their efforts to combat the opioid misuse and overdose epidemic. The first $500 million was appropriated in the financial year (FY) 2017 federal budget. Funding for children was also included for several efforts: (1) for those who may enter the child welfare system if parents with SUD are incarcerated, (2) for building connections with child welfare agencies, and (3) for outreach to families and additional support services for children.

Child Trauma and Violence: Policy Gaps

Despite many years of advocacy and policy efforts, significant gaps remain in the national effort to address the needs of children exposed to trauma and violence. As noted earlier (Fang et al., 2012; The Perryman Group, 2014), the scope and cost of the problems are vast; insufficient funding is the biggest and most significant policy gap. Without sufficient funding, children may not receive timely treatment and support, and the consequences of trauma can be lifelong and severe (Felitti et al., 1998). The same children affected by trauma are often seen in multiple systems without sufficient attention to trauma histories; without attention to the impact of trauma, psychological development can be derailed and problems exacerbated over time. In Box 12.3, we have listed key barriers to treatment services for children affected by trauma.

Gaps in policy are often most apparent at the interface of clinical service delivery. In a 2016 survey (NCTSN, 2016), NCTSN respondents described the main policy and practical barriers to treatment and services for children affected by trauma. The identified barriers were low Medicaid reimbursements, time-limited nature of grant funds, confusing regulations related to private insurance reimbursements, restrictions on reimbursement eligibility due to the child's age or diagnosis, and limited or no funding that specifically supports evidence-based practices. These problems can lead to inadequate treatment and lack of access to care.

Box 12.3 Barriers to Treatment Services for Children Affected by Trauma

- Low Medicaid reimbursement rates
- Time-limited nature of funds
- Difficulties with private insurance reimbursement
- Restrictions on funding due to age or diagnosis
- Limited or no funding for evidence-based practices

Inadequate research funding also continues to be a problem, delaying or preventing important research on the impact of child trauma and the quality of effective treatment and intervention related to diagnosis. The National Institute of Mental Health significantly reduced its focus on trauma and violence research after 1998. Without focused research on child trauma, the understanding of how adult and child trauma differ in symptomology and treatment guidelines has lagged, leading to complications in clinical care, treatment planning, and reimbursement when established diagnosis symptomology (and their related codes required for insurance reimbursement) or SED (serious emotional disturbance) categories (required for Medicaid reimbursement) do not match the trauma experiences of children. At CDC, related research on the impact of gun violence was repeatedly specifically prohibited by congressional Republicans; appropriated funds could not be used to support any research related to gun violence, including research on the psychological consequences of exposure to violence for children. The ban resulted in a major gap in our scientific and clinical knowledge related to the causes of gun violence and the impact on children, families, and communities.

In 2017, some congressional legislation was shaped to address some of these gaps, even while research and services funding was uncertain. As an example, the Trauma-Informed Care for Children and Families Act (S. 774/HR 1757) included language to address the research funding gap, requiring a report on cross-National Institutes of Health (NIH) research activities with respect to child and adult trauma, describing the review process, the relevance of trauma to other health domains, and other information about the NIH involvement in such research. Other gaps addressed in the bill included the identification of best practices related to child trauma treatment and services, authorization within many federal programs to allow spending of funds for training related to child trauma, a law enforcement training center related to child trauma, grant funds for schools related to trauma, expansion of NCTSN funding authorization levels, CDC and Government Accountability Office (GAO) studies related to trauma, and other sections related to Medicaid and workforce issues.

Although not enacted as law, this continued interest in trauma appeared promising, but the concurrent congressional and administrative proposals to reduce Medicaid funding and other domestic spending in FY 2018 contributed to renewed alarm about the impact on children who need treatment and services for problems related to exposure to trauma. These concerns were outlined by several hundred organizations involved in health, mental health, and SUD work in a letter to relevant congressional committees in early 2017 (Arditi, 2017). They noted that 50 percent of Medicaid beneficiaries are children who face severe restrictions in their access to MH and substance use treatment if proposed changes in Medicaid expansion and eligibility were to be enacted. With 75 percent of MH conditions emerging by age 24 (Kessler et al., 2005), and the recognized long-term impact of early childhood adversities (Felitti et al., 1998), restricting access to early MH care could result in both short- and long-term MH and health consequences. They noted also the potential serious impact on school and child welfare programs, leading to more family disruption, out-of-home placements for children (a significant trauma that has its own long-term health effects), and reduced school services.

Value of Science, Practice, and Personal Narrative in Policy Change

The optimal development of effective child trauma and violence policies involves input from multiple perspectives: research, clinical practice, providers in child-serving system (e.g., juvenile justice, education, and child welfare), advocates, patients, survivors, and family members. Scientific and clinical expertise offers data and other evidence to support specific changes, while the experience of those exposed to violence and trauma provides the details about what is at stake and helps ensure that policies are shaped to meet the real needs of survivors. Frontline providers offer real-world examples of professional challenges and barriers to establishing new policies. Experts in the regulatory and economic aspects of health-care delivery are essential to ensure successful implementation, and advocacy experts can offer a historical and political context to help advance and sustain effective policies.

Effectively Communicating with Policymakers

Regardless of the policy issue at hand, effectively informing and influencing public policies requires multiple steps, including identifying the policy issues of interest or importance, determining who has the authority to grant the request, communicating and developing relationships with relevant policymakers and agency officials, identifying an appropriate advocacy approach, providing scientific and clinical expertise to inform the policymaking process, sharing personal and constituent stories of relevance, and participating in policy and political activities to advance your issue (American Psychological Association [APA]PsycAdvocate®, 2012). Stakeholder involvement in policy change is needed within all levels and branches of government, including the executive, legislative, and judicial branch, each having distinct responsibilities for developing, implementing, and evaluating policies and laws. No matter what specific role a stakeholder may have, or the level of government, communicating regularly with policymakers is step one toward influencing policy change. In Box 12.4, we outline guidelines for communication with policymakers.

Box 12.4 Communication Guidelines

Communication with policymakers is increasingly easy to do in the digital age. Regular contact is building a relationship with representatives and communicating the policy changes that are needed. Contact information for members of Congress can be found at www.congress.gov, www.house.gov, and www.senate.gov. Details about executive branch offices and federal agency departments are available at https://www.usa.gov/federal-agencies/.

In practical terms, effective communication with policymakers includes:

- a brief introduction of yourself and the purpose of your outreach;
- expert information (e.g., data/statistics);
- anecdotal information (e.g., federal, state, or district examples);
- specific request; and
- concluding words of appreciation and offer to follow up.

Image 12.1 Rally for the Mental Health Parity and Addiction Equity Act (MHPAEA); September 17, 2008, Washington, D.C. Speaker at podium: Former Congressman Patrick Kennedy, with other speakers: David Wellstone (son of the late Senator Paul Wellstone), Rep. James Clyburn, former Rep. Jim Ramstad, and former Senator Chris Dodd.

Cultivating Champions

All effective policy action or change requires the support of policymakers who are willing to serve as champions for an issue, cause, or particular policy effort. Policymakers can develop an interest in supporting policies to address child violence or trauma for a number of different reasons. Some are committed to an issue because of personal or familial experience with the issue. Recent examples include Senator Tom Harkin and his commitment to the Americans with Disabilities Act and Senators Paul Wellstone, Pete Domenici, Ted Kennedy, and Patrick Kennedy, in relation to MHPAEA, the parity law (see Image 12.1 for a photograph taken at rally for the MHPAEA). Other motivating factors could be interest or pressure from constituents and donors, political interests or priorities, and advocacy from interest groups and stakeholder organizations.

Collaborating with Professional Organizations, Advocacy Groups, and Other Stakeholders

While every citizen has the right to advocate and individual input is valuable, greater power and influence can be attained by collaborating and coordinating with others interested in child violence and trauma policies, allowing for a sharing of ideas, labor, resources, failures, and successes. Further, policymakers are often more likely to respond to the recommendations of larger coalitions and groups that have struggled with differences, developed consensus, and agreed on collective recommendations. In Box 12.5, we list strategies for influencing policy change.

Box 12.5 Strategies for Influencing Policy Change

- Write letters to the editor or op-ed letters in local or national papers.
- Disseminate press releases about your child trauma work or related issues.
- Call policymakers and other decision makers.
- Send personal e-mails or letters by mail.
- Respond to action alerts from advocacy organizations.
- Use social media to raise awareness about policymaker activity.
- Invite policymakers and agency officials to visit your workplace (e.g., clinic, university).

- Participate in or submit testimony for congressional hearings.
- Organize or participate in congressional briefings.
- Attend town hall meetings, political receptions, rallies, and fundraisers.

—(APA PsycAdvocate®, 2012)

A Case Example: NCTSN

The launch and growth of NCTSN illustrates how advocacy, science, legislation, and perseverance can intersect to establish and integrate new federal policies that affect the delivery of services to children affected by trauma.

The idea of the NCTSN—as a national network of child trauma centers collaborating to raise the standard of care, increase access to services, and accelerate the integration of science to frontline providers—grew from a national dialogue among clinicians, researchers, advocates, and state and federal policymakers. Meeting in 1998 in Cape Cod, Massachusetts, these individuals shaped the broad outline and purposes of the network, sparking actions that moved to the federal level in the U.S. Congress and federal agencies. Several members of Congress (Senators Durbin, Kennedy, and Wellstone) requested a GAO report (GAO-02–813) to examine the national reach of services for children affected by trauma and any policy gaps. The findings of the report—that a national policy gap existed—were largely reflected in the title, "Effectiveness of Insurance Coverage and Federal Programs for Children Who Have Experienced Trauma Largely Unknown." Legislation was drafted and finalized to address these gaps, included as part of the Children's Health Act, which then became part of a larger bill to reauthorize the SAMHSA federal agency. This is where it languished, despite efforts by advocates and congressional staff to move it forward. Then, on April 20, 1999, a mass school shooting occurred at Columbine High School in Denver, Colorado, a tragedy that changed the federal landscape and national sensibility about trauma. In response, the U.S. Congress released the SAMHSA reauthorization bill, and it, along with the language to authorize the NCTSN, was enacted into law. This experience illustrates the impact of national events on the consciousness of the public and the willingness of elected officials to act or direct funds in new ways.

Once the NCTSN program became law, and an initial $10 million funding was appropriated to SAMHSA, the administrative federal agency responsible for the NCTSN, the process for establishing clear guidelines for the NCTSN began. This involved writing a "Request for Applications" grant announcement, which detailed the responsibilities and expectations of the 17 grants that would be *funded under this first announcement. Applications came into SAMHSA, and the review process for determining awards began with the review panel meeting in Washington, D.C., as it turned out, on a fateful day: September 11, 2001.*

The 9/11 attacks changed the United States in many deep and profound ways, including initiating a greater interest and understanding of the impact of trauma on children and adults. As the U.S. Congress shaped its response, new funds were directed to the NCTSN, beginning its expansion immediately.

Between that moment and 2017, many other national events have contributed to expanding and changing the NCTSN. At times, proposals were made to narrow permanently the NCTSN's mission as part of a national response to a specific current crisis. Advocates and congressional supporters have fought back these efforts, recognizing the breadth of the mission as a strength of the NCTSN, one that allows the resources and expertise of the thousands of members, affiliates (formerly funded), and partners of the NCTSN to, in essence, rise to any occasion where children are affected by trauma and to provide support and resources.

Because of the growing national awareness of the impact of child trauma, many national mental health and child-serving organizations have integrated an understanding of trauma into their own work, recognizing its potential role in many settings, including foster care, child welfare, juvenile justice, domestic violence, refugee experiences, military families, and educational and medical settings. This growth has created many partnership opportunities for the NCTSN and these organizations, extending the reach of the NCTSN resources. Similarly, far-reaching public awareness campaigns that use the findings of the Adverse Childhood Experiences studies to advance an understanding of trauma have also led many states and organizations to turn to the NCTSN resources for guidance on how to meet the needs of children with trauma histories once they are identified.

As with many federal programs, the future of the NCTSN is not certain within a climate of federal budget cuts for children and families. The same education, awareness raising, advocacy, and partnerships with policymakers and other stakeholders that launched the NCTSN, and many of the programs described in this chapter, are needed to ensure that they continue and the needs of children and families affected by trauma are met.

Conclusion

The history of policy change in the area of child trauma and violence is one of struggle for attention and resources; the outlook for the future is no different. Throughout this chapter, the uncertainty of the future was noted, within a context where serious changes are being proposed that could have a negative impact on services for children affected by trauma. While positive changes have occurred, ongoing attention is needed to maintain and advance improvements in research, evaluation, services, collaboration, systems integration, and education in order to prevent or counteract policy changes that would harm children and families. Federal policies can guide and facilitate the implementation of new strategies that direct funding where it is most needed and advance the state of scientific knowledge about effectiveness. In turn, those who are expert in child trauma and violence can share their expertise with decision makers about what is needed and what is at stake. This requires leadership, experience, and a steadfast commitment to participate in the process of policy change.

References

American Psychological Association. (2012). *American Psychological Association PsycAdvocate® curriculum*. Retrieved from http://www.apa.org/ed/ce/resources/psycadvocate.aspx

Arditi, L. (2017, March 21). Treatment for addiction, mental illness would suffer under GOP plan to change health care law, RI groups tell Congress. *Providence Journal*. Retrieved from http://www.providencejournal.com/news/20170321/treatment-for-addiction-mental-illness-would-suffer-under-gop-plan-to-change-health-care-law-ri-groups-tell-congress

Centers for Disease Control and Prevention. (n.d.). *About the CDC-Kaiser ACE Study*. Retrieved from https://www.cdc.gov/violenceprevention/acestudy/about.html

Child Welfare Information Gateway. (2011). *About CAPTA: A legislative history*. Washington, DC: U.S. Department of Health and Human Services, Children's Bureau.

Community Anti-Drug Coalitions of America. (n.d.). *The Comprehensive Addiction and Recovery Act*. Retrieved from http://www.cadca.org/comprehensive-addiction-and-recovery-act-cara

Copeland, W. E., Keeler, G., Angold, A., & Costello, E. J. (2007). Traumatic events and posttraumatic stress in childhood. *Archives of General Psychiatry, 64*, 577–584.

Fang, X., Brown, D. S., Florence, C. S., & Mercy, J. A. (2012). The economic burden of child maltreatment in the United States and implications for prevention. *Child Abuse & Neglect*, 2, 156–165.

Felitti, V. J., Anda, R. F., Nordenberg, D., Williamson, D. F., Spitz, A. M., Edwards, . . . Marks, J. S. (1998). Relationship of childhood abuse and household dysfunction to many of the leading causes of death in adults. *American Journal of Preventive Medicine, 14*, 245–258.

Fernandes-Alcantara, A. L. (2015, October 14). *Family Violence Prevention and Services Act (FVPSA): Background and funding*. Congressional Research Service: Report 42838. Retrieved from https://fas.org/sgp/crs/misc/R42838.pdf

Finkelhor, D., Turner, H.A., Shattuck, A., & Hamby, S.L. (2013). Violence, crime, and exposure in a national sample of children and youth: An update. *JAMA Pediatrics, 167*(7), 614–621.

Finklea, K.M., Fernandes-Alcantara, A.L., & Siskin, A. (2015). *Sex trafficking of children in the United States: Overview and issues for Congress.* Congressional Research Service: Report R41878. Retrieved from https://fas.org/sgp/crs/misc/R41878.pdf

Friedman, M. (2016, February 13). *PTSD history and overview.* Washington, DC: Department of Veterans Affairs, National Center for PTSD. Retrieved from https://www.ptsd.va.gov/professional/ptsd-overview/ptsd-overview.asp

Futures without Violence. (2012). *How the Affordable Care Act (ACA) affects victims of domestic, sexual, and dating violence.* Retrieved from https://www.futureswithoutviolence.org/userfiles/file/HealthCare/ACA%20and%20DV%20final.pdf

Gilbert, L.K., Breiding, M.J., Merrick, M.T., Thompson, W.W., Ford, D.C., Dhingra, S.S., & Parks, S.E. (2015). Childhood adversity and adult chronic disease: An update from ten states and the District of Columbia, 2010. *American Journal of Prevention Medicine, 48*(3), 345–349.

Gragg, F., Petta, I., Bernstein, H., Eisen, K., and Quinn, L. (2007). New York prevalence study of commercially sexually exploited children: Final report. Rockville, MD: Westat.

Harvard Law School. (2017, February 8). *The impact of President Trump's executive orders on asylum seekers.* Retrieved from https://today.law.harvard.edu/wp-content/uploads/2017/02/Canada-Trudeau-letter-Feb-8-2017.pdf

Institute of Medicine and National Research Council. (2013). *Confronting commercial sexual exploitation and sex trafficking of minors in the United States.* Washington, DC: The National Academies Press.

Kessler, R.C., Berglund, P., Demler, O., Jin, R., Merikangas, K.R., & Walters, E.E. (2005). Lifetime prevalence and age-of-onset distributions of DSM-IV disorders in the National Comorbidity Survey Replication. *Archives of General Psychiatry, 62*, 593–602.

Kosciw, J.G., Greytak, E.A., Giga, N.M., Villenas, C. & Danischewski, D.J. (2016). *The 2015 National School Climate Survey: The experiences of lesbian, gay, bisexual, transgender, and queer youth in our nation's schools.* New York, NY: GLSEN. Retrieved from https://www.glsen.org/article/2015-national-school-climate-survey

Mirhashem, R., Allen, H.C., Adams Z.W., van Stolk-Cooke, K., Legrand, A., & Price, M. (2017, June). The intervening role of urgency on the association between childhood maltreatment, PTSD, and substance-related problems. *Addictive Behaviors, 69*, 98–103.

Murphey, D. (2016, September 6). *Moving beyond trauma: Child migrants and refugees in the United States.* Washington, DC: Child Trends. Retrieved from

https://www.childtrends.org/wp-content/uploads/2016/09/Moving-Beyond-Trauma-Report-FINAL.pdf
National Center for PTSD. (2017). *Goals and objectives*. Retrieved from https://www.ptsd.va.gov/about/mission/goals_and_objectives_of_the_national_center_for_ptsd.asp
National Child Traumatic Stress Network. (2016, July). *NCTSN financing and sustainability survey report*. Retrieved from http://www.nctsn.org/resources/policy-issues
National Children's Alliance. (n.d.). *Fact sheet*. Retrieved from http://www.nationalchildrensalliance.org/sites/default/files/downloads/NCA-Media-Guide.pdf
National Children's Alliance. (2016). *Snapshot 2017: Advocacy, efficacy and funding in CACs*. Retrieved from http://www.nationalchildrensalliance.org/sites/default/files/downloads/Snapshot-2017.pdf
National Low Income Housing Coalition. (2014). *40 years ago: Child Abuse Prevention and Treatment Act passed*. Retrieved from http://nlihc.org/article/40-years-ago-child-abuse-prevention-and-treatment-act-passed
Pear, R. (2017, July 3). Congress moves to stop I.RS. from enforcing health law mandate. *New York Times*. Retrieved from https://www.nytimes.com/2017/07/03/us/politics/congress-moves-to-stop-irs-from-enforcing-health-law-mandate.html
Pear, R., & Kaplan, T. (2017, June 22). Senate health care bill includes deep cuts to Medicaid. *New York Times*. Retrieved from https://www.nytimes.com/2017/06/22/us/politics/senate-health-care-bill.html
The Perryman Group. (2014). *Suffer the little children: An assessment of the economic cost of child maltreatment*. Retrieved from https://www.perrymangroup.com/wp-content/uploads/Perryman_Child_Maltreatment_Report.pdf
Polaris Project. (2016). *2016 hotline statistics*. Retrieved from https://polarisproject.org/resources/2016-hotline-statistics
Prevent Child Abuse America. (2016). *2016 federal public policy agenda*. Retrieved from http://www.preventchildabuse.org/images/docs/2016FPPA.pdf
Putnam, K., Harris, W. W., & Putnam, F. (2013, August). Synergistic childhood adversities and complex adult psychopathology. *Journal of Traumatic Stress, 26*, 435–442.
Raphael, J., & Shapiro, D. L. (2002). *Sisters speak out: The lives and needs of prostituted women in Chicago*. Chicago, IL: Center for Impact Research.
Sacco, L. N. (2015, May 26). *The Violence against Women Act: Overview, legislation, and federal funding*. Congressional Research Service. Retrieved from https://fas.org/sgp/crs/misc/R42499.pdf
Stein, F. (2017a, January 25). *AAP statement on protecting immigrant children*. Retrieved from https://www.aap.org/en-us/about-the-aap/aap-press-room/Pages/AAPStatementonProtectingImmigrantChildren.aspx
Stein, F. (2017b, March 6). *AAP statement on revised immigrant and refugee travel ban executive order*. Retrieved from https://www.aap.org/en-us/about-the-

aap/aap-press-room/pages/AAP-Statement-on-Revised-Immigrant-and-Refugee-Travel-Ban-Executive-Order.aspx

Stoltz, J. M., Shannon, K., Kerr, T., Zhang, R., Montaner, J. S., & Wood, E. (2007). Associations between childhood maltreatment and sex work in a cohort of drug-using youth. *Social Science & Medicine*, *65*, 1214–1221.

Stoltzfus, E. (2017, January 10). *Child welfare: An overview of federal programs and their current funding*. Congressional Research Service. Retrieved from https://fas.org/sgp/crs/misc/R43458.pdf

Substance Abuse and Mental Health Services Administration. (2014). *SAMHSA's concept of trauma and guidance for a trauma-informed approach*. HHS Publication No. (SMA) 14–4884. Rockville, MD: Substance Abuse and Mental Health Services Administration.

Trauma-Informed Care for Children and Families Act. S. 774, 115th Congress (2017).

UN High Commissioner for Refugees. (2016a). *Children on the run: Unaccompanied children leaving Central America and Mexico and the need for international protection*. Washington, DC: UN High Commissioner for Refugees. Retrieved from http://www.unhcr.org/en-us/about-us/background/56fc266f4/children-on-the-run-full-report.html?query=children

UN High Commissioner for Refugees. (2016b). *Global trends: Forced displacement in 2015*. Washington, DC: UN High Commissioner for Refugees. Retrieved from http://www.unhcr.org/en-us/statistics/unhcrstats/576408cd7/unhcr-global-trends-2015.html

U.S. Department of Education. (n.d.). *The Individuals with Disabilities Education Act: Parts B and C*. Retrieved from http://idea.ed.gov/

U.S. Department of Health and Human Services, Administration for Children and Families, Administration on Children, Youth and Families, Children's Bureau. (2011). *Child Abuse Prevention and Treatment Act as amended by P.L. 111–320, the CAPTA Reauthorization Act of 2010*. Retrieved from https://www.acf.hhs.gov/sites/default/files/cb/capta2010.pdf

U.S. Department of Health and Human Services, Administration for Children and Families, Administration on Children, Youth and Families, Children's Bureau. (2012). *The Children's Bureau legacy: Ensuring the right to childhood*. Retrieved from: https://cb100.acf.hhs.gov/sites/default/files/cb_ebook/cb_ebook.pdf

U.S. Department of Health and Human Services, Administration for Children and Families, Administration on Children, Youth and Families, Children's Bureau. (2017). *Child maltreatment 2015*. Retrieved from https://www.acf.hhs.gov/cb/resource/child-maltreatment-2015

U.S. Department of Health and Human Services, Family and Youth Services Bureau. (2016). *Family Violence Prevention and Services Program*. Retrieved from https://www.acf.hhs.gov/fysb/programs/family-violence-prevention-services/about

CHAPTER 13

Infant and Early Childhood Trauma

Policy Opportunities and Systemic Responses

Cindy Oser, Julie Cohen, Patricia A. Cole, Janie Huddleston, and Lindsay Usry

Introduction

Babies and young children are no strangers to violence. Being the age group most likely to be poor increases young children's chances of living in communities characterized by social disorganization that gives rise to violence. Infants and toddlers are also the age group most likely to experience maltreatment, including the personal violence of abuse.

The nature of early brain development makes infants and toddlers particularly vulnerable to the effects of living in violence's shadow. Living with trauma and chronic stress at an early age can disrupt the architecture of the developing brain. Research shows that early adverse experiences—which are not confined to neighborhoods or families without resources—have lifelong consequences for later health and functioning in life. There is a hopeful message for public policies that seek prevention rather than reaction, promotion of resilience rather than remediation. The early years of life are the most promising period for promoting strong, emotional health and safe, stable, nurturing relationships that can buffer the effects of trauma on the development of young children.

Policies to promote the well-being of babies and young children must be multigenerational, considering their relationships with adult caregivers—usually their parents—which shape their development. A parent's mental well-being and own past trauma can affect the ability to parent and form the close relationships babies need to thrive. Adults also are the victims of both community and domestic violence, which in turn affects the children. The dearth of services to address adult issues such as mental health problems or substance abuse is a barrier to addressing or preventing the effects of trauma on young children. Parents and other caregivers, who may be a critical buffer between a young child and the effects of violence and trauma as well as the first layer of promoting resiliency, must be included in any solution to prevent or heal trauma in young children.

Public policies directed at long-term solutions to end violence and reduce the impact of trauma need to be developed for the full continuum of targeted strategies. These policies need to address the promotion of healthy emotional development of young children, prevent the consequences of exposure to trauma, and ensure appropriate treatment for children and families who do suffer from traumatic experiences.

This chapter provides an overview of trauma and its impact on the health and development of young children, the extent of the problem, and why it is a policy concern. We highlight policy case examples to describe systemic responses to trauma and the growth of trauma-informed practice approaches and propose a framework for considering policies to address early childhood trauma. Finally, we discuss potential policy solutions and opportunities at the federal, state, and community level that would (1) reduce exposure to trauma, (2) promote healing in children and families exposed to violence and trauma, (3) increase capacity of those who serve children and families to apply a trauma-focused lens on their practice, and (4) document the problem and track trends to improve accountability and make progress in addressing early childhood trauma.

The Problem

There are a variety of terms used to discuss the experience of traumatic events and the effects of those experiences in childhood, including childhood trauma, complex trauma, toxic stress, traumatic stress, chronic stress, posttraumatic stress disorder (PTSD), child traumatic stress, and Adverse Childhood Experiences (ACEs). For the purposes of this chapter, we will use the term "trauma."

Exposure to trauma is widespread among young children and families in the United States, producing a range of consequences across developmental domains, even for children in the first year of life. Trauma exposure is particularly prevalent among children in certain settings such as the mental health, child welfare, and juvenile justice systems (Cooper, Nasi, Dababnah, Aratani, & Knitzer, 2007). There are a variety of circumstances and events that may be traumatic for young children, including physical trauma, child abuse and neglect, accidents, forced separation from a parent or caregiver, homelessness, natural disasters, medical trauma, exposure to domestic or community violence, serious accidents, and loss of a caregiver (Cohen, Oser, & Quigley, 2013). It is not uncommon for young children to be exposed to multiple traumatic stressors. Young children may react to trauma differently than older children or adults. Even experiences the child doesn't remember can have lifelong effects (SAMHSA, 2013). For example, an infant who is in the home where the parents are addicted to heroin may not remember the details of the drug use, but the baby will suffer from the lack of responsive parenting and may carry the scars of abandonment for many years.

Young children are exposed to trauma at disturbing rates. Among healthy, typically developing children, an estimated 26 percent will witness or experience a trauma event before they reach age four (Briggs-Gowan, Ford, Fraleigh, & McCarthy, 2010; Crusto, 2014). Among vulnerable children—those who are at risk for poor health outcomes because they live in socioeconomically disadvantaged communities and have fewer health resources—the incidence of trauma events range from 49 percent to 75 percent (Briggs-Gowan et al., 2010; Crusto, 2014; Roberts, Campbell, Ferguson, & Crusto, 2013). Young children (birth to five years old) face the greatest risk for abuse and neglect, most often by parents or primary caregivers. More than 700,000 children experienced substantiated maltreatment in 2014, including 192,000 infants and toddlers. Over 30 percent (31.2%) of children entering foster care are babies and toddlers (U.S. Department of Health and Human Services, 2014). Children in their first year of life had the highest rate of victimization (24.4 per 1,000 children of the same age in the national population), and they spend the greatest amount of time in care once admitted (U.S. Department of Health and Human Services, 2014).

African American children had the highest rate of victimization (15.3 per 1,000 children in the population of the same race or ethnicity), and American Indian and Alaskan Native children had the second highest rate (13.4 per 1,000 children; U.S. Department of Health and Human Services, 2016). American Indian and Alaskan Native children experience trauma at higher rates than other children in the United States; they are

2.5 times more likely to experience trauma compared to their nonnative peers (Lechner, Cavanaugh, & Blyler, 2016).

Why Is Trauma a Concern for Infants and Young Children?

Trauma in early childhood is an issue of extreme importance for our society. Trauma can have a significant impact on individuals at any age, but it can take a unique and serious toll on very young children due to their rapidly developing bodies and brains. A common misconception is that very young children, particularly preverbal infants and toddlers, are unaffected by and unable to remember traumatic experiences. This is a pervasive and faulty belief because young children cannot describe their experiences to us in a way we readily understand, and because young children are sometimes quite resilient, they may appear to "bounce back" or appear unaffected to an untrained eye. This is far from the truth. During the early years of life, children are *particularly* vulnerable to their environments and stress experienced by their caregivers and constantly drawing in information from each and every interaction and experience. Their brains are developing at a rate faster than at any other point in development, and this development is greatly impacted by the child's experiences, both good and bad.

In addition to brain development, exposure to trauma affects lifelong health and well-being. According to the Adverse Childhood Experiences (ACE) Study, traumatic experiences are associated with chronic illness such as heart disease and cancer, as well as substance use disorder, mental health problems, victimization of various forms, suicide, and, ultimately, early death (Felitti et al., 1998). Adults who experienced high levels of trauma as a child are more likely to have depression or other mental health problems, use drugs, be incarcerated, and suffer from chronic illnesses; children of those adults are more likely to experience ACEs, like having an incarcerated family member, living in a house with substance use, having a parent with a mental health problem, or losing a parent during childhood. These children then grow into adults with high ACE scores, and the cycle continues. Therefore, it is important that policies to address childhood trauma also take into account the needs of parents and families, who are positioned to buffer the effects of trauma on that child.

In addition to the physical and mental health ramifications, trauma in childhood has been linked to lower educational attainment, lower occupational attainment and earnings, and lower worker productivity (including higher rates of absenteeism and sick days) in adulthood (Institute of Medicine & National Research Council, 2013). Estimated costs of trauma, looking solely at the economic cost of first-time cases of child maltreatment in the United States (not capturing the impact of other forms of trauma), have been estimated at nearly $5.9 trillion in lifetime spending, $2.7 trillion in lost gross domestic product, and $27.9 million lost in person-years of employment (The Perryman Group, 2014).

Systemic Responses to Early Childhood Trauma

There is a growing recognition that exposure to adversity, violence, and trauma can affect the future health, development, and learning of infants and young children. The federal government as well as some states and communities have created and implemented practice-oriented responses to trauma. The most effective approaches address policy responses at the same time so that changes in attitudes and direct responses to trauma can be supported by rules, regulations, and financing that incorporate the principles of trauma-informed care. In other words, creating a trauma-informed system of care requires attention to the provision of services to individuals to establish physical and psychological safety, promote recovery from traumatic exposure, and prevent adverse outcomes. Creating a trauma-informed system of care also requires a framework of policies that support both the provision of trauma prevention and treatment and the system infrastructure itself—the workforce, financing, oversight, and accountability mechanisms.

States and communities have developed a range of responses to reduce the impact of trauma on the well-being of children and families. The immediate purpose of these efforts is to provide emergency relief and serve as first responders to traumatic events such as domestic violence, house fires, and natural disasters (flooding, tornados, hurricanes, etc.). However, states and communities recognize the longer-term impact, including the cost of not intervening, of exposure to traumatic events, and are seeking ways to promote resilience and well-being in all children, prevent deleterious effects of exposure to trauma, and intervene as early as possible with children and their families who have experienced trauma.

The federal government has also created structures to support implementation and research on trauma-informed care (e.g., the National Child Traumatic Stress Network; see Chapter 12) and encouraged or required the use of trauma-informed practices in relevant federal grant opportunities.

Changing Perspectives Affect Policy Responses

Clinical perspectives about trauma, and the impact of trauma, have changed over time; policy, especially early childhood policy, has been much slower to incorporate trauma-informed perspectives. Early conceptualizations of trauma and posttraumatic stress arose from the experience of war: in the Civil War, traumatic exposure was known as "Soldier's Heart," in World War II as "shell shock," in the Korean and Vietnam Wars as "combat stress," and more recently in Afghanistan and Iraq, as PTSD. Clinical thinking changed from a view of trauma as a transient situational disturbance; symptoms were thought to be temporary, and therefore, they would pass on their own and the affected individual would recover without treatment or intervention.

Clinical thinking has changed dramatically. Research has demonstrated that trauma is present far beyond just the battlefield and the soldier and in women as well as men. The *Diagnostic and Statistical Manual* (*DSM-5*) states that "PTSD is more prevalent among females than among males across the lifespan" due to a greater likelihood of exposure to rape and other forms of interpersonal violence (American Psychiatric Association, 2013). Animal research studies on the immediate and long-term effects of the stress response helped to inform and advance human clinical research on early life stress, parent–child attachment, and exposure to trauma (Nelson & Carver, 1998; Rincon-Cortes & Sullivan, 2014). Ongoing research and practice revealed that trauma, including single and multiple exposures, also affects infants and very young children as victims and as witnesses to violence and trauma. Early exposure to trauma and stress places young children at higher risk for mental health disorders later in life (Hart, Gunnar, & Cicchetti, 1996). Growing awareness led to the identification of treatable trauma-related mental health disorders. PTSD first entered the *DSM* with the *DSM-IV* (American Psychiatric Association, 1994) in 2000, and the *DSM-5* includes PTSD for children under age six as well as adults. The DC:0–5™: Diagnostic Classification of Mental Health and Developmental Disorders of Infancy and Early Childhood (DC:0–5) includes PTSD with criteria for children under age five; the diagnosis should be made with caution in infants under 12 months old (ZERO TO THREE, 2016).

In the 1990s, there was an emerging recognition that trauma coexisted with mental health and substance abuse disorders in men and in women.[1] The 1990s was also the "decade of the brain," and with the release of *From Neurons to Neighborhoods* in 1994, connections were made between early experience (including exposure to trauma) and brain development

(National Research Council and Institute of Medicine, 2000). The first reports from the ACE study were also published during this time (Felitti et al., 1998).

Advances in clinical trauma perspectives have also led to changes in policy and practice, although more slowly, and not as widespread. The release of findings from the ACE study, for example, inspired the creation of ACE collaboratives in some states, and ACE survey data were collected to inform strategic priorities, budget development, and program improvement. The American Academy of Pediatrics issued a policy statement in 2012 on exposure to adversity and toxic stress (Committee on Psychosocial Aspects of Child and Family Health et al., 2012) and published guidance to assist pediatricians to create trauma-informed practices (American Academy of Pediatrics, 2017).

Direct service programs in child welfare, early intervention for children with developmental disabilities, and mental health agencies implemented trauma screening to identify children and caregivers who had experienced or been exposed to trauma. Service delivery protocols were created to assure that practice was consistent with trauma-informed care (Gilkerson et al., 2013). As new evidence-based trauma treatments such as Child Parent Psychotherapy were implemented, some states such as Nebraska issued new guidance to clarify how to bill for such services.

Box 13.1 Infant and Early Childhood Mental Health

Infant and early childhood mental health is the developing capacity of the child from birth to five years of age to form close and secure adult and peer relationships; experience, manage, and express a full range of emotions; and explore the environment and learn—all in the context of family, community, and culture. It is important to note that while we use the term "infant and early childhood mental health (IECMH)" in this chapter, it is also commonly referred to as "infant mental health."

Another area of clinical work has influenced the spread of trauma-informed practice and has great potential for guiding trauma policy: infant and early childhood mental health (IECMH), which we define in Box 13.1. Over the past three decades, the field of IECMH has strengthened, bolstered by a growing research base. A consensus definition of this term was coined by ZERO TO THREE as the capacity of a child from birth to age five to (1) experience, express, and regulate emotions; (2) form close, secure interpersonal relationships; and (3) explore his or her environment and learn all within the context of family and cultural expectations (Cohen, Oser, & Quigley, 2012).

Trauma informed early childhood policy should adhere to the full continuum of targeted strategies focused on promotion, prevention, and treatment:

1. **Promotion**: Strategies that aim to encourage positive IECMH development may include public awareness campaigns that encourage parents to speak to their preverbal children and "help lines" for parents to seek advice on child development.
2. **Prevention**: Prevention services, delivered in diverse settings, seek to identify risk factors, mitigate the impacts of ACEs, and intervene in child–caregiver dynamics that threaten healthy development; they may include parenting education, home visiting services, and referrals to community and social services.
3. **Treatment**: Effective, evidence-informed treatment provides services and supports intended to directly address mental health disorders. Children's parents or primary caregivers are typically involved in treatment, which may include such services as Child Parent Psychotherapy, Parent–Child Interaction Therapy, and Attachment and Biobehavioral Catch-Up.

Public Policy Responses to Trauma

The current view of trauma embraces the concepts that the consequences of trauma can persist, that recovery resolves the symptoms but fundamental changes endure, and that even very young children experience and suffer from trauma. Unfortunately, public policy has not always kept pace with changes in trauma-informed practice. Policies in and across child-serving systems must shift from "it's a personal problem" to addressing trauma as a public health problem necessitating a much broader public policy discussion.

The federal government has convened workgroups and appointed task forces to consider and make recommendations to alleviate the "epidemic" of violence. The work of these groups helped to solidify the connection between exposure to violence and consequences on mental health and development across the life span. The reports, and their recommendations, also inspired new research and intentional focus on trauma-informed systems building. Recommendations were directed at the child welfare, substance abuse and mental health systems, the juvenile justice system, to services for military families, and to law enforcement. One of the first public policy efforts to focus on trauma was the Indian Child Welfare Act (ICWA) of 1978. The ICWA is a federal law that seeks to keep American Indian children with American Indian families. Congress passed ICWA in 1978 in response to the alarmingly high number of Indian children being removed from their homes by both public and private agencies. The intent of Congress under ICWA was to "protect the best interests of Indian children and to promote the stability and security of Indian tribes and families" (25 U.S.C. § 1902).

The federal government also incorporated a trauma-informed approach into several major grant programs for children, including the Early Childhood Comprehensive Systems (ECCS) program's strategy on mitigation of toxic stress and trauma in infancy and early childhood across multiple systems, the Project LAUNCH (Linking Actions for Unmet Needs in Children's Health), state, community, and tribal grants to promote wellness among children birth to age eight, and the Maternal, Infant and Early Childhood Home Visiting (MIECHV) program. For example, the federally funded ECCS program (Health Resources and Services Administration, 2016) began in 2003 as a cross-system effort to build seamless service delivery systems for children from birth to kindergarten entry. There were initially five areas of focus for the ECCS state grants: access to medical homes, promotion of mental health, early care and education, parenting education, and family support. In 2013, in response to the growing recognition of the impact of trauma on children's health and development, ECCS funds were directed at three priority areas, including "mitigation of toxic stress and trauma during infancy and early childhood across two or more early childhood systems." States took advantage of this funding to create coordinated plans for addressing trauma in public health, child welfare, early care and education, and home visiting. Perhaps the most comprehensive trauma-related federal effort was created in 2000 when Congress established the National Child Traumatic Stress Network to support clinical practice, research, and training.

Clinicians, advocates, and researchers continue to push for trauma-informed policy at the federal, state, community, and tribal levels. More recently, specific policy recommendations and grant programs have called for trauma-informed approaches and evidence-based practices. For example, in 2013, a joint guidance letter was issued by the U.S. Departments of Health and Human Services, Administration for Children and Youth, Centers for Medicaid and Medicare Services, and Substance Abuse and Mental Health Services. The letter was intended to "encourage the integrated use of trauma-focused screening, functional assessments and evidence-based practices in child-serving settings for the purpose of improving child well-being." Unique for its cross-agency perspective, the letter was broadly disseminated to state Medicaid directors, substance abuse and behavioral health directors, childcare developmental block grant administrators, state health departments, and so forth.

Given the cross-system impact of trauma, it is useful to have a framework to guide the development of policies for early childhood trauma-informed care. Although frameworks have been described for trauma-informed practice, these typically describe clinical approaches or address organizational considerations such as identifying leadership for transformation within the organization, hiring or training a trauma-informed workforce, and preventing secondary trauma in staff members (Menschner & Maul, 2016). Key practice elements for implementing trauma-informed care have been described for child welfare, pediatrics, primary health care, human services, hospital-based violence intervention programs, and Part C Early Intervention (Administration for Children and Families, 2017; American Academy of Pediatrics, 2017; Children's Hospital of Philadelphia, 2017; Gilkerson et al., 2013; National Network of Hospital-Based Violence Intervention Programs, 2016). As developmentally appropriate trauma-informed treatment were developed and tested and implemented, organizations often found that policies needed to be adjusted, for example, creating a way to pay for treatment where both the parent and the child were included in the intervention. Payment reform is just one opportunity for early childhood trauma policy improvement.

We propose a policy framework that approaches early childhood trauma with a systemic response and that addresses four elements: (1) reducing exposure, (2) supporting children and promoting healing, (3) increasing capacity in the workforce, and (4) documenting the problem and tracking trends. This policy framework takes into account the unique needs of infants and young children, along with their families, and thus represents a developmentally appropriate trauma policy framework. In the next section, we describe possible policy solutions and opportunities for moving forward to create meaningful early childhood trauma-focused policy that supports evidence-informed practice.

Moving Forward—Trauma-Focused Early Childhood Policy

Exposure to violence and trauma among children and their families has reached epidemic proportions (Office of Juvenile Justice and Delinquency Prevention, 2012). For infants and young children, exposure to trauma overwhelms their ability to cope, and without a source of safe, stable, nurturing relationships, this can have devastating effects on lifelong health, development, and learning. Evidence-based, trauma-specific services are being developed, evaluated, and implemented in health care, education, social services, child welfare, and juvenile justice. However, more work must be done to create policies—legislation, rules, regulations, and budgets—that support practice changes that are developmentally appropriate for infants, young children, and their families.

Principles of trauma-informed early childhood policies

- Acknowledge the unique needs of very young children with an intentional focus on children from birth to five years old and their caregivers.
- Support developmentally appropriate assessments and services.
- Include a continuum of supports and services (promotion, prevention, and treatment).
- Address the needs of special populations, such as infants and toddlers in the child welfare system.
- Support cross-system collaborations.

Any trauma-informed early childhood policy should be written with these principles in mind.

Strategic Policy Directions for Trauma-Informed Early Childhood Policy

In the previous section, we suggested that trauma-informed early childhood policy could be framed by four components and should seek to (1) reduce exposure to trauma, (2) promote healing in children and families exposed to violence and trauma, (3) increase capacity of those who serve children and families to apply a trauma-focused lens on their practice, and (4) document the problem and track trends in trauma exposure in order to improve accountability and make progress on this issue. What would this look like for infants, young children, and families affected by trauma? What policies are needed at the federal, state, and community level to support this vision? The following section provides policy case examples and opportunities to create trauma-informed early childhood policy.

A Framework for Trauma-Informed Early Childhood Policy

Component 1—Reduce Exposure: Ensure Safe, Stable, Nurturing Homes and Communities for Young Children

Infants and young children process all experiences through relationships with adults. These early connections can help buffer the effects of exposure to trauma, build resilience, and change the child's physical response to stress. Reducing exposure promotes emotional well-being, and this can best be accomplished by ensuring that every child has at least one safe, stable, nurturing relationship in their early years of life. In the policy landscape, this can be achieved by creating policies that support parents in being fully capable of meeting their children's physical and emotional needs. This means promoting mental and physical well-being of parents and families and promoting community stability.

It is beyond the scope of this chapter to present all possible opportunities to create safer, healthier and more family-supportive communities. In addition to the early childhood policy opportunities presented later in this chapter, advocates and others interested in trauma-informed policy should consider improvements in the social determinants of health—the conditions in which people are born, grow, live, work, and age—including the availability of healthy food choices, safe public places for families to gather and play with their children, convenient transportation, environmental protections such as lead abatement and clean water, employment and job training, and so forth (World Health Organization, 2017). Communities can identify strengths and areas of growth and build upon those to support young children and families. Specific programs, supported by federal policy, have been implemented to address this component. The MIECHV program, described next, provides an example of how policy can support Component 1.

How Can Policy Help Reduce Trauma Exposure? Policy Case Example: MIECHV Program

MIECHV was established in 2010—authorized by the Social Security Act, Title V, Section 511 (42 U.S.C. 711), as added by Section 2951 of the Patient Protection and Affordable Care Act (P.L. 111–148)—to provide grants to states and tribal entities to support voluntary, evidence-based, home visiting services to at-risk families. The program is administered by the Health Resources and Services Administration (HRSA) Maternal and Child Health Bureau in collaboration with the Administration for Children and Families (ACF). MIECHV programs are in 774 at-risk communities in all 50 states, Washington, D.C., 25 tribal communities, and several territories (ZERO TO THREE, 2015). As of September 2013, MIECHV was serving approximately 80,000 parents and children. States, territories, and tribal entities receive funding through MIECHV and are given the flexibility to shape the program to serve the particular needs of their communities. At least 75 percent of MIECHV funding must be used for program models that have been rigorously tested and proven to make a positive difference in the health and well-being of families and communities. States may use the remaining 25 percent of MIECHV funding for "promising approaches" that are also rigorously evaluated. Three percent of funds are set aside for the Tribal Home Visiting program and an additional 3 percent for research and evaluation.

MIECHV grantees are accountable for meeting several benchmarks including improved maternal and newborn health; prevention of child injuries, child abuse, neglect, or maltreatment and reduction of emergency department visits; improvement in school readiness and achievement; reduction in crime or domestic violence; improvements in family economic self-sufficiency; and improvements in the coordination and referrals for other community services and support. The federal MIECHV program provided an impetus to reduce exposure to trauma through evidence-based home visiting; MIECHV helps families provide safe, stable, nurturing homes for their young children. Because of MIECHV funding, more women had healthy pregnancies, participating mothers experienced less stress and improved their parenting skills, and their children received scheduled well-child checkups (Reauthorization of the MIECHV Program, 2017).

Policy opportunities

1. Support parents as they raise their young children.
2. Create a national Paid Family Leave program.
3. Create a public health initiative that supports parents of young children through home visiting, developmental or mental health consultants in pediatric practices, and community peer-to-peer groups.
4. Expand communities' capacity to support young brain development through early care and learning programs.
    a. Extend Early Head Start to eligible infants and toddlers in poverty.
    b. Invest to ensure that all families can access quality, affordable child care, with a major funding surge to improve the quality of infant-toddler care.
5. Support strategies for building strong, violence-free communities that support strong families, including such efforts as Promise Neighborhoods (U.S. Department of Education, n.d.) and Promise Zones (U.S. Department of Housing and Urban Development, n.d.) that support community-wide strategies of promoting strong child and family development, community strategies for economic development, and building social supports, including collective impact approaches.

Component 2—Support Children, Promote Healing: Increase Access to Services and Supports

Promoting healing among children who have been exposed to trauma requires ensuring access to evidence- and trauma-informed screening, assessment, diagnosis, and treatment. Exposure to trauma and chronic stress takes a physical toll on children's development and functioning. Unfortunately, the symptoms of trauma-exposed children often go unrecognized because few parents and providers fully understand how children's mental health manifests in their behavior. For this reason, a fully responsive and trauma-informed safety net for young children requires infant and early childhood mental health expertise to be infused in all child-serving settings, with teachers, doctors, and family support professionals who understand the signs of trauma and the appropriate ways to respond. Once children are identified as having a need, they must have access to effective, developmentally appropriate evidence-based treatment, with a clinician who understands that their needs differ greatly from those of an adult who has experienced trauma and understands that the mental health and caregiving practices of their parents are critical to their recovery. The Safe Babies Court Teams program is an example of how policy can support Component 2.

How Can Policy Promote Healing? Policy Case Example: ZERO TO THREE Safe Babies Court Teams

Safe Babies Court Teams (SBCT) is a research-based systems-change approach grounded in the science of child development. Since 2005, ZERO TO THREE has led the development of the SBCT approach, including collecting cross-site data and training judges. The SBCT is a community-level, judicially led team that provides families with tailored interventions to meet their specific needs.

The SBCT approach is designed to protect babies from further harm and address the issues in the child welfare system that prevent families from being successful. The Infant-Toddler Court Team works at the community level to ensure that the families receive the services and supports they need and also eliminate any barriers in the system that would prevent families from successful reunification efforts. The team typically involves a variety of community providers, including teachers, child advocates, attorneys and court-appointed special advocates, mental health clinicians, pediatricians and other health-care providers, substance abuse counselors, early intervention, members of the faith community, and others.

Another important component of the approach is the Family Team meeting. These meetings happen monthly. Families attend and can invite other individuals of their choice (e.g., friends, faith leaders). Child welfare staff, attorneys, foster parents, community service providers, and the community coordinator also attend. The Family Team works together to create a safe space for the families to talk about their own trauma and service needs. Families are empowered to address their own needs and assist in creating the healing journey toward reunification with their children.

SBCT has worked with over 975 infants and toddlers and more than 1,100 parents. Because of the success of SBCT, 97 percent of the 186 children received needed services and 99.05 percent of the 186 infant and toddler cases examined were protected from further maltreatment while under court supervision (Hafford, McDonnell, Kass, DeSantis, & Dong, 2009). In addition, children monitored by the SBCT project reached permanency 2.67 times faster than the national comparison group (McCombs-Thornton, 2012). The SBCT approach has led to policy changes in child welfare, mental health, and the judiciary.

Policy opportunities

1. Invest in the bedrock of brain connections by promoting the mental health of infants, young children, and families.
    a. Expand availability and accessibility of IECMH services, including in early childhood programs such as child care and prekindergarten.
    b. Ensure that IECMH services are adequately funded.
2. Reorient the child welfare system to ensure stable relationships and sound development for infants and toddlers experiencing maltreatment.
    a. Enact federal legislation to allow Title IV-E foster care maintenance funding to be used for preventive and reunification services and the infrastructure to ensure effective use of those funds.
    b. Promote states' adoption of child welfare policies and practices oriented toward supporting the healthy development of infants and young children (ZERO TO THREE, 2012).
    c. Expand SBCT to establish a network of community-level, judicially led teams that provide families with tailored interventions to meet their specific needs.

Component 3—Increase Capacity: Develop a Sufficient and Highly Qualified Workforce

Knowledgeable, skilled, and culturally responsive professionals who understand trauma and respond effectively to young children can play a significant role in how children are affected by their exposure to violence and trauma. Early childhood professionals and others who work with the families of young children may lack sufficient knowledge of the impact of trauma on children. They may not recognize that the behaviors they see in young children are actually symptoms of fear and anxiety. Professionals in health care, early education, home visiting, early intervention, child welfare, and so forth may need additional skills and training to work with young children (and possibly with their parents) who experience toxic stress. Even professionals trained in mental health and similar fields do not necessarily have specialized knowledge to deliver evidence-based trauma treatments to infants, young children, and families. In most parts of the country, there is a shortage of qualified infant and early childhood mental health providers. Policy must address this shortage in order to ensure the timely and culturally appropriate access children and families need. The following policy case examples illustrate how workforce development can inspire policy change and support Component 3.

How Can Policy Help Increase Workforce Capacity? Two Policy Case Examples from Louisiana

Louisiana-Tulane Parenting Education Program

In the state of Louisiana, the Department of Children and Family Services (DCFS) provides services to child protection–involved families by contracting with a network of Family Resource Centers across the state. In the Greater New Orleans area, these services are provided by the Tulane Parenting Education Program (T-PEP) Family Resource Center, within the Tulane University School of Medicine, Department of Psychiatry and Behavioral Sciences. T-PEP provides DCFS-referred families (biological, foster, and adoptive) a variety of parenting education services, assessments, and interventions. The goal of the program is to improve family functioning and create safety for children and families involved with DCFS. In addition to providing these direct services to families in the Greater New Orleans area, DCFS also contracts with T-PEP to provide consultation to the other Family Resource Centers around the state.

The program provides a licensed clinical social worker and a licensed psychologist from Tulane's faculty to provide consultation services to eight DCFS-supported Family Resource Centers throughout the state. Consultation is provided to Family Resource Center staff and any interns working with a given Family Resource Center. Consultants meet by telephone with workers for 1.5-hour sessions twice a month. All T-PEP staff (social workers and parent educators) are supervised by a Tulane faculty member, who provides weekly supervision and review of all monthly reports submitted to DCFS. Consultation addresses specific intervention techniques like Visit Coaching and the Nurturing Parents Program, as well as other issues of concern including attachment, child-centered foster care, effects of trauma, domestic violence, and parental mental illness. In an effort to improve consultation services, T-PEP assisted DCFS in Baton Rouge in the development of a survey to assess participant satisfaction and gather ideas to improve the services.

T-PEP has increased training efforts with existing partners and stakeholders with the hope that efforts will translate into a more sensitive and trauma-informed community approach to working with maltreated children and families. Because of the success of T-PEP, a total of 997 individuals have been served (as of September 2015; T-PEP, 2015). A number of sites in other states and countries are hoping to replicate all or a portion of this model. Tulane faculty have been providing consultative support and training to other sites including New Mexico, Minnesota, Nevada, Scotland, and England.

State-Initiated Child-Parent Psychotherapy

State Medicaid agencies and managed care providers are required to consider provider supply and capacity, and in most states, the availability of qualified infant mental health providers is extremely limited. In order to increase the capacity of licensed mental health providers in Louisiana to provide evidence-based treatment services for young children, 0–6, who have experienced traumatic events and/or mental health, attachment, and/or behavioral problems, since 2014, several managed health-care groups asked national child-parent psychotherapy (CPP) trainers and faculty in the Department of Psychiatry at Louisiana State University Health Sciences Center to provide 18 month CPP Learning Collaboratives with 3 in-person sessions and twice a month case consultation calls. With this initiative, the managed care groups supported the dissemination strategy of the National Child Traumatic Stress Network to support uptake of best practices through an intensive focus on "learning-by-doing." After completing the training, clinicians are eligible to join the national roster of trained CPP clinicians, which greatly enhances the availability of therapeutic services for young children throughout the state. Given that Louisiana is ranked very high for children living in poverty, which contributes to higher developmental risk for young children, the availability of increased services for this population serves a crucial need for both prevention and early intervention. Further, these efforts will contribute to a more sensitive and trauma-informed approach for supporting maltreated infants, young children, and their families.

How Can Policy Help Increase Service Capacity? Policy Case Example: Federal Legislation Supporting IECMH

In November 2016, IECMH gained unprecedented attention at the federal level, with the passage of the 21st Century Cures Act (P.L. 114–255; 21st Century Cures Act, 2017). This bill included the Helping Families in Mental Health Crisis Act of 2016 and a provision entitled Infant and Early Childhood Mental Health Promotion, Intervention, and Treatment (Section 10006). Inclusion of this provision represents the first instance of IECMH being addressed in national mental health policy. The provision, although a minor part of the overall bill, was a landmark for the IECMH field and required more than one year's persistent advocacy by ZERO TO THREE, along with mental health clinicians and other advocates, to be realized.

The Infant and Early Childhood Mental Health Promotion, Intervention, and Treatment provision authorizes the creation of grants, which can be used at the state and community level to support a variety of services across the continuum of promotion, prevention, assessment, diagnosis, and treatment. Grants may be used to train mental health professionals in evidence-based IECMH treatment methods or clinical consultation skills or to provide professional development to other child-serving providers to expand their capacity to recognize and address IECMH concerns. Grants may also support direct services to children and their families. Notably, the legislation recognizes the unique need to address support for the mental health of very young children in the context of the close relationships with the adults who care for them and specifically mentions as allowable grant using multigenerational therapy and other services to support the caregiving relationship.

The Infant and Early Childhood Mental Health Promotion, Intervention, and Treatment provision is an example of federal legislative policy that recognizes the needs of young children as well as the broad range of services that are needed to fully support IECMH at the population and individual levels. At the writing of this chapter, the IECMH provisions are awaiting federal appropriations. This legislation, and the grant programs therein, provides an opportunity to expand and sustain IECMH services and increases the number of skilled clinicians available to address the unique mental health needs of infants and young children.

Policy opportunities

1. Create a well-qualified IECMH workforce that can promote emotional health in young children and families, prevent the consequences of exposure to violence and trauma, and treat PTSD.

2. Invest in training for selected mental health providers on specific, developmentally appropriate, and evidence-based trauma treatments such as Child Parent Psychotherapy, Attachment and Biobehavioral Catch-Up, and Parent Child Interaction Therapy.

Component 4: Document the Problem and Track Trends

Understanding the scope and nature of the problem is critical to bolstering support and taking action to address it. It is important to collect and report data on the prevalence of early childhood trauma as well as the prevalence of conditions resulting from trauma. These data can be used to convey to decision makers who or what is affected, how widespread or concentrated the issue is, and to drive conversations about how to best address the problem. In addition to quantifying the scope of the problem, there needs to be effective communication of the data and research findings and support for policymakers to translate data into action. Iowa's work using ACEs data to take action on reducing early childhood adversity is an example of how policy can support Component 4.

How Can Policy Help Document the Problem? Policy Case Example: Iowa Adverse Childhood Experiences

The Adverse Childhood Experiences (ACE) study illustrated how strongly negative experiences in childhood can disrupt a child's development and lead to an array of health and social challenges over the course of a lifetime. In 2011, a presentation on the ACE study prompted several central Iowa organizations to take action to address its findings leading to the formation of the ACEs 360 Steering Committee. The committee brought a diverse group of organizations together to collaborate on efforts to measure ACEs data in Iowa, raise awareness across the state, and identify successful interventions to help minimize the risk of ACEs (Cohen et al., 2013). Four subcommittees were formed: Policy, Partnering and Convening, Communication, and Data and Research.

The Policy subcommittee works to raise awareness of the ACE study findings among Iowa legislators. Subcommittee members work to integrate information on ACEs into meetings with policymakers and have established the topic as relevant to state policy. In 2015, the subcommittee along with other Iowa groups established a five-year vision and common legislative agenda for responding to ACEs in Iowa. Thirty-four legislators were educated on ACEs during the session. In 2016, the Iowa ACEs Policy Coalition held two advocacy days at the Iowa State Capitol;

participants came together from across the state and various sectors to advocate for a range of preventive and early intervention strategies. Key legislative requests for the 2016 session included expanding the 1st Five Healthy Mental Development Initiative statewide, creating a statewide system of care for children's mental health, and ensuring access to preventative and early identification services for children in the transition to managed care.

In Iowa and other states and communities, measuring and reporting ACE data has helped to increase awareness of the incidence and impact of childhood adversity, and established a baseline for data-based policy decision-making. This data, in combination with the ACE-related research shared among research institutions, states, and communities, has provided advocates with a platform to bring stakeholders together and to catalyze community and state policy action.

Policy opportunities

1. Collect data to quantify the impact of early childhood trauma through existing data collection (e.g., child maltreatment metrics tracked by federal agencies, national databases, child protection agencies, the Center for Disease Control and Prevention's Behavioral Risk Factor Surveillance System) or new data collection (e.g., community ACE surveys, data systems established to capture results from trauma screening in early care and education and primary care) and use these data to drive policymaking decisions.
2. Build the evidence base by conducting robust evaluations of programs designed to prevent and address childhood trauma so that effective strategies can be scaled up and future investments may be directed to proven approaches.
3. Promote understanding of childhood trauma among decision makers at all levels. Use local data and the existing body of research to educate legislators, judges, law enforcement, the business community, and others about the science of early childhood trauma and then understand how trauma impacts children, families, and long-term societal stability and how policy can promote safety for children.
4. Create opportunities and strategies for engaging community members in data collection and building the evidence base. Provide regular updates at the community level to document trends in violence and experiences that affect infants and young children. Utilize strategies such as Parent Cafes to engage parents in discussions of how violence is affecting their ability to raise their children, and identify practical, neighborhood-based ways to address these issues. Provide leadership training for parents and other community members so that they can effectively present their stories to policymakers and other decision makers.

Strategic Questions

The following questions may be useful to policymakers, advocates, clinicians, and families as they consider systemic responses to early childhood trauma:

Leadership

- Who are the trauma champions? If none, how will we nurture leadership for this work?
- Who might take the lead and provide coordination for our planning efforts?
- What kind of advocacy messages can you use that will make the case for trauma-informed services?
- What funded projects currently exist that might provide direction to these efforts? Can we garner additional federal funding for trauma services and supports?

Reduce exposure (prevention)

- How can we get community residents, including parents of young children, involved in planning for safe and stable neighborhoods?
- Do current violence reduction efforts include attention to the impact on very young children?
- How might we train our first responders (police officers, firefighters, Community Emergency Response Teams, etc.) and nontraditional first responders (infant toddler educators, judicial court system staff, public health nurses, home visitors, etc.) in early childhood trauma-informed care?

Support children and promote healing (promotion and treatment)

- What are the existing trauma services and supports for expectant parents, infants, young children, and families?
- What gaps in trauma services currently exist?
- Should all young children and their families be screened for trauma as a required and billable service? When and how does this occur, and how are referrals for treatment handled?
- What policies are needed to support resilience of infants, young children, and their families?
- Does our state or community have a plan for embedding trauma services in related children's programs (early learning and development, special education and early intervention, child welfare, home visiting, pre-K, Head Start/Early Head Start)?
- How might our programs build empathy in young children?

Increase capacity of the workforce

- Who among our state, communities, and programs provides trauma training to individuals who work with children in child welfare, special education and early intervention, home visiting, schools, and Head Start/Early Head Start?
- What trauma-informed, evidence-based approaches are currently used? Which ones need to expand, and who will be trained?
- How do our programs provide reflective supervision to prevent secondary trauma to providers?

Document the problem and track trends

- What do we know about the extent of trauma and trauma-exposure among the youngest children in our state or community? How has this changed over time?
- What do families in our community feel is their top priority when it comes to raising their children?
- Does our state or community have a mechanism for reviewing the trauma services that are provided and for reporting on the progress made?
- How are trauma services and supports funded?

Conclusion

Addressing the impact of trauma on infants and young children requires attention to policy as well as changes in practice. Trauma-informed early childhood policy acknowledges the unique needs of young children and includes a continuum of collaborative, developmentally appropriate supports and services. We propose a framework for trauma-informed policy that reduces exposure to trauma, promotes healing in children and families exposed to trauma, increases capacity among those who serve children and families, and documents the problem and tracks trends. Federal, state, and community policies that address these four components can alleviate suffering in young children and lay the groundwork for a healthy future.

Note

1. See https://www.nasmhpd.org/content/federal-partners-committee-women-and-trauma-report for a discussion of alcohol and drug problems in women and women with severe mental illness who are at high risk for substance abuse—as well as other forms of abuse and deprivation—due to poverty and victimization.

References

Administration for Children and Families. (2017). *Resource guide to trauma-informed human services*. Retrieved from https://www.acf.hhs.gov/trauma-toolkit?utm_source=blog&utm_medium=blog/

American Academy of Pediatrics. (2017). *Becoming a trauma informed practice*. Retrieved from https://www.aap.org/en-us/advocacy-and-policy/aap-health-initiatives/resilience/Pages/Becoming-a-Trauma-Informed-Practice.aspx

American Psychiatric Association. (1994). *Diagnostic and statistical manual of mental disorders* (4th ed.). Washington, DC: Author.

American Psychiatric Association. (2013). *Diagnostic and statistical manual of mental disorders* (5th ed.). Washington, DC: Author.

Briggs-Gowan, M., Ford, J., Fraleigh, L., & McCarthy, K. (2010). Prevalence of exposure to potentially traumatic events in a healthy birth cohort of very young children in the northeastern United States. *Journal of Traumatic Stress, 23*(6), 725–733.

Children's Hospital of Philadelphia. (2017). *Health care toolbox: Working with the child welfare system*. Retrieved from https://www.healthcaretoolbox.org/

Cohen, J., Oser, C., & Quigley, K. (2012). *Making it happen: Overcoming barriers to providing infant-early childhood mental health*. Retrieved from http://www.zerotothree.org/public-policy/federal-policy/early-child-mental-health-final-singles.pdf

Cohen, J., Oser, C., & Quigley, K. (2013). Igniting the policy conversation: Bringing a trauma-informed approach to early childhood system building. *ZERO TO THREE Journal, 34*(2), 24–33.

Committee on Psychosocial Aspects of Child and Family Health, Committee on Early Childhood, Adoption, and Dependent Care, Section on Developmental and Behavioral Pediatrics, Garner, A. S., Shonkoff, J. P., Seigel, B. S . . . Wood, D. L. (2012). Early childhood adversity, toxic stress, and the role of the pediatrician: Translating developmental science into lifelong health. *Pediatrics, 129*, e224–e231.

Cooper, J., Nasi, R., Dababnah, S., Aratani, Y., & Knitzer, J. (2007). *Strengthening policies to support children, youth, and families who experience trauma*. Retrieved from http://www.nccp.org/publications/pdf/text_737.pdf

Crusto, C. (2014). *Childhood trauma: A public health problem that requires a robust response*. Retrieved from http://www.rwjf.org/en/culture-of-health/2014/07/remember_the_financi.html

Felitti, V., Anda, R., Nordenberg, D., Williamson, D. F., Spitz., A. M., Edwards, V., . . . Marks, J. S. (1998). Relationship of childhood abuse and household dysfunction to many of the leading causes of death in adults. *American Journal of Preventive Medicine, 14*, 245–258.

Gilkerson, L., Graham, M., Harris, D., Oser, C., Clarke, J., Hairston-Fuller, T., & Lertora, J. (2013). Trauma-informed Part C early intervention: A vision, a challenge, a new reality. *Zero to Three, 34*(2), 34–44.

Hafford, C., McDonnell, C., Kass, L., DeSantis, J., & Dong, T. (2009). *Evaluation of the court teams for maltreated infants and toddlers: Final report*. Submitted to the Office of Juvenile Justice and Delinquency Prevention, U.S. Department of Justice by James Bell Associates, Arlington, VA.

Hart, J., Gunnar, M., & Cicchetti, D. (1996). Altered neuroendocrine activity in maltreated children related to symptoms of depression. *Developmental Psychopathology*, *8*, 201–214.

Health Resources and Services Administration, Maternal and Child Health. (2016). *Early childhood comprehensive systems*. Retrieved from https://mchb.hrsa.gov/earlychildhoodcomprehensivesystems

Hearing on the Reauthorization of the Maternal, Infant, and Early Childhood Home Visiting (MIECHV) Program: Hearing before the Committee on Ways and Means, House, 150th Congress. (2017).

Institute of Medicine and National Research Council. (2013). *New directions in child abuse and neglect research*. Washington, DC: The National Academies Press.

Lechner, A., Cavanaugh, M., & Blyler, C. (2016). *Addressing trauma in American Indian and Alaska Native youth*. Washington, DC: Mathematica Policy Research.

McCombs-Thornton, K. L. (2012). The effect of the ZERO TO THREE court teams initiative on types of exits from the foster care system: A competing risk analysis. *Children and Youth Services Review, 34*, 169–178.

Menschner, C., & Maul, A. (2016). *Key ingredients for successful trauma-informed care implementation*. Retrieved from http://www.chcs.org/resource/key-ingredients-for-successful-trauma-informed-care-implementation/

National Network of Hospital-Based Violence Intervention Programs. (2016). *Trauma informed care: Interview with Dr. Theodore Corbin*. Retrieved from http://nnhvip.org/trauma-informed-care/

National Research Council, & Institute of Medicine, Committee on Integrating the Science of Early Childhood Development. (2000). *From neurons to neighborhoods: The science of early childhood development*. Washington, DC: National Academy Press.

Nelson, C., & Carver, L. (1998). The effects of stress and trauma on brain and memory: A view from development cognitive neuroscience. *Developmental Psychopathology, 10*, 793–809.

Office of Juvenile Justice and Delinquency Prevention. (2012). *Report of the attorney general's national task force on children exposed to violence*. Retrieved from https://www.justice.gov/defendingchildhood/cev-rpt-full.pdf

The Perryman Group. (2014). *Suffer the little children: An assessment of the economic costs of child maltreatment*. Retrieved from https://www.perrymangroup.com/wp-content/uploads/Perryman_Child_Maltreatment_Report.pdf

Rincon-Cortes, M., & Sullivan, R. (2014). Early life trauma and attachment: Immediate and enduring effects on neurobehavioral and stress axis development. *Frontiers in Endocrinology*, *5*, 1–15.

Roberts, Y., Campbell, C., Ferguson, M., and Crusto, C. (2013). The role of parenting stress in young children's mental health functioning after exposure to family violence. *Journal of Traumatic Stress, 26*(5), 605–612.

Substance Abuse and Mental Health Services Administration. (2013). *Project LAUNCH briefing sheet.* Retrieved from http://www.healthysafechildren.org/sites/default/files/launch_briefing_book.pdf

Tulane Parenting Education Program (T-PEP) Family Resource Center Region 1 Annual Performance Report October 1, 2014–September 30, 2015.

21st Century Cures Act. 42 U.S.C §399Z—2. Infant and early childhood mental health promotion, intervention, and treatment (2015–2016).

U.S. Department of Education. (n.d.). *Promise neighborhoods.* Retrieved from https://ed.gov/programs/promiseneighborhoods/index.html

U. S. Department of Health and Human Services, Administration for Children and Families, Administration on Children, Youth, and Families, Children's Bureau. (2014). *The AFCARS report: Preliminary FY 2014 estimates as of July 2015.* Retrieved from https://www.acf.hhs.gov/sites/default/files/cb/afcarsreport22.pdf

U.S. Department of Health and Human Services, Administration for Children and Families, Administration on Children, Youth and Families, Children's Bureau. (2016). *Child maltreatment 2014.* Retrieved from http://www.acf.hhs.gov/programs/cb/research-data-technology/statistics-research/child-maltreatment

U.S. Department of Housing and Urban Development. (n.d.). *Promise zones.* Retrieved from https://portal.hud.gov/hudportal/HUD?src=/program_offices/comm_planning/economicdevelopment/programs/pz/overview

World Health Organization. (n.d.). *Social determinants.* Retrieved from http://www.who.int/social_determinants/sdh_definition/en/

ZERO TO THREE. (2012). *A developmental approach to child welfare services for infants and toddlers: A self-assessment tool for states and counties administering child welfare services.* Retrieved from https://www.zerotothree.org/resources/217-a-developmental-approach-to-child-welfare-services-for-infants-and-toddlers

ZERO TO THREE. (2015). *Home visiting fact sheet: Meeting families where they are.* Retrieved from https://www.zerotothree.org/resources/456-home-visiting-fact-sheet-meeting-families-where-they-are

ZERO TO THREE. (2016). *DC:0–5™: Diagnostic classification of mental health and developmental disorders of infancy and early childhood.* Washington, DC: Author.

About the Editors and Contributors

Joy D. Osofsky, PhD, is a clinical and developmental psychologist and the Paul Ramsay Chair of Psychiatry and Barbara Lemann Professor of Child Welfare at Louisiana State University Health Sciences Center in New Orleans. She has published widely and authored or edited *Treating Infants and Young Children Impacted by Trauma: Interventions That Promote Healthy Development* (2017), *Clinical Work with Traumatized Young Children* (2011), *Young Children and Trauma: Intervention and Treatment* (2004), and *Children in a Violent Society* (1997). In 2017, she co-authored *Questions Every Judge and Lawyer Should Ask about Infants and Toddlers in the Child Welfare System* (National Council of Juvenile and Family Court Judges). Osofsky is past president of Zero to Three: National Center for Infants, Toddlers and Families and the World Association for Infant Mental Health. She played a leadership role in the Gulf Region following Hurricane Katrina and the Deepwater Horizon Oil Spill as codirector of the Louisiana Rural Trauma Services Center in the National Child Traumatic Stress Network (NCTSN) and clinical director for Child and Adolescent Services for Louisiana Spirit, Louisiana's Crisis Counseling Program. She serves as codirector of the Mental and Behavioral Health Capacity Project, part of the Gulf Region Health Outreach Program following the Gulf Oil Spill, and coprincipal investigator of the NCTSN Terrorism and Disaster Coalition for Child and Family Resilience, an NCTSN center. In 2007, Osofsky received the Sarah Haley Award for Clinical Excellence for trauma work from the International Society for Traumatic Stress Studies and in 2010 a presidential commendation from the American Psychiatric Association for her work in the aftermath of Hurricane Katrina. In 2014, she was recognized with the Reginald Lourie Award for leadership in infant mental health and outstanding contributions to the health and welfare of children and families.

Betsy McAlister Groves, MSW, LICSW, is a licensed clinical social worker and founding director of the Child Witness to Violence Project at Boston Medical Center, a program that has received national recognition for its work with young children affected by domestic and community violence. This program is one of four sites comprising the Early Trauma Treatment Network within the National Child Traumatic Stress Network. Within the Network, she serves on the Policy Task Force, and was cochair of the Domestic Violence Workgroup, leading efforts to create resources for parents and professionals on children affected by domestic violence. While at Boston Medical Center, Groves served as codirector of the Child Protection Team in the Department of Pediatrics. Her practice and research interests are on the impact of community and family trauma on young children, and on engaging the health and education systems in identifying and responding to children affected by trauma. She holds academic appointments as associate professor of pediatrics at Boston University School of Medicine and lecturer at the Harvard University Graduate School of Education, where she is coordinator of their Child Advocacy Program and teaches courses on childhood trauma. She served on the Massachusetts Governor's Council for Domestic Violence and Sexual Assault for 17 years and in 2010 was appointed by Attorney General Eric Holder to the National Advisory Commission for the US. Department of Justice—Office of Violence against Women. She has served as a consultant to the American Academy of Pediatrics, the National Council of Juvenile and Family Court Judges, Healthy Families America, and Futures without Violence. She is the author of *Children Who See Too Much: Lessons from the Child Witness to Violence Project*, and has published extensively on topics related to child exposure to domestic violence, early childhood trauma, and intervention.

Riana Elyse Anderson, PhD, is an assistant professor at the University of Southern California's Suzanne Dworak-Peck School of Social Work in the Department of Children, Youth, and Families. She is the developer and director of the EMBRace (Engaging, Managing, and Bonding through Race) racial socialization intervention.

Laura Marie Armstrong, PhD, is an assistant professor in the Department of Psychological Science and graduate faculty in the Health Psychology program at the University of North Carolina, Charlotte. She is also a licensed psychologist in North Carolina. Her research focuses on the development of self-regulation across infancy and childhood, with an emphasis on emotion regulation, caregiver–child interactions, and family conditions that support or undermine these processes.

Cecily Basquin is a second year student at University of North Carolina, Charlotte, in the Health Psychology PhD program. Her research focuses on family health decision making.

Christopher Blodgett, PhD, is a Washington State University faculty member and a licensed clinical psychologist. He is the director of the CLEAR Trauma Center at Washington State University. Trauma-informed work in schools using the CLEAR model now includes multiple schools in Washington, Oregon, Alaska, New York, and California.

Diane Elmore Borbon, PhD, MPH, is policy program director for the UCLA-Duke University National Center for Child Traumatic Stress. Previously she served as associate executive director of the APA Public Interest Government Relations Office and Health Policy Fellow in the Office of Senator Hillary Clinton. She is president of the International Society of Traumatic Stress Studies (ISTSS) and associate editor for *Psychological Trauma: Theory, Research, Practice, and Policy.*

Judge Constance Cohen (Ret.) served as an associate juvenile judge from June 1994 until her retirement in July 2014. She is currently teaching, consulting, and enjoying time with family. She also served as an adjunct professor at DMACC and Drake University Law School. Prior to law school, Judge Cohen was an educator for 12 years.

Julie Cohen, MSW, is associate director of the ZERO TO THREE Policy Center. She has worked at ZERO TO THREE for more than 17 years and specializes in early childhood policy, specifically infant and early childhood mental health. Most recently, she worked as part of an international expert task force to produce the DC:0–5™: Diagnostic Classification of Mental Health and Developmental Disorders of Infancy and Early Childhood.

Patricia A. Cole, MA, is senior director of federal policy at ZERO TO THREE. She leads the organization's work in developing and promoting a strong start for infants and toddlers through federal policies in a range of areas, including early care and learning, child welfare, and infant-early childhood mental health. She has over 30 years of experience in policy at the federal and state levels, including serving as senior staff on the U.S. Senate Subcommittee on Children, Family, Drugs and Alcohol.

Rachel Davis, MSW, is a managing director at Prevention Institute, overseeing the Institute's violence prevention and trauma work, spanning child abuse and maltreatment, domestic and sexual violence, community violence, community trauma and mental health. She has directed the UNITY initiative, previously funded by the CDC to advance a public health approach to violence prevention.

Aimee Drouin Duncan, PhD, has worked for 10 years in the human services and education policy, practice, and research arenas. Her research examines the developmental outcomes of young children at environmental risk, namely, poverty, abuse, and neglect.

Ellen Gerrity, PhD, is an associate professor, Psychiatry Department, Duke University Medical Center, and associate director, UCLA-Duke University National Center for Child Traumatic Stress. Dr. Gerrity has worked in traumatic stress research, practice, and public policy for over 35 years, including as an NIMH research administrator and as senior mental health policy advisor for the late U.S. Senator Paul Wellstone.

Tonya Cross Hansel, PhD, LMSW, is a social worker and clinical associate professor in the Department of Psychiatry at Louisiana State University Health Sciences Center. Her work focuses on disaster mental health, research and program evaluation, and ways to support individual and community strengths following traumatic events.

Brenda Jones Harden, PD, is a professor in the Department of Human Development and Quantitative Methodology, University of Maryland College Park. Her research examines the developmental and mental health needs of young children at environmental risk. A particular focus is preventing maladaptive outcomes in these populations through early childhood, parenting, home visiting, and infant mental health programs.

Janie Huddleston, director of the Quality Improvement Center for Research-Based Infant-Toddler Court Teams at ZERO TO THREE, brings years of experience with system change, child welfare, education, and early learning to this position. She decided after 16 years with the Arkansas Department of Human Services, in various positions including the director of the Division of Early Care and Education, director of the Division of Children- and Family Services, and deputy director for the Department to focus her career on promoting the health and development of infants and toddlers.

Marva L. Lewis, PhD, is associate professor at the Tulane University School of Social Work with a clinical appointment in the Department of

Child Psychiatry in New Orleans, Louisiana. She is a Zero to Three fellow and founder and director of the Center for Natural Connections, which provides community-based interventions promoting hair combing interaction as a naturalistic and culturally valid method to strengthen parent–child attachment.

Ann S. Masten, PhD, is Regents Professor and Irving B. Harris Professor of Child Development at the University of Minnesota. She is an internationally recognized leader in developmental resilience science and the protective influences of relationships for children and families who experience trauma.

Neena McConnico, PhD, LMHC, serves as program director for the Child Witness to Violence Project at Boston Medical Center and faculty and consultant on the Boston Defending Childhood Initiative. She has served as a member of an advisory team and core faculty for Futures without Violence, helping to plan, design, and disseminate two national curricula, *Preventing and Responding to Childhood Trauma: New Strategies for Schools and Communities* and *Building Competence and Resilience in Children and Parents: The Advocate as Change Agent.*

Nawal Muradwij, MA, is a graduate from the Master's program in Clinical Psychology at Teachers College, Columbia University. She is also a current doctoral student in the Clinical Psychology program at John Jay College of Criminal Justice and the Graduate Center at the City University of New York.

Angela J. Narayan, PD, LP, is an assistant professor in clinical child psychology at the University of Denver and an assistant adjunct professor in the Department of Psychiatry at the University of California, San Francisco. Her current research interests focus on understanding pregnancy as a key period of developmental transformation and an opportunity to buffer the intergenerational transmission of risk and promote resilience in pregnant women exposed to childhood adversity.

Cindy Oser, RN, MS, is director of Infant and Early Childhood Mental Health Strategy at ZERO TO THREE. Oser is experienced in directing state and national initiatives and most recently was the staff leader on an international expert workgroup to produce the Diagnostic Classification of Mental Health and Developmental Disorders of Infancy and Early Childhood (DC:0–5™).

Howard J. Osofsky, MD, PhD, is the Kathleen and John Bricker Chair and Head, Department of Psychiatry at Louisiana State University School of Medicine in New Orleans. Dr. Osofsky has published widely and his career is marked by a strong commitment to the community and in developing health services systems for the region and state. He has played an important role in developing community, state, and national psychosocial preparedness programs for first responders and mental health professionals to improve responses following disasters and terrorism.

Howard Pinderhughes, PhD, is an associate professor in the Department of Social and Behavioral Sciences at the University of California, San Francisco. Dr. Pinderhughes is the author of *Race in the Hood: Conflict and Violence among Urban Youth* and his forthcoming book, *Dealing with Danger: How Inner City Youth Cope with the Violence That Surrounds Them*, examines the production of youth violence and how urban adolescents think about, experience, and make decisions about the use of violence. He works with cities around the country on the development and implementation of comprehensive strategies to prevent violence.

Anthony H. Speier, PhD, is an associate professor of clinical psychiatry in the Department of Psychiatry at Louisiana State University Health Sciences Center (LSUHSC). He is the former Assistant Secretary of the Louisiana Office of Behavioral Health. Dr. Speier served as state-wide director for disaster behavioral health in Louisiana for 20 years and was responsible for directing the public-sector behavioral health response to Hurricane Katrina. He is Senior Advisory to disaster and terrorism-related initiatives.

Holly M. Strain, MPH, serves as director of Government Relations at Capitol Decisions, Inc. She has successfully advocated for the inclusion of provisions to increase access to mental health and addiction treatment in several laws, including the Mental Health Parity and Addiction Equity Act, the Affordable Care Act, and the Comprehensive Addiction and Recovery Act.

Richard Tedeschi, PhD, is professor of psychology at the University of North Carolina at Charlotte and core faculty for the Health Psychology PhD program. He has published books on posttraumatic growth, an area of research that he developed examining personal transformations in the aftermath of traumatic life events. Tedeschi serves as a consultant to the American Psychological Association on trauma and resilience and is past president of the North Carolina Psychological Association.

Erika Tullberg, MPA, MPH, is on the faculty at NYU School of Medicine, where she is also a member of the Center for Stress, Trauma and Resilience. Her work is focused on children and families that have experienced abuse and maltreatment, how trauma impacts parenting and child safety, and secondary traumatic stress experienced by child welfare staff.

Lindsay Usry, MPH, is a senior policy analyst in the Policy Center at ZERO TO THREE. She is also on the faculty of Tulane University School of Medicine and was formerly the Director of Special Projects for their Institute of Infant and Early Childhood Mental Health. Her work focuses on the translation and dissemination of research on infant and early childhood mental health to inform policy.

Larry Wissow, MD, MPH, is the James P. Connaughton Professor of Community Psychiatry, Division of Child and Adolescent Psychiatry, at the Johns Hopkins University School of Medicine.

Index

Note: *Italicized* page numbers indicate tables, figures, and boxed material.